ADMINISTRATIVE DECENTRALIZATION

ADMINISTRATIVE DECENTRALIZATION

Strategies for Developing Countries

John M. Cohen
Stephen B. Peterson

This work is published for and
on behalf of the United Nations

KUMARIAN
PRESS

Administrative Decentralization: Strategies for Developing Countries

Published 1999 in the United States of America by Kumarian Press, Inc.,
14 Oakwood Avenue, West Hartford, Connecticut 06119-2127 USA.

Production and design by The Sarov Press, Stratford, Connecticut.
Index by Barbara J. DeGennaro.
The text of this book is set in Bembo 11.5/14.2.

Printed in Canada on acid-free paper by
Hignell Printing Limited.
Text printed with vegetable oil-based ink.

∞ The paper used in this publication meets the minimum requirements
of the American National Standard for Information Sciences—Permanence of
Paper for Printed Library Materials, ANSI Z39.48–1984.

Library of Congress Cataloging-in-Publication Data
Cohen, John M.
    Administrative decentralization : strategies for developing
countries / John M. Cohen, Stephen B. Peterson.
      p.   cm.
    Includes bibliographical references and index.
    ISBN 1–56549–097–5 (cloth : alk. paper). — ISBN 1–56549–096–7
(pbk. : alk. paper)
      1. Decentralization in government—Developing countries.
2. Developing countries—Politics and government. I. Peterson,
Stephen B. II. Title.
JF60.C643 1999
352.2'83—dc21
                                           99–14051

---

03   02   01   00   99   5   4   3   2   1   First Printing 1999

Contents

Preface

A BOOK INVOLVES many debts and the authors thank several individuals and institutions for their patience, support, and encouragement. Dwight Perkins, Director of HIID when the book was written, provided Steve a year sabbatical which was used in part to work on the manuscript. Dwight also encouraged John to squeeze in the research between his other pressing assignments. Jeff Sachs, the current Director of HIID, encouraged and supported the completion and publication. The United Nations Secretariat provided initial funding and assistance in publication, and we are indebted to the UN for getting us both back to studying decentralization. Eng. Luis Castro and Miguel Ramirez Barber provided extensive information on Mexico's 100 Cities Program and an anonymous reviewer made several useful insights.

The publication of a book brings closure to an intellectual effort and in this case it brings closure to John Cohen's distinguished career. John ardently believed that research in development administration was best done by doing. He practiced what he preached and served nearly twenty years overseas advising governments in administration. Despite the very difficult environments in which he worked, John was forever an optimist. He recognized that management and institutional constraints could not be overcome overnight and that patience, creativity, and experience were needed to improve public management. John was a prolific writer and students of development administration would do well to review his insights. He strongly felt that public management was neglected in development thinking and in schools of public policy. His plea to address the need for public management should not go unheeded.

I have lost a co-author, a colleague, and a close friend. The development administration profession has lost a very important voice. John was a remarkable man and I am deeply indebted to him for the wisdom he imparted and the experiences he made possible. I was fortunate to have had the rare privilege of working with John for so many years.

STEPHEN PETERSON

ADDIS ABABA

Introduction

SINCE THE END OF WORLD WAR II, government decision makers, development professionals and academics have sought to formulate strategies for designing and implementing administrative decentralization reforms. Chapter 1 reviews those that have been promoted over the past four decades and evaluates the impact of those that have been implemented in developing countries.

Chapter 1 highlights four important and current issues in administrative decentralization. The first relates to the administrative and financial capacity of governments to produce and provide public goods and services. Here, neo-classical economic theory and new management approaches urge that public sectors be downsized, governments reengineered, and the provision and production of many public goods be transferred to quasi-public or private institutions.[1] The second issue, which is related to the first, concerns the recommendations of experts that Non-Governmental Organizations (NGOs), civil associations, and other community organizations can and should take over responsibility for the provision and production of a wide range of collective goods and services.[2] The third issue relates to the problems of accountability that hamper the effective and efficient provision of public goods and services. This is a significant problem, for it is increasingly recognized that accountability is critical to good governance.[3] The fourth issue relates to sub-national conflict, democratization, and local-level involvement in development interventions. Increasingly, administrative decentralization reforms are being seen as central to devolving responsibilities to elected regionally-based local government units, thereby facilitating a transition to good governance, ensuring that the public sector responds to the needs and views of rural and urban people, and defusing tensions created by ethnic, religious, or regional movements arguing for secession.[4]

Chapter 2 reviews the major concepts and terms related to strategies of administrative decentralization. It clarifies the *forms* of decentralization: political, spatial, administrative, and market. It then elaborates the major *types* of administrative decentralization: deconcentration, devolution, and delegation. The chapter clarifies the boundaries of the study and the focus on *administrative decentralization*.

After reviewing frameworks of administrative decentralization, Chapter 2 elaborates the one that has dominated thinking since the early 1980s: the *Type:Function Framework*.[5] This is a descriptive framework that focuses on spatial and structural relationships. It has several limitations. First, it is based on definitions rather than on theoretical principles.[6] Second, the framework tends to generate an excessive number of guidelines that can easily overwhelm those promoting reform.[7] Third, the framework is centered on zero-sum authority relationships among central and local-level governmental units and institutions. It proposes decentralization as a solution because it is an obverse solution (the opposite or so it is thought, to centralization) and fails to recognize that the administrative decentralization of any public sector task requires a partnership among central and non-central government units and agencies, as well as with private institutions and organizations carrying out functional roles relative to the task.[8] The framework fails to give specific attention to the roles that must be performed at the center if administratively decentralized tasks are to be effectively, efficiently, and accountably performed. Finally, the framework focuses on end-state structures rather than on transition processes. Critical questions are neglected related to the environment of reform, namely political commitment, administrative and financial capacity, and task specificity.[9]

A theoretical breakthrough beyond the limitations of the Type:Function Framework is needed if governments are to implement effective administrative decentralization. Towards this end, Chapter 3 reviews recent efforts to respond to political pressures to redefine the public sector to make it more accountable, effective, and efficient. These are found in the literature on organizations, public choice, fiscal federalism, and public finance, and are focused on four development issues: economic growth, financial limits of the state, spatial concentration of development, and bureaucratic reform.

Based on the review and analysis of existing approaches to decentralization, Chapter 4 presents a new framework: the *Administrative Design Framework*. This framework is inclusive, and sets decentralization in a broader context of administrative design. The framework does not view administrative designs as zero-sum. This is important because the administrative reform strategies in most countries involve a complex mix of centralization and decentralization. The defining feature of this new framework, however, is that it goes beyond the spatial and structural aspects of administrative decentralization by examining the concentration of organizational and institutional roles that implement public sector tasks. The central thesis underlying the framework is that providing tasks through a pluralist rather than a monopolist administrative design promotes accountability, which is the most important administrative principle. Breaking the *monopoly of central design* and expanding the options of administrative design are two of the major challenges facing decision-makers in developing countries.

At its core, the framework identifies and elaborates three administrative design strategies governments can pursue singly or in combination:

- *Institutional Monopoly* (centralization)
- *Distributed Institutional Monopoly* (deconcentration and devolution)
- *Institutional Pluralism* (delegation)

Organizational roles are the key to understanding the differences among these three strategies. Institutional Monopoly exists when roles are concentrated at the spatial center in one organization or institution. It is commonly termed "centralization." Distributed Institutional Monopoly exists where roles are distributed spatially but are either concentrated in one organization or institution operating at one or more hierarchical levels (deconcentration) or are shared among a hierarchy of organizations and institutions, each of which holds a monopoly over the assigned roles (devolution). Institutional Pluralism exists when roles are shared by two or more organizations or institutions, which can be at the spatial center, distributed, or a combination of both.

The Administrative Design Framework provides development professionals with a powerful methodology for assessing and designing accountable administrative systems as well as for understanding an important emerging trend in administration. How and why this is the case is the central focus of Chapter 4.

Chapter 5 demonstrates the application of the Administrative Design Framework in regard to the efforts of three governments to design and implement administrative decentralization reforms.

The first case study in Chapter 5 is Kenya's District Focus Strategy, which is based on a centrally controlled strategy of Distributed Institutional Monopoly. This case illustrates the path many countries take as they seek to maintain central control while promoting the provision of public sector tasks through deconcentration reforms. It also demonstrates that the kind of administrative design strategy pursued by Kenya is likely to continue to be as frustrating and unproductive as Chapter 1 and 2's analysis suggests. The case illustrates how politicians can frame Distributed Institutional Monopoly as a strategy that promotes local authority and participation while using it, in fact, to strengthen central control.

The second case study may be the most significant. It focuses on a different kind of Distributed Institutional Monopoly, one that a number of countries are likely to turn to as they adopt devolutionary strategies to deal with demands by ethnic, religious, and nationalist movements for greater regional autonomy. This is the trend toward federalism, confederation, or substantial unitary devolution. It is likely that extreme forms of devolution may eventually be attempted in such countries as Somalia, the former Yugoslavia, Sudan, Sri Lanka, and Iraq. Yet there is little evidence on the extent to which these kinds of Distributive Institutional Monopoly are likely to work in weak states. For this reason, the second case reviews efforts by the Government of Ethiopia to establish a federal system comprised of ethnic-based states and districts administered by local-level governments holding substantially devolved responsibilities. As such, Ethiopia is an example of a future pattern of administrative decentralization that is likely to be considered by internally fragmented states.

The promise of Institutional Pluralism is illustrated in the chapter's third case study. Mexico's new and innovative 100 Cities Program seeks to strengthen selected urban governments so that they can decide upon and manage the development of their local economy. The case study illustrates how creative strategies of delegation help the Mexican government to ensure that specific public sector tasks related to the production and provision of urban-focused goods and services, and the roles associated with those tasks, are carried out. While Mexico excludes its largest cities from participation in the Program because it is designed to serve second and third tiers of urban areas, the case study is relevant for governments struggling to better serve urban areas.

The use of all three cases to illustrate the Administrative Design Framework is risky. Kenya is at a crossroads. Political dynamics raise questions as to how long the Government can continue to dominate urban and rural areas through its strategy of tightly controlled deconcentration and limited devolution. The Ethiopian experiment is instructive, even though some experts think it unlikely that successful devolution will occur because the center is weak and major ethnic-based parties are withholding legitimacy from the government's new constitution and elections. Finally, Mexico, too, faces severe constraints to the full transfer of administrative and fiscal resources to local governments. The 100 Cities Program appears to have strong supporters, but the effects of the 1994–95 financial crisis may delay its implementation. Previous (though unrelated) reforms and innovative programs have proved to be more rhetoric than reality, and many questions remain about whether there is sufficient capacity and political will to move forward this administrative redesign in the targeted cities.

Chapter 6 concludes by offering general guidelines for applying the Administrative Design Framework, particularly in regard to Institutional Pluralism. The guidelines relate to the mobilization of leadership support, the importance of legal frameworks, the careful specification of functional roles required to carry out decentralized tasks, the specification and sequencing of those roles, and the importance of building partnerships and linkages among a range of institutions and organizations carrying out functional roles. The last section of the chapter reviews what remains to be learned about the strategies for introducing Institutional Pluralism.

Despite the emphasis in Chapters 3–6 on Institutional Pluralism, and the assertion that it is a strategy that can assist a number of developing countries to address major public sector administrative reforms, the study seeks to avoid advocating any one administrative design strategy or type of administrative decentralization. As such, the study attempts to avoid normative bias toward either centralization or decentralization. Further, it rejects the arguments of naive proponents of administrative and political decentralization that extreme devolution and delegation coupled with substantial political empowerment at the grassroots is the only solution to the difficulties of producing and providing collective goods and services on an efficient, effective, and equitable basis.

The decision to avoid such biases is a product of several important lessons learned during the 1980s, which are reviewed in the study. One of the most important of these is that in certain task environments, the conditions are such that administrative decentralization strategies are likely to be less efficient, effective, or equitable than centralized strategies. The other is that even in task environments where administratively decentralized interventions make sense, strong central governments are required to ensure their success.

INTRODUCTION
NOTES

1. For example: David Osborne and Ted Gaebler, *Reinventing Government: How the Entrepreneurial Spirit is Transforming the Public Sector* (New York: Plume Press, 1993); Richard E. Foglesong and Joel D. Wolfe, *The Politics of Economic Adjustment: Pluralism, Corporatism, and Privatization* (New York: Greenwood Press, 1989); John J. Dilulio, Jr., ed., *Deregulating the Public Service: Can Government Be Improved?* (Washington, D.C.: The Brookings Institution, 1994); Michael Barzelay, *Breaking Through Bureaucracy: A New Vision for Managing in Government* (Berkeley: University of California Press, 1994); John Nellis, Sunita Kikeri, and Mary Shirley, *Privatization: The Lessons of Experience* (Washington, D.C.: The World Bank, 1992).
2. For example: K. Wellard and J. G. Copestake, *Non-Governmental Organizations and the State in Africa* (London: Routledge, 1993); M. Edwards and D. Hulme, *Making a Difference: NGOs and Development in a Changing World* (London: Earthscan, 1992).
3. The importance of accountability comes from such classic studies as: Richard A. Musgrave, *The Theory of Public Finance* (New York: McGraw-Hill, 1959).
4. For example: Samuel P. Huntington, "The Clash of Civilizations?" *Foreign Affairs*, LXXII, 3 (1993), pp. 22–49; Gidon Gottlieb, "Nations Without States," *Foreign Affairs*, LXXIII, 3 (1994), pp. 100–12; I. William Zartman, ed., *Collapsed States: the Disintegration and Restoration of Legitimate Authority* (Boulder: Lynne Rienner Publishers, 1994).
5. The principal studies generating this Framework are: Shabbir G. Cheema and Dennis A. Rondinelli, eds., *Decentralization and Development: Policy Implementation in Developing Counties* (Beverly Hills: Sage Publications, 1983); Dennis A. Rondinelli, John R. Nellis, and Shabbir G. Cheema, *Decentralization in Developing Countries: A Review of Recent Experience* (Washington, D.C.: The World Bank, Staff Working Paper No. 581, 1984); Jerry M. Silverman, *Public Sector Decentralization: Economic Policy and Sector Investment Programs* (Washington, D.C.: The World Bank, African Technical Department, Technical Paper No. 188, 1992).
6. This point is well made by James S. Wunsch: "The lack of a 'theory' to explain when, how, and why to decentralize has been important ... [in explaining why decentralization efforts are] generalized, superficial, and not surprisingly, largely ineffective." "Sustaining Third World Infrastructure Investments: Decentralization and Alternative Strategies," *Public Administration and Development*, XI, 1 (1991), p. 15.
7. The most advanced statement of the Type:Function Framework is presented in a World Bank monograph: Silverman, *Public Sector Decentralization*. This study's guidelines are lengthy and complex, even though they are narrowly focused on financial functions related to administrative delegation of public sector tasks to private firms.

8. Such points are well made by Herbert H. Werlin in his: "Elasticity of Control: An Analysis of Decentralization," *Journal of Comparative Administration*, II, 2 (1970), pp. 185–209; "Linking Decentralization and Centralization: A Critique of the New Development Administration," *Public Administration and Development*, XII, 3 (1992), pp. 223–35.
9. For example, the critiques of: Joel Samoff, "Decentralization: The Politics of Intervention," *Development and Change*, XXI, 3 (1990), pp. 513–30; D. Slater, "Territorial Power and the Peripheral State," *Development and Change*, XX, 3 (1989), pp. 501–31.

The Evolution of Decentralization Concepts

> ... more and more governments see decentralization as a way forward,
> as a desirable policy. On the other hand, the implementation of that
> policy has mostly failed to live up to expectations.
>
> Malcolm Wallis, "Local Government and Development," p. 128.

FOR MORE THAN FOUR DECADES, optimistic colonial powers, newly independent countries, and Western aid agencies have sought to assist the governments of late developing countries to formulate, adopt, and implement decentralization reforms and programs. This long period is marked by at least three phases of attention, each of which emphasized different but cumulative objectives. In the early 1960s proponents of decentralization focused on using the intervention to assist colonies in beginning a transition to independence, achieving political equity, and responding to rising demand for public goods and services. A few countries pursued federal solutions and considered decentralization strategies in regard to state-central relations and intrastate governance. But most newly independent countries considered decentralization within the unitary state model, for none of the colonial powers had federal or confederal systems.

The second phase in decentralization occurred from the mid-1970s to the early 1980s. Aid agencies urged governments of both long independent and newly emerging countries to introduce decentralization reforms and programs in order to promote development objectives, such as improved management and sustainability of funded programs and projects, equitable distribution of economic growth, and facilitation of grassroots participation in development processes. Again, their advice was largely tailored for unitary states, even though some large countries, such as India, Mexico, and Nigeria, had federal systems with constitutionally devolved power to state or regional governments.

Finally, since the mid-1980s, aid agencies have used structural adjustment conditionalities to pressure governments to adopt administrative decentralization reforms and programs. In part, this is being done to promote the emergence of civil societies, to support the growth of democratic institutions, and to respond to ethnic, religious, or nationalist demands for regional self-government and greater autonomy.[1] But it is being done primarily to facilitate more efficient and effective production and provision of public goods and services and to establish market-oriented economies in which public sector tasks can be privatized

During the years covered by these three phases, extensive attention was given by government officials, aid agency professionals, and academics to debates over the advantages and disadvantages of centralized versus decentralized approaches to carrying out public tasks. Discussion related to this debate took place in four areas: tasks of central government, forms of decentralization, types of decentralization, and guidelines to design administrative decentralization. First, considerable thought was given to the tasks central governments can and should perform in the development process. Here attention focused on what economic, social, and security tasks related to the production and provision of collective goods and services should be provided by states, how such goods and services can best be administered and financed, and what strategies might be followed by states that are weakened by limited administrative and financial capacity. Second, careful assessment was given to the advantages and disadvantages of four *forms* of decentralization: political, spatial, administrative, and market. The focus was largely on the capacity of central unitary or federal governments to maintain national unity and promote equitable economic growth while simultaneously increasing democratic participation in development processes and providing goods and services to rural and urban citizens more efficiently and equitably. Third, of these four forms of decentralization, most of the attention was given to elaborating the major *types* of administrative decentralization. Among those that are most clearly identified and elaborated are: deconcentration, devolution, and delegation. Fourth, a number of implicit and explicit guidelines were generated to assist those designing and implementing particular types of administrative decentralization. To date, progress in specifying such guidelines has been limited.

The considerable progress that has been made in building the knowledge base just described has had costs. First, an extremely large body of literature has emerged on the topic of decentralization, one that is marked by extensive theoretical, analytical, prescriptive, and geographical scope. Second, this literature is complex, inconsistent, and conflicting. As a result, it is extremely difficult for government decision-makers to draw upon its findings, insights, and recommendations.

Given the renewed interest in administrative decentralization as a way of dealing with a host of problems currently faced by the governments of many developing countries, the time has come for a new consolidating study, one that not only clears out the underbrush and clarifies decentralization concepts and strategies, but one that offers an improved framework for assisting government decision-makers seeking to design and implement administrative decentralization interventions. Such is the objective of this book.

In addressing these topics, this book confines its attention to administrative design issues applicable to developing countries. It does not cover such topics as: (1) advantages and disadvantages of decentralization in Western countries, such as the United States and Great Britain;[2] (2) debates over decentralized and centralized planning in the Newly Independent States of Eastern Europe and the former Soviet Union;[3] (3) theoretical discussions about decentralization as a technical organizational strategy;[4] or (4) decentralization as a type of voluntary organizational approach to community development.[5] To attempt to include these additional topics in this study would make it unmanageable.

Most of the research on administration in developing countries carried out during the 1960s focused on describing the patterns of governmental structures that were emerging. These studies made some attempt to formulate ways of classifying key characteristics. In order to ensure efficient, effective, and equitable supply of collective goods and services, they also sought to specify the size of area that should be covered under each type of decentralization.[6] In addition, during this period a number of academic and professional studies began to focus on such topics as central-local relationships and the advantages or disadvantages of different types of administrative decentralization for the legal, managerial, financial, inter-organizational, and resource roles required to effectively support decentralization interventions.[7] Finally, initial specification of guidelines on when and how to deconcentrate or devolve administrative authority began in the early 1960s through funding provided by the United Nations.[8]

By the late 1970s, studies emerged that identified and distinguished four different *forms* of decentralization: *political, spatial, administrative, and market*. Further, particular efforts were made to specify and elaborate the *types* of administrative decentralization, which were generally agreed to be *deconcentration, devolution, and delegation*. Much of the writing on these forms and types focused on analyzing their strengths and weaknesses and seeking to generate guidelines for promoting more effective design and implementation of decentralization interventions. These resulted in comparative public administration studies[9] and aid agency handbooks for staff.[10]

Further, research supported by aid agency professionals frustrated by the difficulties of implementing projects and programs targeted at the rural poor made strong arguments about the benefits that would result from strengthening local-level institutions through devolution and promoting popular participation in development processes.[11] This research influenced aid agencies and led them to put increased pressure on countries receiving their assistance to: (1) promote processes of democratic decentralization; (2) administratively devolve specified governmental responsibilities to local-level governmental units; (3) establish independent Project Implementation Units staffed by officers seconded from line ministries; and, in some cases, (4) delegate some project and program responsibilities to participatory-based NGOs. Most typically, such pressures were reinforced by conditions placed on receiving foreign aid.[12]

As a result, a number of governments experimented with a mix of decentralization strategies. The objectives of national leaders who introduced them were varied. Some used the innovation to strengthen control while seeking to gain some of the advantages of national unity and developmental efficiencies that decentralization proponents claimed would emerge from lower-level production and provision of public goods and services. This was most often done through administrative deconcentration dressed up in rhetoric that incorrectly implied local empowerment through devolution and delegation.[13] Others experimented with more devolution interventions and participatory strategies, largely to satisfy aid agencies, which were providing an ever larger percentage of the capital budgets of their country, or, in some cases, to satisfy opposition parties or local pressure groups that were pressing for more grassroots participation in governance and development processes.[14]

By the early 1980s, a number of aid agencies had carried out evaluations of efforts to promote administrative decentralization strategies.[15] These, in conjunction with deductive logic, led to the publication of several overarching sets of recommendations.[16] The case studies found that most interventions had not been successful, although it may be that this finding was the result of "negative social science." But most of those responsible for pessimistic conclusions argued that decentralization strategies should not be abandoned. Rather, they urged that future efforts be based on a more realistic view of administrative decentralization's potential and limitations in given political and bureaucratic environments.[17]

In addition, the USAID-funded Berkeley Decentralization Project, which ran from 1979 to 1982, expanded understanding of the organizational requirements for carrying out administrative decentralization, namely: leadership, commitment, effective linkages, resource mobilization capacity and technical skills, problem solving and conflict resolution capacities, adaptability, and some incorporation of community participation.[18] These deeper organizational and comparative administration insights are important and will be drawn upon in Chapter 2 and 3's formulation of a new framework for designing and implementing decentralization reforms and programs.

The progress that was made in the 1970s and early 1980s in understanding administrative decentralization was consolidated in two influential publications.[19] These were funded by aid agencies seeking to both learn from experience and to be more realistic about the introduction of decentralization strategies. From these studies a framework emerged which has gradually become the de facto model for most academics and professionals working on issues of administrative decentralization. For the purposes of clarity and exposition, in this book the stature of this framework has been made quite visible by labeling it the Type:Function Framework. It will be discussed at length in the second half of this chapter.

Concerns in the early 1990s about central administrative capacity, fiscal constraints, and limited accountability at all levels of government provided the basis for a third phase of government and aid agency interest in administrative decentralization strategies based on delegation to the private sector firms and organizations. Additional pressures came from professionals using 1970s arguments to urge decentralization reforms to facilitate such objectives as improved government effectiveness in the delivery of goods and services, the promotion of revenue collection, and popular participation. Participation was pushed as much for its potential to make the public sector more accountable as for its relationship to democratization.

Currently, major aid agencies are beginning to argue that there are important links between democracy and civic pluralism, political and administrative decentralization, and public sector reform. Specifically, administrative decentralization supported by increasing local participation is seen as one aspect of a strategy for ending the inefficient and ineffective heritage of statist-based command economies while downsizing bloated, costly, and ineffective public sectors. It is also seen as key to the emergence of responsive local government leaders and more effective service to local clients. For these reasons, a growing number of aid agencies are involved in studying these linkages.[20] Most notably, USAID has made democracy and administrative decentralization one of its major aid objectives,[21] the World Bank is increasingly focusing on the relationship between democracy, civic associations, and economic growth,[22] and the European Community and its member states are experimenting with projects related to the relationship between democracy, participation, decentralization, and development.[23]

It is not uncommon to find in the emerging studies arguments that political and administrative decentralization, coupled with increased local-level participation, can lead to increased public sector efficiency and accountability in the production and provision of goods and services.[24] Some reports identify specific types of interventions, ranging from local planning groups, citizen advisory groups, and town meetings to local ombudsmen and quality commissions.[25] At present there is little evidence on the relationship among decentralization, participation, and accountability. But there is no question that a good deal of government and aid agency effort at the turn of the century and beyond is going to be given to the problems of public sector accountability. This is why the new framework presented in Chapter 3 gives substantial attention to the relationship between administrative decentralization and accountability, albeit through strategies less dependent on democracy and participation.

By the mid-1990s a new problem attracted Western governments and aid agencies to strategies of administrative decentralization: sub-national ethnic or religious conflict. Such conflict threatens peace and stability within countries and beyond their borders; it also is a major cause of human rights abuses. The emergence of such problems and the rise of human rights abuses has accelerated since the break up of the Soviet Union and the end of the Cold War. This trend is reinforced by persuasive arguments that in the latter half of the twentieth century the world has been moving from nation-state-based ideological conflict to cultural conflict.[26] It is also reinforced by assertions of some analysts that the late 1990s and the next century will be marked by anarchy as:

. . . nations break up under the tidal flow of refugees from environmental and social disaster, wars are fought over scarce resources, especially water, and war itself becomes continuous with crime, as armed bands of stateless marauders clash with the private security forces of the elites.[27]

Further, a growing number of specialists are discussing concepts such as "states-plus-nations" and "historical homelands," the basis of which requires a rethinking of the potential of decentralization strategies to help address these emerging threats to the legal and territorial basis of established states.[28]

Clearly, the message emerging from events in countries as diverse as Chad, Iraq, the former Yugoslavia, Rwanda, Burundi, Indonesia, Sudan, Sri Lanka, Somalia, and Iraq is that their governments need to consider decentralization strategies that might assist in holding together fragmented groups within their borders. Looking at such strategies has led to increased attention to administrative decentralization interventions, particularly federalism and confederalism. Currently, efforts to constitutionally establish devolved regions along ethnic lines are being attempted in Ethiopia and efforts to build a new nation marked by ethnic diversity are being attempted by South Africa.[29] However, there is little evidence on the extent to which these strategies might work. A recent United Nations Development Program (UNDP) workshop concluded that strong national identity was a major prerequisite to successful decentralization.[30] Currently, this appears to be the case in South Africa but not in Ethiopia.[31]

Another important issue that is giving rise to increased attention to administrative decentralization is the question of "patterns of financing and government accountability." It is highly likely that during the late 1990s and beyond, many local urban governments are going to be increasingly unable to provide basic services for rapidly growing populations. A rising number of studies testify to this.[32] The Latin American experience suggests that the financing of decentralization requires considerable attention. The central finding of a United Nations workshop, held in Bolivia in 1993, was that a great deal of attention needs to be given to reevaluating the idea of "fiscal federalism," where each level of government is an autonomous fiscal entity.[33] In addition, the workshop called attention to the question of how to support non-central provision of public tasks without increasing the national budget deficit.[34] Clearly, a framework is needed that helps government decision-makers and aid agency professionals find ways to ensure that public tasks are adequately funded.

Closely related to the financing issue is the current movement toward free market economies, largely promoted through the strategy of structural adjustment.[35] An extensive literature argues for coupling removal of central controls over the market with delegation or contracting of government responsibilities for goods and services to either lower-level governmental units or to market surrogates. For example, strong arguments in support of financial decentralization and privatization of government tasks were made by the World Bank in 1984 and 1988. To some extent, this neoclassical economic argument is reinforced by growing skepticism about the capacity of central government bureaucracies to effectively promote equitable economic development. As a result, Western aid agencies also argue for substantial public sector reform, including downsizing the civil service, administrative delegation, or contracting of public tasks to quasi-public institutions and private sector firms.[36]

Since the early 1980s there has been an increasing call by aid agencies and populist forces for governments to transfer some tasks to NGOs, particularly those operating at the grassroots level.[37] These calls are especially strong in Sub-Saharan Africa, where many governments lack the leadership, civil service personnel, and budgetary resources to carry out public tasks on an equitable, nationwide basis.[38] Some supporters calling for delegation to NGOs argue that village or barrio-level committees can out perform governments because they function on a participatory, democratic basis. Critics, however, note that recent evidence suggests it is naive to overestimate the potential of NGOs to take on responsibilities where the government has been unsuccessful. Further, they argue that much more needs to be learned about the interaction between these organizations and governments.[39] In the meantime, it is likely that during the second half of the 1990s pressures will continue to be placed on governments to allow either *de facto* or *de jure* administrative delegation of their tasks to NGOs.

The 1990s are also marked by growing support for the argument that decentralization can help ensure human development, particularly in more remote or previously neglected areas of a country. Development experts increasingly define "human development" in terms of the expansion of citizens' capacities to lead long and healthy lives, acquire knowledge, and enjoy a decent standard of living, all of which require expanded access to basic social services and expansion of income-earning opportunities. The question here is whether devolution or delegation can contribute to reaching such objectives. Recent studies on this question, particularly those on the health, education, and employment supporting infrastructure sectors, reveal mixed results. The general conclusion, as summarized in a recent United Nations study, is that: (1) if adequate authority and a firm financial base are devolved to local-level governmental units, there is likely to be more investment in the basic priority areas of human development, such as education, health, water systems, and related community amenities; but (2) the allocation of such authority and financial resources is so difficult to achieve that devolution strategies for human development may not be as progressive as some proponents believe.[40]

Growing attention is now being given to the question of how to downsize the public sector while making it more efficient and accountable. Discussion takes two directions. The first looks to assigning central government employees to local-level governmental units and charging them with carrying out their public sector tasks at that level. This approach is not considered very promising by many governments, for this kind of downsizing simply transfers central problems to the periphery.[41] It does not resolve the core problem. The second views downsizing as the delegation of public sector tasks to private firms and NGOs. This is leading to renewed attention to what is increasingly labeled "reengineering of government."[42] This widely promoted reform focuses on breaking the "monopoly of central design" and expanding the array of lower-level public institutions, quasi-public institutions, and private institutions that carry out public sector tasks. Here, the objective is to introduce administrative reforms aimed at downsizing the state through the transfer or divestment of the responsibility for the production and provision of many public goods and services to this emerging institutional array. The new framework proposed in Chapter 3 calls this approach to administrative decentralization "institutional pluralism."

Finally, it should be noted that inadequate research and analytical attention have been given to anticipating constraints to these emerging strategies for promoting democracy, reducing conflict, meeting increasing demands for goods and services with declining resources, and reengineering government. Clearly, some aspects of these reforms are not likely to be in the interests of powerful politicians and public servants. The resistance of entrenched political and bureaucratic elites can be generated by many concerns, ranging from ideology and distrust of the market to fears of political instability, increased demands for participation in government decisions, loss of access to rents, or decline in civil service appointment as a source of patronage. On the other hand, increased delegation and divestment may help insecure governments survive by assisting to balance the budget and ensure delivery of essential public goods and services. So too, delegation and divestment can be attractive because they do increase opportunities for corrupt access to rent despite arguments that administrative decentralization promotes greater transparency in governance. However, to date, there are few studies on how administrative decentralization reforms seeking these new objectives of the 1990s can be made more credible to those responsible for adopting and implementing them. Among the major research tasks of the 1990s is to better understand potential political, bureaucratic, and market resistance to these emerging administrative decentralization reforms and to formulate strategies for dealing with them.

In sum, into the next century, governments of developing countries will more seriously consider administrative decentralization strategies and reforms. This is because of growing arguments from aid agencies that decentralization can help such governments address problems caused by the increased complexity of governance, difficulty of building financially and administratively effective central bureaucracies, growing demands for local empowerment, intractable problems of economic development, cyclical recessions, national debt, rising budget deficits, and growing local-level demands for goods and services. New studies related to these topics are currently emerging. Chapters 3–6 of this book are, to a large extent, part of this new effort.

To develop a framework which is relevant to the current and emerging needs of developing countries, it is first imperative to clear out the conceptual and terminological underbrush. Such is the task of Chapter 2.

Second, it is essential to formulate a new framework that encourages those designing and implementing decentralization reforms to focus on critical tasks, issues, problems, and opportunities. This is the objective of Chapters 3–6.

CHAPTER 1
NOTES

1. Civil society is the sphere of social interaction between the household and the state, which is manifest in norms of community cooperation, structures of voluntary association, and networks of public communication. See, for example: Michael Bratton, "Civil Society and Political Transition in Africa," *Institute for Development Research*, XI, 6 (1994). The range of relationships between the state and civil society are reviewed well in: John W. Harbeson, Donald Rothchild, and Naiomi Chazan, eds., *Civil Society and the State in Africa* (Boulder: Lynne Rienner, 1994). In regard to democratization and development, see, for example: John Healey and Mark Robinson, *Democracy, Governance and Economic Policy: Sub-Saharan Africa in Comparative Perspective* (London: Overseas Development Institute, 1994); Robert Pinkney, *Democracy in the Third World* (Boulder: Lynne Rienner Publishers, 1994).

2. For example: A. L. Dwight, "A Concept of Decentralization," *Public Administration and Review*, XXX, 1 (1970), pp. 60–63; D.K. Hart, "Theories of Government Related to Decentralization and Citizen Participation," *Public Administration Review*, XXXII (1972), pp. 603–21; E. Nordlinger and J. Hardy, "Urban Decentralization: An Evaluation of Four Models," *Public Policy*, XX, Special Issue, (1972), pp. 359–96.

3. For example: Nicholas R. Lang, "The Dialectics of Decentralization: Economic Reform and Regional Inequality in Yugoslavia," *World Politics*, XXVII, 3 (1975), pp. 309–35.

4. For example: Manfred Kochem and Karl Deutsch, *Decentralization: Sketches toward a Rational Theory* (Cambridge: Oelgeschlager, Gunn and Hain, 1980).

5. For example: L. Ralston, J. Anderson and E. Colson, *Voluntary Efforts in Decentralized Management: Opportunities and Constraints in Rural Development* (Berkeley: University of California, Institute of International Studies, 1983).

6. For example: United Nations, *Decentralization for National and Local Development* (New York: United Nations, Working Group on the Administrative Aspects of Decentralization for National Development, 1962), especially pp. 90–132.

7. Most notably: Ursula K. Hicks, *Development from Below: Local Government and Finance in Developing Countries of the Commonwealth* (Oxford: Clarendon Press, 1961); United Nations, *Decentralization for National and Local Development*; A. A. Maass, ed., *Area and Power: A Theory of Local Government* (Glencoe: Free Press, 1959); H. Maddock, *Democracy, Decentralization and Development* (Bombay: Asia Publishing House, 1963); H. F. Alderfer, *Local*

Government in Developing Countries (New York: McGraw-Hill, 1964); J.W. Fesler, "Approaches to the Understanding of Decentralization," *Journal of Politics*, XXVII, (1965), pp. 536–66.

8. For example: United Nations, *Decentralization for National and Local Development*; Maddock, *Democracy, Decentralization and Development*.

9. For example: Brian C. Smith, *Field Administration: An Aspect of Decentralization* (London: Routledge and Kegan Paul, 1967); S. Humes and E. Martin, *The Structure of Local Government: A Comparative Survey of 81 Countries* (The Hague: International Union of Local Authorities, 1969); James J. Heaphy, ed., *Spatial Dimensions of Development Administration* (Durham, N.C.: Duke University Press, 1971); Jack Goldsmith, ed., *Comparative Local Politics: A Systems-Functions Approach* (Boston: Holbrook Press, Inc., 1973).

10. For example: United Nations, *Decentralization for National and Local Development*.

11. USAID, in particular, stimulated research on the role decentralization and popular participation could play in facilitating more efficient and effective rural development projects. Typical of the numerous studies produced in the 1970s and early 1980s are: John M. Cohen and Norman T. Uphoff, *Rural Development Participation: Concepts and Measures for Project Design, Implementation and Evaluation* (Ithaca: Rural Development Committee, Cornell University, 1977); David D. Gow, *Local Organizations and Rural Development: A Comparative Reappraisal*, 2 vols. (Washington, D.C.: Development Alternatives, Inc., 1979); David K. Leonard and Dale Rogers Marshall, eds., *Institutions of Rural Development for the Poor: Decentralization and Organizational Linkages* (Berkeley: Institute of International Studies, University of California, 1982); Ralston, Anderson and Colson, *Voluntary Efforts in Decentralized Management*.

12. See the discussion of "decentralization within centralization" in: R. Apthorpe and D. Conyers, "Decentralization, Decentralization and Popular Participation: Towards a Framework for Analysis," *Development and Peace*, III, 2 (1982), pp. 47–59.

13. For example the USAID project supporting the "Awraja Self-Government Reform" introduced by Haile Selassie in the last year of his reign: John M. Cohen and Peter H. Koehn, *Ethiopian Provincial and Municipal Government: Imperial Patterns and Postrevolutionary Changes* (East Lansing: Michigan State University, African Studies Center, 1980), pp. 58–65.

14. Diana Conyers, "Decentralization for Regional Development: A Comparative Study of Tanzania, Zambia, and Papua New Guinea," *Public Administration and Development*, I, 2 (1981), pp. 107–20.

15. Examples of studies commissioned by USAID include:

W. J. Sherwin, *Decentralization for Development: The Concept and its Application in Ghana and Tanzania* (Washington, D.C.: Development Studies Program, 1977); T. Walker, ed., *Building Capacity for Decentralization in Egypt: The Pilot Project and Beyond* (Washington, D.C., Development Alternatives, Inc., 1981); Jerry VanSant, *Supporting Capacity-Building in the Indonesian Provincial Development Program* (Washington, D.C.: Development Alternatives, Inc., 1981).

16. For example: United Nations Centre for Regional Development, *Implementing Decentralization Policies and Programmes* (Nagoya: UNCRD, 1981); United Nations Educational, Scientific and Cultural Organization, *The Decentralization of Educational Administration*, (Bangkok, Regional Office, UNESCO, 1982); E. P. Wolfers et al., *Decentralization: Options and Issues: A Manual for Policy Makers* (London: Commonwealth Secretariat, 1982); K. J. Davey, *Financing Regional Government* (Chichester: John Wiley and Sons, 1983); United States Agency for International Development, *Local Organizations in Development* (Washington, D.C.: USAID, 1984).

17. Collections of these studies have had the most influence. See, for example: United Nations, *Local Government Reform: Analysis of Experience in Selected Countries* (New York: United Nations, 1975); D.C. Rowat, ed., *International Handbook on Local Government Reorganization: Contemporary Developments* (Westport: Greenwood Press, 1980).

18. Leonard and Marshall, *Institutions of Rural Development for the Poor*, pp. 1–39, 193–226; David K. Leonard, "Interorganizational Linkages for Decentralizing Rural Development: Overcoming Administrative Weaknesses," in Shabbir G. Cheema and Dennis A. Rondinelli, eds., *Decentralization and Development: Policy Implementation in Developing Counties*, (Beverly Hills: Sage Publications, 1983), pp. 271–91.

19. Cheema and Rondinelli, *Decentralization and Development*; Rondinelli, Nellis, and Cheema, *Decentralization in Developing Countries*.

20. The questions being researched today are: (1) Is administrative decentralization an intervention that can assist central government to respond to the problems of sub-national ethnicity or religious differences? (2) Given the current trend of weak governments to centralize their power, is it still possible to pursue administrative decentralization strategies that have advantageous results? (3) What is the relationship between decentralization and the emergency of a democratic civil society? (4) Is it possible to have effective administrative decentralization in the absence of democratization and economic development? (5) Is decentralization a way to promote government efficiency, effectiveness, and responsiveness, given the fact that most Third World countries lack the personnel and financial resources to carry out effectively assigned functions? (6) Can increased participation and democratization lead to increased public sector accountability?

(7) What is the relationship between decentralization and the implementation of market oriented economic strategies and policies? (8) How far are most political leaders willing to go in pursuing new forms of divestiture oriented decentralization? And (9) Do aid agencies promote decentralization largely to support economic behavior that leads to contribute to national developmental objectives and to strengthen the implementation of their projects and programs?

21. United States Agency for International Development, *Democracy and Governance* (Washington, D.C.: Directorate for Policy, USAID, November 1991). See, for example, USAID's centrally funded project on Decentralization Finance and Management, carried out by Associates in Rural Development, Inc., and recently commissioned studies such as: Gary Hansen, Heather McHugh and Malcolm Young, "Civil Society and Democratic Development" (Paper Prepared by Center for Development Information and Evaluation, USAID, Washington, D.C., February 1994); United States Agency for International Development, "USAID, Civil Society and Development" (Center for Development Information and Evaluation, USAID, Washington, D.C., December 1992). See also: United States General Accounting Office, "Promoting Democracy: Foreign Affairs and Defence Agencies Funds and Activities: 1991–93" (GAO, Washington, D.C., January 1994).

22. For example: World Bank, *Governance and Development* (Washington, D.C.: The World Bank, April 1992); World Bank, "Planned Study Series on the Relationship between NGOs and the State" (Interoffice memorandum, September 14, 1992); Hans Binswanger, "Decentralization, Fiscal Systems, and Rural Development" (Request for Research Support Budget Funding, World Bank Agricultural Division, March 18, 1994); World Bank, *Assessing AID: What Works, What Doesn't, and Why* (Oxford University Press, 1998).

23. For example, the European Centre for Development Policy Management's occasional papers on democratization, decentralization, and development, such as its: *Democratization in Sub-Saharan Africa: The Search for Institutional Renewal* (Maastricht: ECDPM Occasional Paper, 1992).

24. Theoretical work on accountability comes from such classic studies as: Musgrave, *The Theory of Public Finance*; Wallace E. Oates, *Fiscal Federalism* (New York: Harcourt Brace and Jovanovich, Inc., 1972); Wallace E. Oates, *Studies in Fiscal Federalism* (Brookfield, Vermont: Edward Elgar, 1991).

25. Arguments about participation and public sector accountability are drawn from literature from advanced developed countries. See, for example: Dawn Oliver, *Government in the United Kingdom: The Search for Accountability, Efficiency, and Citizenship* (Oxford: Oxford University Press, 1991); Martin Loughlin, *Administrative Accountability in Local Governments* (London: Joseph

Rowntree Foundation, 1992); Michael Fagence, *Citizen Participation in Planning* (Oxford: Pergamon Press, 1977).

26. Huntington, "The Clash of Civilizations?"

27. The influential opinions of one analyst are found in: Robert D. Kaplan, "The Coming Anarchy," *Atlantic Monthly* (February 1994), pp. 44–49, 52, 54, 58–64.

28. For example: Gottlieb, "Nations Without States"; Zartman, ed., *Collapsed States*; Forest D. Colburn, *The Vogue of Revolution in Poor Countries* (Princeton: Princeton University Press, 1994).

29. John M. Cohen, *Transition Toward Democracy and Governance in Post Mengistu Ethiopia* (Cambridge: Harvard Institute for International Development, Development Discussion Paper No. 493, June 1994), pp. 9–17. Initial analysis on the South African case is found in: Martin Linsky, "The Realities of Making Democracy in Southern Africa," *Boston Globe* (February 25, 1995).

30. United Nations Development Program, *Workshop on the Decentralization Process: Bern, Switzerland 20–23 April 1993* (Report on Workshop, New York, Management Development Program, 1993), p. 2.

31. Linsky, "The Realities of Making Democracy in South Africa"; Bertrand Le Gendre, "Ethiopia Takes a Step Towards Democracy," *Manchester Guardian* (August 16, 1995).

32. For example: William Dillinger, *Decentralization and Its Implications for Urban Service Delivery* (Washington, D.C.: World Bank, Urban Management Program Paper No. 6, May 1994).

33. Naciones Unidas, *Descentralizacion en America Latina: Santa Cruz de la Sierra, Bolivia 3–5 Noviembre 1993* (Nueva York: Departamento de Apoyo al Desarrollo y de Servicios de Gestion, 1994), p. 101.

34. *Ibid.*, p. 135.

35. Recent trends on these relationships are well reviewed in: John Healey and Mark Robinson, *Democracy, Governance and Economic Policy*; Foglesong and Wolfe, *The Politics of Economic Adjustment*.

36. A good summary of arguments and literature in this area, relative to decentralization, is found in: Robert Klitgaard, *Adjusting to Reality: Beyond "State Versus Market" in Economic Development* (San Francisco: International Center for Economic Growth, 1991), pp. 139–67.

37. Edwards and Hulme, *Making a Difference*.

38. For example: A. Fowler, *NGOs in Africa: Achieving Comparative Advantage in Relief and Micro-Development* (Institute of Development Studies, Discussion Paper No. 249, University of Sussex, 1988); Wellard and Copestake, *Non-Governmental Organizations and the State in Africa*; P. Landell-Mills,

"Governance, Cultural Change and Empowerment," *Journal of Modern African Studies*, XXX, 4 (1992), pp. 543–67.

39. For example, a study carried out at the village level in The Gambia found that while NGOs increasingly provide collective goods and services at the field level, they are not in themselves a solution to administrative decentralization. Daniel Davis, David Hulme, and Philip Woodhouse, "Decentralization by Default: Local Governance and the View from the Village in The Gambia," *Public Administration and Development*, XIV, 3 (1994), pp. 253–69.

40. See both the text and bibliography in Jeni Klugman, *Decentralization: A Survey of Literature from a Human Development Perspective* (New York: United Nations, Human Development Report Office, Occasional Paper No. 13, July 1994). This study provides particularly useful insights and case studies related to questions of efficiency, resource availability, participation, and equity in regard to decentralized health, education, water and sanitation, and housing tasks.

41. For example, Venezuela devolved health and educational responsibilities for more than 300,000 public servants funded at a cost of $2.8 million to financially troubled local-level governmental units. There are technical difficulties as well. In 1993 Brazil faced difficult problems while transferring some 47 percent of its budget to administratively weak regional and local authorities. *Ibid.*, p. 65, 87.

42. The concept was largely invented for dealing with problems of the United States government but is increasingly being applied to the problems of late developing countries. Osborne and Gaebler, *Reinventing Government*.

Current Frameworks of Decentralization

The lack of a 'theory' to explain when, how, and why to decentralize has been important ... (in explaining why decentralization efforts are) generalized, superficial, and, not surprisingly, largely ineffective.

James S. Wunsch,
"Sustaining Third World Infrastructure Investments," p. 15.

THIS CHAPTER PRESENTS the current frameworks used to analyze decentralization and to make recommendations for administrative reform.

1. LEGAL MODELS AND PUBLIC SECTOR TASKS

Constitutional law specialists typically avoid the conceptual problem by confining decentralization to legal models of governmental relations. Their principal distinction is between unitary systems and "non–centralized" federal-based systems, such as federations, confederations, consociations, unions, leagues, and condominiums.[1] For such specialists, federal-based systems are, by definition, decentralized to at least one level, with each level having some constitutionally or legally specified sovereignty over identified public sector tasks in a well-defined territorial jurisdiction. Unitary systems need not be legally decentralized, but most are through a hierarchy of lower-level units that have specified geographical jurisdictions. In unitary systems, the center maintains ultimate sovereignty over public sector tasks decentralized to lower-level units.

Of the 116 late developing countries classified by the World Bank as having decentralized systems, 106 are generally considered unitary, though it must be recognized that some major countries on this list are federal, such as Brazil, India, Malaysia, Mexico, Nigeria, Pakistan, and Venezuela.[2] With the collapse of Senegambia, there are currently no confederations in the developing world.[3] It should be noted, however, that some scholars find federal principles in a number of states, leading to the claim that a substantial number of late developing countries can be classified as federal.[4]

The legal approach then elaborates the two systems by their subnational levels, most typically described as state (confederal or federal) or region/province/department (unitary). Many different titles are given under the two systems to the local and sub-local units: districts, sub-districts, locations, sub-locations, municipalities, towns, wards, hamlets, and so on. The careless use of these labels generates much confusion in the literature on decentralization. Beyond this, the literature based on constitutional law distinctions is complex and involuted. The legal approach has particular difficulty dealing with the increasing number of situations in which the production and provision of public goods and services are delegated to quasi-public or private organizations. Clearly, elaborating the concept of decentralization merely on the basis of a constitutional law model is inadequate.

More useful classifications result when the analyst moves from a simple description of "legal characteristics" to an elaboration of the distribution of governmental power. This approach has deep historical roots in political theory.[5] Since the turn of the century, the concepts of "centralization" and "decentralization" have had increasingly well-established meanings. The former refers to the concentration of administrative power in the hands of a few, and the latter refers to processes through which that power is spread to a larger range of actors and organizations.[6] It is to an elaboration of the forms and types of concentration and sharing of power that this chapter now turns.

2. FORMS OF DECENTRALIZATION

Several different ways of classifying forms of decentralization have been promoted over the past few decades by those making a clear distinction between centralization and decentralization. What is common to these classification systems is that they recognize the need for a definition that is grounded on more than legal concerns. Six approaches to identifying forms of decentralization can be identified in the literature.

The first approach classifies forms on the basis of historical origins. A focus on history has led one specialist to assert there were four basic decentralization patterns: French, English, Soviet, and Traditional.[7] Today, this system of classification is viewed as both too simplistic and analytically weak.

A second approach distinguishes the forms of decentralization by hierarchy and function.[8] According to this view "territorial decentralization" refers to the transfer of centrally produced and provided public goods and services to local-level units in the government hierarchy of jurisdictions. "Functional decentralization" refers to the transfer of such central responsibilities to either parastatals under the control of the government or to units outside governmental control, such as NGOs or private firms. The problem with this classification is that it is too rudimentary to facilitate clarity over design and implementation issues, such as legal basis, structural organization, division of powers, or administrative, financial, and budgetary procedures. Further, the emphasis on territory highlights a major misconception about decentralization: that decentralization is largely focused on the process of transferring public sector tasks out of the capital city and into the hinterland. This spatial view of decentralization is naive and obscures the complexities of the concept. The notion of functional decentralization is more useful, for it underlies the current view, discussed shortly, that administrative decentralization is the expansion of the array of institutions and organizations carrying out collective public sector tasks and that this can happen in the capital city as well as in other urban areas and the countryside.

The third approach identifies forms of decentralization by the problem being addressed and the values of the investigators. This approach is best illustrated by the work of the Berkeley Decentralization Project, which was primarily interested in finding ways of bringing more effective development programs and projects to the rural poor. Given this problem, the Berkeley group identified eight forms of decentralization: (1) devolution, (2) functional devolution, (3) interest organization, (4) prefectoral deconcentration, (5) ministerial deconcentration, (6) delegation to autonomous agencies, (7) philanthropy, and (8) marketization.[9] In formulating this set of forms, most of the Berkeley group was not interested in addressing larger generic issues related to the concept of "decentralization."[10] Rather, it focused on studying the linkages of the center and the periphery on a sector-by-sector basis. In studying these linkages it formulated an idiosyncratic set of forms that ensured, on a project-by-project basis, that development interventions addressed the vulnerability of the rural poor and the threat to them by central and local elites seeking their own interests. The problem with this approach to addressing particular weaknesses of over-centralization is that it is eclectic and dependent on the administrative, political, economic, and value rationale of the analysts addressing the problem.[11]

A fourth approach focuses on patterns of administrative structures and functions that are responsible for the production and provision of collective goods and services. One of the first of these was presented in 1962 by the United Nations. It identified four forms of decentralization: local-level governmental systems, partnership systems, dual systems, and integrated administrative systems.[12] The problem with this approach is that it is not analytical enough to deal with the increasing diversity of structural and functional designs that marks the last three decades.

A fifth approach takes a narrow definition of decentralization, typically based on the experience of a single country. Under this view, transferring responsibility, manpower, and resources to central government field offices is not decentralization. Rather, decentralization only occurs when local-level government units are: (1) established by legislation, typically in the form of a charter that gives the unit legal personality, defined as established by law with the right to sue and be sued; (2) located within clearly demarcated jurisdictional boundaries within which there is a sense of community, consciousness, and solidarity; (3) governed by locally elected officials and representatives; (4) authorized to make and enforce local ordinances related to devolved public sector tasks; (5) authorized to collect legally earmarked taxes and revenues; and (6) empowered to manage their budget, expenditure, and accounting systems, and to hire their own employees, including those responsible for security.[13]

The sixth approach, and the one used in Chapters 3–6 of this book, classifies *forms* of decentralization on the basis of objectives: political, spatial, market, and administrative. Then it gives specific attention to three *types* of administrative decentralization: deconcentration, devolution, and delegation.[14]

"Political" decentralization typically identifies the transfer of decision-making power to citizens or their elected representatives. "Spatial" decentralization is a term used by regional planners involved in formulating policies and programs that aim at reducing excessive urban concentration in a few large cities by promoting regional growth poles that have potential to become centers of manufacturing and agricultural marketing. "Market" decentralization focuses on creating conditions that allow goods and services to be produced and provided by market mechanisms sensitive to the revealed preferences of individuals. This form of decentralization has become more prevalent due to recent trends toward economic liberalization, privatization, and the demise of command economies. Under it, public goods and services are produced and provided by small and large firms, community groups, cooperatives, private voluntary associations, and NGOs. Finally, "administrative" decentralization is focused on the hierarchical and functional distribution of powers and functions between central and non-central governmental units. This form of decentralization is key to this book, though Chapters 3 and 4 set it in a broader analytical context than is currently the case.

It is important to note that forms affect each other. Decisions made about spatial decentralization will affect the efforts of governments to pursue a particular type of administrative decentralization. Or, for example, a decision by a government to pursue a particular type of administrative decentralization will affect patterns of political forms of decentralization. That is, in the real world, as opposed to the analytical world, it is difficult to fully separate these four forms of decentralization. The analytical forms are useful in that they define a perspective but they are difficult to separate out because each affects the others in subtle ways that vary greatly from among task environments.

The failure to distinguish forms is one of the major reasons for the confusion in the literature on decentralization. Clarity is difficult to achieve even when efforts are made to distinguish forms. Several examples might help clarify the complexities found in relationships among forms. First, effective spatial decentralization generally leads to a demand for administrative decentralization. As urban and rural areas grow and diversify it becomes more difficult and costly for central government to control, produce, and provide collective goods and services throughout a country. This is a very common problem, since most regions in late developing countries have populations and demands equal to those that characterized their entire country at independence. Second, market decentralization tends to emerge in situations where central delivery is difficult to achieve and sustain, and private firms or non-public organizations can deliver them better. Third, while administrative decentralization is not the same as political decentralization, it can, under enlightened central leadership, lead to democratization and greater political participation. But for this to happen, central leadership must be committed to tolerating the emergence of civil society, devolving decision-making authority, and promoting the democratic election of lower-level officials and councils.

3. TYPES OF ADMINISTRATIVE DECENTRALIZATION

Most of the literature on decentralization is focused on only one of these four forms of decentralization: *administrative*. The most widely accepted conceptual definition of this type is based primarily on public policy, administration, and finance concerns.[15] It defines "administrative decentralization" as:

... the transfer of responsibility for planning, management, and the raising and allocation of resources from the central government and its agencies to field units of government agencies, subordinate units or levels of government, semi-autonomous public authorities or corporations, area-wide regional or functional authorities, or non-governmental private or voluntary organizations.[16]

There are three types of administrative decentralization: *deconcentration, devolution, and delegation.*[17]

i. Deconcentration

"Deconcentration" is the transfer of authority over specified decision-making, financial, and management functions by administrative means to different levels under the jurisdictional authority of the central government. At its core, it involves ministries retaining power over key tasks at the center while transferring the implementation roles related to such tasks to staff located in ministerial field offices. Typically, deconcentrated activities are those that the center, for political reasons, believes only it can or should control or closely supervise but that require field-level implementation in order to be effectively carried out. The weakest rationale for such deconcentration is to transfer work loads downward. Stronger reasons relate to the ability of field personnel to allow the center to be more responsive to the needs and interests of citizens.

In the literature on administrative decentralization, the French prefect system is often given as an example of deconcentration, largely because it is based on the Napoleonic adoption of military hierarchy and control to administrative governance. It is typically argued that central governments prefer this approach to reaching lower administrative levels because it gives them greater political, administrative, and technical control. It is also argued that aid agencies prefer it because this provides a delivery system that lowers the cost of project and program implementation since they do not have to invest in building or providing such structures. Generally, with such a transfer of tasks comes authority allowing field staff some latitude to plan, make routine decisions, and adjust the implementation of central directives to local conditions within guidelines set by the central government.

As noted, most developing countries are marked by a deconcentrated hierarchy of generalist field officers serving directly under the central government and charged with overseeing the processes of governance in the jurisdictions in which they serve. These individuals typically play a political role and represent state authority. They are responsible for law and order. In some countries they are further charged with promoting coordination of government activities and overseeing devolved local-level governmental units, if any, in their jurisdiction. The principal function this hierarchy serves is to have a public servant in each jurisdiction who represents the state itself, thereby promoting political stability in insecure and fragmented societies.[18]

The degree of central coordination, effectiveness, and efficiency largely depends on who holds technical authority over deconcentrated field staff of the line ministries. Under the "integrated prefectoral" model, the executive officer or council president has both administrative and technical supervision of central ministry field agents.[19] Under the "unintegrated prefectoral" model, these representatives have administrative powers but not technical supervisory powers over field agents.[20] This is because line ministries typically resist transferring technical jurisdiction over their field agents. Such resistance is particularly common with ministries charged with the provision of infrastructure, agriculture, health, education, safety, and welfare tasks.[21] Such ministries insist on retaining authority to ensure that their policies, standards, and programs are correctly implemented — governors, commissioners, district officers, or council presidents notwithstanding. The weight of evidence is clear: unintegrated prefectoral systems are very difficult to manage and generate major administrative inefficiencies. This is significant because most countries pursuing deconcentration can be classified under the category of unintegrated prefectoral model.

ii. Devolution

"Devolution" occurs when authority is transferred by central governments to autonomous local-level governmental units holding corporate status granted under state legislation. Some specialists refer to devolution as "local government," creating terminological problems. Devolution does not define *ex ante* constitutionally divided powers within a federal or confederal system of government, where states, as is the case of India, hold legally defined and shared powers. However, it is possible to talk about devolution when a unitary system decides to adopt a new constitution based on states, regions, or municipalities holding extensive devolved powers. This latter situation is likely to become more common given the pressures on governments to deal with rising demands for sub-national rights by ethnic and religious groups in particular geographic areas. Given these demands, it is likely that some troubled unitary states will consider specifying ethnically or religiously defined local-level governmental units and devolving to them substantial decision-making and administrative authority. This appears to be the case in Ethiopia, where Haile Selassie's deconcentrated system of local-level administration is being recast as a federation based on regional units holding considerable governmental powers and responsibilities.[22] Finally, the term devolution does apply to decisions by established units of a federal or confederal system to devolve authority to lower-level governmental units, as is the case with Brazil and Nigeria, which grant substantially autonomous municipalities or other local-level governmental units specified, chartered powers.[23]

Devolution by developing countries that are unitary is not common, largely because many developing countries are characterized by weak governments wary of losing political or administrative control to local-level governmental units. Even in developing countries that are federal or confederal, significant limitations are placed on the devolution of power and responsibility. But devolution is quite common in regard to the administration and governance of urban areas. Indeed, it is not uncommon to find devolved municipal or township units functioning in a unitary state pursuing a deconcentrated strategy of public sector administration.

That is, devolution is most commonly associated with chartered municipalities and townships operating within specified jurisdictional boundaries. Requirements for this type of administrative decentralization were used earlier to illustrate the sixth approach to defining the concept of decentralization, an approach that often and misleadingly defines devolution as "decentralization writ large."

Briefly, devolution requires that there be national legislation and supporting regulations that: (1) grant specific local-level units corporate status; (2) establish clear jurisdiction and functional boundaries for such units; (3) transfer defined powers to plan, make decisions, and manage specified public tasks to such units; (3) authorize such units to employ their own staff; (4) establish rules for the interaction of such units with other units of the governmental system of which they are a part; (5) permit such units to raise revenue from such specifically earmarked sources as property tax, commercial agricultural production tax assessments, license fees, public utility charges, or from grants and loans provided by the central ministries; and (6) authorize such units to establish and manage their own budgetary, accounting, and evaluation systems.[24]

These laws and regulations governing devolution are typically monitored and enforced by central administrative bodies, frequently through a ministry of local government or interior. Financial activities of devolved local-level units are also monitored and otherwise regulated by the ministry of finance. Challenges to actions by devolved units are typically handled through established court systems. Where effective, devolution can expand the opportunity for a wider range of public sector tasks to be better coordinated and more effectively carried out. The British local government system is typically given as an example of devolution.

An uncommon variant of devolution occurs when a particular local-level unit holding discretionary authority further devolves it to specific projects or firms. Devolution is also found in regard to specific units holding corporate status and carrying out public services and maintenance, most notably with regard to roads.[25]

iii. Delegation

"Delegation" refers to the transfer of government decision-making and administrative authority for clearly defined tasks to organizations or firms that are either under its indirect control or are independent. Most typically, delegation is done by the central government to semi-autonomous organizations not wholly controlled by the government but legally accountable to it. Examples of the types of organizations to which delegation is made include state-owned industrial or manufacturing enterprises, public utilities, housing and transport authorities, and urban or regional development corporations. In the early 1980s, it was not uncommon for a given government to have established and delegated authority to hundreds of such semi-autonomous organizations.[26] Since then, fully privatizing such organizations has been a major objective of aid agency structural adjustment conditions.[27]

Delegation has also been common with regard to special regional planning or area-specific development authorities and to complex development projects. Typically, these types of government-related institutions are involved in agricultural marketing, public utilities, energy, communications, port, and transport sectors. The diversity that marks this pattern of delegation is well illustrated by integrated rural development authorities, which were quite common in the 1970s. These projects were funded by aid agencies which, upon realizing the inter-governmental complexities affecting their investments, pushed governments to delegate powers to "enclave" project management units, or PMUs.[28]

If they have the legal authority, deconcentrated or devolved government units can delegate to private firms. Such delegation is usually undertaken when public sector units recognize that they have limitations that make it difficult for their staff to provide the required public goods and services. Examples of this pattern of public–private contract are numerous: in Sudan the field agents of the Ministry of Health contract with local-level firms to keep urban areas free of accumulated refuse; in Nepal town governments use private contractors to collect local taxes; and in Tunisia and Sri Lanka municipal markets are rented to private vendors who manage them for all merchants.[29]

These kinds of contractual arrangements are frequently made because government units lack sufficient managerial and technical capacity or equipment, such as skilled accountants, engineers, computers or specialized vehicles. It is generally expected that those holding delegated responsibilities cover their capital and recurrent costs through user charges or from aid agency or NGO grants. But in practice many such organizations and firms have not been well managed and their budget deficits and defaulted loan payments are often covered by central governments under guarantee agreements.

Delegation is not restricted to private firms. Development experts increasingly recommend delegation to such independent interest groups as professional associations, trade unions, community groups, cooperatives, private voluntary associations, NGOs, and women or youth clubs.[30] For example, in some countries professional associations are delegated responsibility to license, regulate, and supervise their members. Another common example is found in urban slums, where local dweller associations are delegated the tasks of implementing and managing sites-and-service housing schemes. The major condition for delegation to such a group is that they have an established organization managed by members as well as an administrative or technical capacity to effectively carry out the delegated responsibilities.

"Privatization," which is sometimes referred to as "public-private partnership" or "market decentralization," is a sub-type of delegation. It occurs when a government divests itself of responsibility for carrying out a given public sector task or providing a given service.[31] Arguments in support of privatizing government tasks are that non-public sector firms can provide goods and services more efficiently, effectively, and accountably because they are not hampered by bureaucratic politics and practices or burdened by complex administrative procedures relating to budgeting, disbursing, accounting, and auditing.[32] As a result, they are thought to be better capable of meeting targets and schedules. Finally, because under such arrangements users are charged for the contracted goods and services, such firms are under pressure to meet the requirements of users.

Some distinguish "deregulation" as a type of privatization. Deregulation is the removal of legal controls restricting private production or provision of goods and services formally held under a monopoly by the government or its delegate. By deregulating a government makes it possible for private firms and NGOs to serve the public, thereby helping to relieve the government of some financial and administrative burdens, reduce the size and presence of the public sector in the economy, and, hopefully, produce and provide better quality goods and services to the public. An example of deregulation is where a chartered municipality gives up its monopoly control over refuse collection and allows private firms to compete for the provision of that service.

In sum, this book argues there are only three types of administrative decentralization: deconcentration, devolution, and delegation.[33]

4. TASK PERFORMANCE FUNCTIONS

Given the increased complexity of administrative decentralization, it is essential to move beyond form and type if a framework is to be developed that can provide guidelines for decentralization. The principal approach that has emerged for doing this focuses on the *functions* that must be performed relative to a decentralized task.

The functional focus begins by distinguishing among the kinds of decisions that need to be made with regard to public sector tasks. The types of decisions that are typically required include: (1) the kinds of collective goods and services the public sector should ensure are produced and provided; (2) the financing of selected public goods and services; (3) the quality, quantity, location, and distribution of public goods and services; (4) the projects and programs through which such public goods and services should be produced and provided; (5) the regulation that should take place if the provision of public goods and services is devolved or delegated; and (6) the monitoring of the provision of public goods and services. These types of decisions need to be made by both central decision-makers selecting a type of administrative decentralization for particular goods and services and those in public or private institutions who the center makes responsible for their production and provision.

The focus on these kind of decisions during the late 1970s and early 1980s gradually led to a more systematic approach based on identifying the key management functions that must be performed by whatever central, non-central, or private sector institution or organization is charged with providing public goods and services. A focus on these kinds of functions lies at the heart of the currently dominant framework for analyzing administrative decentralization. This *de facto* framework is labeled here as: the *Type-Function Framework*. The origins of this analytical view were reviewed in Chapter 1. Support for it was consolidated during the 1980s. If any one study consolidates this framework, it is found in the study carried out by Jerry M. Silverman for the World Bank study.[34]

While focusing primarily on African problems, Silverman identifies five functions that have comparative utility and are central to the effective and efficient provision of public goods and services: (1) planning; (2) financial policy formulation and generation of revenue; (3) expenditure programming and management; (4) staffing; and (5) operations and maintenance. To this list, other studies generally add two additional functions: (6) project and program implementation; and (7) management information.[35] While complex, these functions have clear meanings in the literature on comparative public administration.[36]

5. MATRICES BASED ON TYPES AND TASK FUNCTIONS

The Type:Function Framework is summarized in Figure 1 (see next page).[37] This framework has substantial utility for analysis, design, and implementation purposes, largely because it is sensitive to both the types of administrative decentralization governments can consider and the central functions that are essential to the provision of public tasks by central, non-central, or private sector institutions and organizations. Also the framework can be used to look at the administrative decentralization of specific activities, sectoral activities, or large-scale government-wide activities.

Today, most analysts explicitly or implicitly use the Type:Function Framework for reviewing choices over strategies of administrative decentralization, describing the legal and institutional requirements for types relative to functions, or formulating guidelines for designing and implementing selected interventions.

The major criticism of the framework is ideological in nature. This critique charges that the framework is a pragmatic, official, Western aid agency view that is excessively grounded in neo-Liberal concerns about efficiencies and insensitive to equitable growth, democracy, social struggle, and state power.[38] While this critique was persuasively engaged by those central to elaboration of the framework,[39] the fact remains that the framework gives inadequate attention to politics, authority, accountability, and the diversity of actual task environments.[40]

A more pragmatic criticism centers on the fact that the matrix can generate so many general guidelines that it becomes very difficult to separate the wheat from the chaff. This point is well illustrated in the 1992 World Bank monograph cited earlier.[41] The guidelines filling the matrix in that study are narrowly focused on financial functions related to administrative delegation of public sector tasks to private firms. They are further tailored to the problems of administrative decentralization in Sub-Saharan Africa. Quite significantly, even with these qualifications on the matrix's scope, the Bank's guidelines are too numerous and complex to be summarized here.

Task Functions	TYPES OF ADMINISTRATIVE DECENTRALIZATION		
	Deconcentration	Devolution	Delegation
Planning			
Fiscal Policy and Revenue Generation			
Budgeting and Expenditure Management			
Staffing			
Program and Project Implementation			
Information Management			
Operations and Maintenance			

FIGURE 1: Standard Matrix-based Framework Comparing Types of Decentralization to Major Government Functions

Adapted from: Jerry M. Silverman, *Public Sector Decentralization: Economic Policy and Sector Investment Programs* (Washington, D.C.: The World Bank, African Technical Department, Technical Paper No. 188, 1992), pp. 62–67.

6. ALTERNATIVES TO THE TYPE:FUNCTION FRAMEWORK

Two current frameworks provide alternative ways of analyzing administrative decentralization. The first challenges core notions about the role of the state and introduces politics and social struggle into the analysis of decentralization, a role that critics charge is down-played or ignored in the writing of those who formulated the dominant framework.[42] This alternative framework is most often labeled "people centered development" or "New Development Administration." The second framework draws on neo-classical economic theories of rational choice. To a large extent, it also obscures political forces, concentrating instead on the role of individuals in demanding, producing, and providing collective goods and services. Both frameworks were formulated in the early 1980s. Neither has effectively challenged the Type:Function Framework's dominance or offered much programmatic guidance to governments, largely because they do not speak to the needs of comparative public administration specialists charged with the actual task of designing and implementing administrative decentralization interventions.

Building on emerging case studies of traditional associations and NGOs that suggest that they promote development more effectively than central or local-level governmental institutions, the New Development Administration school idealistically argues that over-centralization should be aggressively addressed by central governments and the foreign aid community and, wherever possible, initiatives should be introduced that concentrate on funding people-centered initiatives carried out by the private sector, NGOs, community-based organizations, and traditional associations.[43] Supporters of this view urge governments and aid agencies to promote minimal government, deregulation, delegation to traditional associations, popular participation, use of NGOs, and privatization.[44]

Proponents of the New Development Administration view are aware of the existence of studies that demonstrate that strong central support and improvement are critical to successful implementation of devolution or delegation reforms.[45] They also recognize that despite trends away from central planning and toward multiparty government,[46] decision-makers in many late developing countries, and particularly the personalized states of Africa,[47] are opposed to reforms that would transfer central powers and responsibilities to local-level units. Still, they are naive in failing to recognizing the difficulties of implementing devolution and delegation reforms.

It is useful to briefly review the issues that New Development Administration proponents neglect to consider. First, devolution and delegation are not always desirable ends, particularly in countries marked by wide inter-regional economic disparities and ethnic, religious, or nationalist cleavages. Second, certain political conditions need to exist before devolution or delegation can be promoted as an administrative strategy. The most discussed of these requirements are strong national unity, central-periphery consensus that administrative decentralization is appropriate, clarity of goals as to the type, direction, and purpose of decentralization reforms and programs, commitment of national leadership to these interventions, and potential for adequate manpower and financial resources in the non-central and private sector institutions and organizations to which tasks are decentralized. Third, for many governments, devolution and delegation strategies are: (1) difficult for their weak bureaucracies to effectively introduce, staff, and monitor; (2) fraught with political and legal difficulties related to allocation of financial authority, supervision of revenue, and expenditure practices; (3) sustainable to corruption by those receiving decentralized power and financial resources; (4) supportive of trends toward ethnic, religious, or nationalist autonomy or secession; and (5) subject to being captured by local elites, skewing benefits away from the poor majority. Clearly, the problem with the New Development Administration Framework is that it fails to recognize that effective decentralization requires strong political centers and pragmatic realism about the willingness and capacity of governments to relinquish central control and pursue dramatic delegation or devolution reforms.[48]

The second alternative framework comes out of the literature on public choice theory. This approach narrowly focuses on the provision of goods and services while eschewing consideration of public finance and public administration issues.[49] In essence, it defines administrative decentralization as a situation where public goods and services are produced and provided through market mechanisms responding to individual preferences. At the heart of the framework is a commitment to privatization and deregulation. The major assumptions underlying the approach are: (1) financially and administratively handicapped central governments are incapable of effectively and efficiently producing and providing goods and services to ever growing rural and urban populations; (2) there is increasing local-level demand for such goods and services; (3) local-level governmental units have limited capacity to provide such goods and services to increasingly complex urban and small town environments; and (4) market mechanisms are the only option left for producing and providing goods and services on a sustainable basis. The problems with this framework, however, is that the language in which its ideas are cast is too complex for most government decision-makers to understand, its rejection of government is too threatening to those government officials who do consider its arguments, and acknowledged experts in the field find it limited and unhelpful.[50] As a result, the framework is largely confined to debates between academics. Neither of these two alternative frameworks challenges the current dominance of the Type:Function Framework. This is because it is more applied and useful than its two competitors. This is also because it is neither naively populist or excessively analytical. Further, the Type:Function Framework speaks directly to government decision-makers, professionals, and practitioners in terms they understand, and is more realistic about the long-term location of political and administrative power in late developing countries. In addition, proponents of the Type:Function Framework have in recent writing incorporated some of the central ideas of the alternative frameworks, particularly those related to public choice theory, deregulation, and privatization.[51]

ISSUES NOT WELL ADDRESSED BY THE DOMINANT FRAMEWORK

It is increasingly clear that the Type:Function Framework, despite its widespread use, is inadequate for guiding those designing and implementing devolution and delegation interventions that serve governmental needs in the 1990s and the next decades. This section reviews these inadequacies.

1. Transition Strategies

The Type:Function Framework leads analysts to consider the types of administrative decentralization as end-states and to give inadequate attention to process. This is important because the decentralization of any public sector task involves a number of actors operating in conditions that are dynamic and constantly changing. This point was well made by the Berkeley Decentralization Project:

... decentralization must be seen as a process, not a condition, (so it is) futile, in policy terms, to compare states by the extent of decentralization or to rank them on a (single) continuum. What is at issue is a question of dimensionality... Hence we emphasize the verbs — to decentralize or to make decentralizing moves, or to introduce decentralizing policies, and not adjectives such as decentralized state or even a decentralized delivery system.[52]

35

To some extent, the neglect of process results from the fact that the framework is based on a typology. Most social science typologies are used to describe conditions and structures rather than processes and operations. Neglect of process also results from the framework's tendency to lead analysts to assume that when a given public sector task is transferred to a specific institution or organization, all of the functions related to the task go with it. That is, the framework gives inadequate attention to the fact that the some of the *roles* required to carry out a decentralized task can be performed at the center as well as at the local-level or in the private sector. Indeed, as argued in Chapter 4, some task-related roles must be performed at the center if efficiency, effectiveness, and accountability are to be achieved in the implementation of public sector tasks.

Because the Type:Function Framework does not break functions down into roles carried out by a range of actors, it tends to see the transfer of responsibility as inclusive and final. For example, chartered municipalities will be responsible for the provision of solid waste plants serving their jurisdiction. However, taking such an end-state view fails to recognize the gradualism that is essential to the long-term success of any administrative innovation or reform. The need for such gradualism has been increasingly recognized over the past decade, largely through the growing recognition of the distinction between process and blueprint models of administration.[53]

The types of administrative decentralization represent more than an end-state and should be seen as such. Decentralization interventions should increasingly draw upon an array of institutions and organizations that can carry out roles related to the public sector task being decentralized. As such, the process of organizing and revising this array over time requires a framework that focuses on *processes* as much as on the end-state, for the institutions and organizations performing such roles will change over time. Whatever type of administrative decentralization strategy is followed, it will be achieved through a long process that involves recombining governmental and non-governmental institutions and organizations in ways that carry out roles critical to efficiently, effectively, and accountably performing public sector tasks. That is, successful administrative decentralization should be based on an array of institutions and organizations performing task related roles. Because of changing political, economic, and social objectives, the patterns of this array should be dynamic and changing over time. From this perspective, the definition of the end-state is less meaningful for a government than the task of getting a process of administrative decentralization moving.

2. Political Commitment, Authority, and Accountability

An influential literature drawn from East Asia and Latin America has generated the impression that public sectors in late developing countries are comprised of strong and relatively autonomous governmental institutions that, when committed to reform and innovation, can impose their decisions on society. Because of the strength of the statist-generated image of "strong bureaucratic authoritarianism," an image that often does not hold up under research scrutiny,[54] the Type:Function Framework has not been particularly sensitive to distinctions or variations in the managerial, technical, and financial capacity of institutions and organizations to which public sector tasks can be deconcentrated, devolved, or delegated. As a result, those formulating guidelines based on the framework often fail to carefully distinguish between countries marked by limited political capacity to support decentralization initiatives and those marked by moderate to strong political capacities.

As noted in the above critique on the New Development Administration framework, it is well established in the literature that the introduction and sustainability of administrative decentralization interventions and reforms requires both committed central leaders and central institutional capacity to support these interventions and reforms. Political leaders of unstable states are generally reluctant to transfer their control and authority over public sector tasks to non-central or private sector institutions and organizations. The evidence suggests that at best such leaders and senior decision-makers will only give lip service to administrative decentralization and confine their efforts to deconcentration strategies that strengthen central penetration rather than build and draw upon local-level capacities.

Attempts to decentralize administration often run counter to the centralizing dynamics of modern organizations, so there may be an inherent contradiction for late developing countries that seek simultaneously to modernize and decentralize.[55] Further, governments have an "approach-avoidance" complex about decentralization. On the one hand, government leaders recognize its potential to resolve a variety of organizational and economic development problems. On the other hand, they are aware of its potential to threaten their control over the allocation of resources in society.[56] Finally, a concerned center may conclude that administrative decentralization is antithetical to the interests of the rural poor because it usually favors the local elite and can facilitate the extraction of local resources by line ministries.[57]

In sum, there is a need for centers to find ways to administratively decentralize while maintaining sufficient authority, accountability, and responsibility to enhance their capacity to ensure that administratively decentralized public sector tasks are carried out. Clarifying how to best divide authority and responsibility between the center and local-level units to ensure the accountability of this expanding array of institutions is very difficult to do. This problem has been recognized since the early 1980s.[58]

3. Levels of Administrative and Financial Capacity

Many late developing countries are characterized by weak public sector institutions that lack the personnel and financial resources required to implement their strategic and policy decisions.[59] As pressures build to devolve or delegate public sector tasks to non-central or private sector institutions and organizations, heroic assumptions are being made by some analysts using the Type:Function Framework about the personnel and financial capacity of non-central and private sector institutions and organizations.

There is a lack of public sector capacity in late developing countries:

> Weak administrative capacity limits central governments' ability to improve (goods and service) ... delivery in many developing countries, even if larger amounts of financial resources become available. Among the most serious administrative problems are ... weak planning and managerial capability at all levels of administration ... inefficient managerial and supervisory practices in the field, and severe shortages of trained personnel.[60]

While this point is recognized to some extent by the Type:Function Framework, it is not given sufficient attention. As a result, many specialists view the design and implementation of decentralization interventions as one of augmenting capacity rather than one of recombining capacities. Augmentation is clearly a problem for states with limited administrative and financial capacity.

Further, the evidence suggests that the more limited the capacity of a state's public sector to administer or finance public sector tasks, the fewer administrative decentralization options are open to it. Such states cannot solve the problem of producing and providing goods and services by transferring them to non-central institutions and organizations, largely because the probability is that if they did so, their administrative and financial capacities will be even lower. In such cases, it may be best for weak governments and/or governments with limited capacities to delegate tasks related to collective goods and services to the private or non-governmental sector and focus instead on providing the major macro functions required for stability and economic development, such as foreign affairs, fiscal and monetary policy, and infrastructure provision. However, in such situations it is likely that private sector institutions will also lack the managerial and financial capacity to carry out functions central to the provision of collective goods and services.

4. Coordination, Linkages, and Partnerships

The Type:Function Framework fails to give attention to the importance of institutional and organizational collaboration relative to administratively decentralized public sector tasks. This problem is addressed in Chapters 3 and 4, which argue that a major objective of deconcentration, devolution, and delegation should be to expand the array of central, non-central, and private sector institutions and organizations carrying out roles to execute public sector tasks. The expansion of this array creates a number of intra- and inter-institutional and organizational coordination and linkage problems that must be addressed as part of any decentralization strategy. The problems of coordination and linkages are well discussed in the comparative public administrative literature.[61] But for reasons related to the static nature of the Type:Function Framework, as well as the tendency to view administrative decentralization in spatial terms, institutional and organizational collaboration is briefly acknowledged but largely neglected as a major concern in manuals on administrative decentralization.[62]

Much of the literature on bureaucratic coordination and linkages related to administrative decentralization is focused on deconcentration.[63] As such, it is largely concerned with how line ministry headquarters staff relate to their field agents, how civil servants in one line ministry or agency interact with those in other government institutions, and how field agents interact with centrally controlled officials who are administratively in charge of local-level units in which they serve, such as governors, commissioners, or district officers.

Additional literature is focused on central government delegation to parastatals.[64] As noted earlier, this book is not focused on state-owned enterprises. Nevertheless, it should be noted that the dismal performance of many of these public enterprises has led to Western pressures to privatize them. While this slow process of divestment unfolds, there is also considerable pressure on governments to better monitor, evaluate, and audit these administratively decentralized parastatals. This means greater attention to inter-institutional linkages and coordination between the central ministries responsible for oversight of particular parastatals; the parastatals holding delegated administrative authority and responsibility; and the ministry of finance, whose budget often bears the brunt of mismanaged and inefficient parastatals. Administrative approaches for doing this, such as performance contracts[65] and updating the skills of public enterprise managers, are examples of the kinds of linkages that need to be better thought through in the administrative decentralization literature. Yet there is little on this issue in advice and guidelines generated by the Type:Function Framework.

There are some studies on administrative devolution to municipal authorities. But this literature rarely extends to the coordination or linkages required to facilitate the devolution of public sector tasks to non-central institutions. As a result, there are few case study-generated guidelines that can assist governments to strengthen such coordination. In part, this is due to the fact that insecure central governments distrust local elites and see municipal authorities as breeding grounds for future political candidates and opposition movements.

The literature gives even less attention to issues of coordination, linkage, and partnership in situations where central or non-central roles related to public sector tasks have been delegated to private sector organizations, such as firms and NGOs. If, as noted above, administrative strategies for facilitating late development through administrative decentralization requires redefining the public sector and expanding the array of such institutions and organizations carrying out roles related to specific tasks, it is imperative that any framework devote more attention to issues of coordination, linkages, and partnerships.

The current focus on local-level authorities, parastatals, private firms, and non-governmental institutions is leading to a great deal of thinking about how this institutional pluralism can be coordinated into service networks based on a diversity of political and economic organizations that co-produce and co-provide sets of collective goods and services and are allowed to compete and collaborate with each other. Such multi-organizational service networks are at the frontier of administrative decentralization. Because the boundaries between such institutions and organizations are unlikely to be clear, significant problems of coordination and linkage will emerge. The Type:Function Framework is not particularly helpful in addressing this problem.

5. Task-related Roles

The draftsmen of the Type:Function Framework recognized that some functional roles and responsibilities required to carry out decentralized public sector tasks probably had to remain in central hands. But they did not devote much attention to this possibility nor to the advantages of task-related role responsibilities being shared by a range of institutional and organizational role players. Hence, a major problem with the framework's focus on functions leads some analysts to conclude that the institution or organization to which a public task is administratively de-centralized is responsible for nearly all of the specified functions. That is, the framework can lead professionals who use it to focus on building up the capacity of institutions or organizations receiving responsibility to carry out nearly all of the functions related to the task. This tendency is reinforced by the anti-central focus of many professionals, which leads some designers and implementors of devolution and delegation reforms to try to avoid giving the center any functional responsibility. Finally, the effects of these biases blinds some decision-makers to one of the key principles of decentralization: a strong center playing supporting roles is critical.

TOWARD A NEW FRAMEWORK

Addressing the decentralization issues of the 1990s and beyond requires embedding established knowledge about the types and functions of administrative decentralization in a deeper context centered on strategies of administrative design.[66] Doing this has several effects. First, it allows for the formulation of a framework that recognizes that strategies for facilitating development requires that the public sector be redefined so that public institutions can leverage resources rather than simply control them. Second, it allows for addressing the five problems with the Type:Function Framework that were just presented. Third, it focuses more attention on such major considerations about design and implementation factors as: (1) the characteristics of the political and administrative environment; (2) the specificity of the public sector task to be decentralized; (3) the levels of efficiency, effectiveness, and accountability that are sought; (4) the actors and means essential to carry out roles related the task; and (5) the possible changes in actor, institutional, or organizational responsibilities that can and should take place as the decentralization initiative is executed and made sustainable. Fourth, it facilitates design considerations related to breaking the monopoly of centralized design by expanding the number of institutions and organizations involved in carrying out decentralized tasks, facilitating the capacity of the public sector to broker access to resources for such institutions and organizations, building partnerships between inherently unequal central and local-level institutions, paradoxically strengthening both the center and the periphery, and obtaining the commitment and flexibility of governmental leaders and senior decision-makers. It is to formulating a new framework based on these tasks that this study now turns.

CHAPTER 2
NOTES

1. Daniel J. Elazar, *Federal Systems of the World* (Essex: Longmans, 1991), p. xvi; Daniel J. Elazar, *Exploring Federalism* (Tuscaloosa: University of Alabama Press, 1987), pp. 34–64.

2. Jerry M. Silverman, *Public Sector Decentralization: Economic Policy and Sector Investment Programs*, pp. 68–70. Looking at a broader range of countries, Daniel J. Elazar lists 22 that are federations, confederations, unions, and regions with constitutional protection: *Federal Systems of the World*, pp. 395–97.

3. E. B. Richmond, "Senegambia and the Confederation: History, Expectations and Disillusions, *Journal of Third World Studies*, X, 3 (1993), pp. 172–94.

4. See, for example: Elazar, *Exploring Federalism*, pp. 33–64.

5. See A. A. Maass who notes: "Since the time of Aristotle political science has been concerned centrally with the distribution and division of governmental power." *Area and Power*, p. 9.

6. For example, see: Martin Landau and Eva Eagle, "On the Concept of Decentralization," paper prepared for the Managing Decentralization Project, Institute for International Studies, University of California, Berkeley; James W. Fesler, "Centralization and Decentralization," in *International Encyclopedia of the Social Sciences*, edited by David L. Sills (New York: Macmillian, 1968), pp. 370–79.

7. Harold F. Alderfer, *Local Government in Developing Countries*, pp. 1–16.

8. Diana Conyers, "Decentralization and Development: A Review of the Literature," *Public Administration and Development*, IV, 2 (1984), p. 187.

9. Leonard and Marshall, *Institutions of Rural Development for the Poor*, p. 30.

10. Two members of the group did give attention to conceptual issues: Landau and Eagle, "On the Concept of Decentralization."

11. The Berkeley project constructed a list that displays the diversity of such reasons and shows why different forms will be identified by different researchers following this approach. Administrative reasons: better responsiveness to local conditions; bureaucratic coordination and integration; innovation and adaptability; project maintenance; appropriateness to service-oriented tasks; and consumer participation and effective demand making. Political reasons: unity and stability; integration and support building; diminishing, strengthening or compromising with the control of local elites over local activities; and diminishing conflict at the center. Economic reasons: spatial distribution of economic activities; mobilization of local resources; and support for small and local activities. Value reasons:

participation; democracy; and self-reliance. Stephen Cohen, John Dykman, Erica Schoenberger, and Charles Downs, "A Framework for Policy Analysis" (Paper Prepared for Decentralization Project, University of California at Berkeley, Institute of International Studies, 1981), p. 39.

12. United Nations, *Decentralization for National and Local Development*, pp. 9–14.

13. This narrow view is best illustrated by: Mawhood, "Decentralization: the Concept and the Practice," in his edited book *Local Government in the Third World: The Experience of Tropical Africa* (Chichester: Wiley, 1983), p. 2. A more recent example is found in: Samuel Stephen Mushi, "Strengthening Local Government in Africa: Organizational and Structural Aspects," in *Seminar on Decentralization in African Countries: Banjul, Gambia 27–31 July 1992* (New York: United Nations Department of Economic and Social Development and African Association for Public Administration and Management, 1993), pp. 27–31.

14. Distinctions between these forms and types of decentralization are well made in: Dennis A. Rondinelli, *Decentralizing Urban Development Programs: A Framework for Analyzing Policy* (Washington, D.C., USAID, Office of Housing and Urban Programs, 1990), pp. 9–15.

15. The most commonly cited sources on the this approach are: Fesler, "Centralization and Decentralization," pp. 370–79; B. C. Smith, "The Measurement of Decentralization," *International Review of Administrative Sciences*, XLV (1979), 214–22, and his *Decentralization: The Territorial Dimension of the State* (London: George Allen & Unwin, 1985), pp. 1–17.

16. Dennis A. Rondinelli and John R. Nellis, "Assessing Decentralization Policies: A Case for Cautious Optimism," *Development Policy Review* IV, 1 (1986), p. 5.

17. On the distinction between "devolution," "deconcentration," and "delegation" see: Rondinelli, Nellis, and Cheema, *Decentralization in Developing Countries*, pp. 13–31. See also: Leonard and Marshall, *Institutions of Rural Development for the Poor*, pp. 27–37.

18. Philip Mawhood, "Decentralization and the Third World in the 1980s," *Planning Administration*, XIV, 1 (1987), pp. 10–22.

19. In integrated prefectoral systems, which closely resemble the French system, "... the prefect is part of the chain of command between headquarters and the field for all government services, whether they be administrative or technical. The prefect embodies the authority of all ministries as well as the government generally and is the main channel of communications between technical field officials and the capital." Smith, *Field Administration*, p. 45. One specialist adds: "The prefect is the hierarchical superior of the technical field directors in his province ... (and) is the sole channel of

communication between the functional departments in the capital and those in the field." Robert C. Fried, "Prefectoral Linkages of Nation and Locality," in Jack Goldsmith, ed., *Comparative Local Politics: A Systems-Functions Approach*, (Boston: Holbrook Press, Inc., 1973), pp. 236–37.

20. The unintegrated prefectoral system more closely resembles the Italian model. Fried points out that the unintegrated prefectoral system is costly for developing countries because it does not provide for "common housekeeping services," which is a serious drawback for a country where recurrent administrative expenditures consume an extremely high share of government revenues, in that every ministry field office has its own offices, motor vehicles, and so on. The unintegrated system, however, does permit somewhat greater flexibility and adaptability to unique geographical conditions. Fried, "Prefectoral Linkages of Nation and Locality," p. 239; Heaphey, *Spatial Dimensions of Development Administration*, pp. 28–29.

21. Rondinelli and others argue these are often "network-based services that require large investments in capital equipment, and that must be linked together in a system in order to operate effectively, those that have high political saliency or sensitivity, those from which an important group such as the poor or a minority would be excluded if they were provided privately, or those with strong implications for public health, safety or welfare." Dennis A. Rondinelli, James S. McCullough, and Ronald W. Johnson, "Analyzing Decentralization Policies in Developing Countries: A Political-Economy Framework," *Development and Change*, XX, 3/4 (1989), p. 75.

22. Compare: Cohen and Koehn, *Ethiopian Provincial and Municipal Government*; and Cohen, *Transition Toward Democracy and Governance in Post Mengistu Ethiopia*.

23. D. Olowu, "Local Government Innovation in Nigeria and Brazil, *Public Administration and Development*, II, 4 (1982), pp. 345–57; L. DeMello, "Local Government and National Development Strategies," *Planning and Administration*, IX, 2 (1982), pp. 96–112; A. Govoyega, "Local Government Reform in Nigeria," in Mawood, *Local Government in the Third World*, pp. 225–47.

24. For a review of these central controls relative to devolution see: Olowu, "Central-Local Government Relations," in Seminar on Decentralization in African Countries: Banjul, Gambia, 27–31 July 1992. New York: United Nations Department of Economic and Social Development and African Association for Public Administration and Management, 1993, pp. 53–76; F. Sherwood, "Devolution as a Problem of Organizational Strategy" in R. T. Daland, ed., *Comparative Urban Research* (Beverly Hills: Sage, 1969), pp. 60–87.

25. See for example: Harry Friedman, "Local Political Alternatives for De-centralized Development," in Cheema and Rondinelli, eds., *Decentralization and Development*, pp. 35–58; Philip Mawhood, ed., *Local Government in the Third World* (Chichester: John Wiley & Sons, 1983).

26. For example, in the early 1980s Mexico had 500, Brazil more than 400, Tanzania 400, Pakistan and India 200 each, and Sri Lanka 100 semiauto-nomous organizations. M. M. Shirley, *Managing State Owned Enterprises* (Washington, D.C.: World Bank, Working Paper No. 577, 1983).

27. For example: Sunita Kikeri, John Nellis, and Mary Shirley, *Privatization: The Lessons of Experience* (Washington, D.C.: The World Bank, 1992).

28. Among the best known of these is the East Pakistan Academy for Rural Development which oversaw the Comilla IRD project: Arthur F. Raper, *Rural Development in Action: The Comprehensive Experiment at Comilla, East Pakistan* (Ithaca: Cornell University Press, 1970); and the Chilalo Agricul-tural Development Unit which managed a large SIDA agricultural project in Ethiopia: John M. Cohen, *Integrated Rural Development: The Ethiopian Experience and the Debate* (Uppsala: Scandinavian Institute of African Studies, 1987). The problem with PMUs is that they are short-term delegation interventions that prove difficult to both administer and phase back into government when funding ends. For this reason the practice of inducing governments to delegate to PMUs has been curtailed by most aid agen-cies. See, for example: World Bank, *Handbook on Technical Assistance* (Washington, D.C.: Operations Policy Department, 1993), pp. 175–79; John D. Montgomery, "Decentralizing Integrated Rural Development Activities," in Cheema and Rondinelli, eds., *Decentralization and Develop-ment: Policy Implementation in Developing Countries* (Beverly Hills: Sage Publications, 1983).

29. J. S. McCullough, "Institutional Development for Local Authorities: Fi-nancial Management" (Consultant Report for Ministry of Local Government, Housing, and Construction, Colombo, 1984); H. P. Minis and S. S. Johnson, "Case Study of Financial Management Practices in Tunisia" (Report Prepared for Research Triangle Institute, 1982); M. Lewis and T. R. Miller, "Public-Private Partnership in African Urban Develop-ment" (Paper Prepared for USAID, Washington, D.C., 1986); S. J. Cointreau, "Environmental Management of Urban Solid Wastes in Developing Coun-tries: A Project Guide" (Paper Prepared for the World Bank, Washington, D.C., 1982).

30. For example: Norman T. Uphoff and Milton J. Esman, *Local Organization for Rural Development: Analysis of Asian Experience* (Ithaca: Cornell Univer-sity, Center for International Studies, 1974); Leonard and Marshall, *Institutions of Rural Development for the Poor*; Ralston, Anderson, and Colson,

Voluntary Efforts in Decentralized Management; Milton J. Esman and Norman T. Uphoff, *Local Organizations: Intermediaries in Rural Development* (Ithaca: Cornell University Press, 1984); Norman T. Uphoff, *Local Institutional Development: An Analytical Source-book with Cases* (West Hartford: Kumarian Press, 1986).

31. Privatization is described as a type in: Rondinelli, McCullough, and Johnson, "Analyzing Decentralization Policies in Developing Countries," pp. 72–74. In regard to specific examples of "privatization" see: James Ferris and Elizabeth Graddy, "Contracting Out: For What? With Whom?", *Public Administration Review,* XLVI, 4 (1986), pp. 332–44; Gabriel Roth, "Can Road Maintenance be Privatized?" (Paper prepared for Services Group, Arlington, 1987). Cynthia C. Cook, Henri L. Beenhakker and Richard E. Hartwig, *Institutional Considerations in Rural Roads Projects* (Washington, D.C.: The World Bank, Staff Working Paper No. 748, 1985).

32. Arguments in support of privatization are found in: Gabriel Roth, *The Private Provision of Public Services in Developing Countries* (New York: Oxford University Press, 1987). Theoretical support is found in: V. Ostrom, C. M. Tiebout, and R. Warren, "The Organization of Government in Metropolitan Areas: A Theoretical Inquiry," *American Political Science Review,* LV (1961), pp. 831–42; J. M. Buchanan and G. Tullock, *The Calculus of Consent* (Ann Arbor: University of Michigan Press, 1962); M. Olson, *The Logic of Collective Action* (Cambridge: Cambridge University Press, 1965); E. S. Savas, ed., *Alternatives for Delivering Public Services: Toward Improved Performance* (Boulder: Westview Press, 1977).

33. Rondinelli takes a different but consolidating position. In his most recent writing he asserts privatization–deregulation is a fourth type, which includes Silverman's principal agency. Rondinelli, *Decentralizing Urban Development Programs,* pp. 11–15.

34. Silverman, *Public Sector Decentralization,* pp. 25–40.

35. Different studies specify such functions or activities differently. For example, Norman Furness identifies eight types of activities and initiatives: industrial, regional planning, administrative, spatial, functional, political, legislative, and corporate. "The Practical Significance of Decentralization," *Journal of Politics,* XXXVI, 4 (1974), pp. 958–82.

36. They are elaborated in some detail in: *Ibid.,* pp. 25–40.

37. The matrix is laid out in: Silverman, *Public Sector Decentralization,* pp. 62–67.

38. D. Slater, "Territorial Power and the Peripheral State."

39. Dennis A. Rondinelli, "Decentralization, Territorial Power and the State: A Critical Response," *Development and Change,* XXI, 3 (1990), pp.

491–500.

40. Joel Samoff, "Decentralization."

41. Silverman, *Public Sector Decentralization.*

42. Most notably: Slater, "Territorial Power and the Peripheral State," pp. 501–31; Samoff, "Decentralization," pp. 513–30.

43. Representative of this literature are: Guy Gran, *Development by People: Citizen Construction of a Just World* (New York: Praeger, 1983); Esman and Uphoff, *Local Organizations: Intermediaries in Rural Development*; David C. Korten and Rudi Klauss, eds., *People Centered Development: Contributions Toward Theory and Planning Frameworks* (West Hartford: Kumarian Press, 1984); Milton J. Esman, "The Maturing of Development Administration," *Public Administration and Development* VIII, 2 (1984), pp. 125–39; James S. Wunsch and Dele Olowu, eds., *The Failure of the Centralized State: Institutions and Self-Governance in Africa* (Boulder: Westview Press, 1990); David C. Korten, *Getting to the 21st Century: Voluntary Action and the Global Agenda* (West Hartford: Kumarian Press, 1990).

44. Examples of arguments for delegation to the private sector are found in: Edwards and Hulme, *Making a Difference*; S. T. Bruyn and J. Meehan, eds., *Beyond the Market and the State: New Directions in Community Development* (Philadelphia: Temple University Press, 1987); and delegation to local and traditional associations: Esman and Uphoff, *Local Organizations*, L. Adamolekun, "Promoting African Decentralization," *Public Administration and Development*, XI, 3 (1991), pp. 285–92; Uphoff, *Local Institutional Development.*

45. A clear statement on this problem is found in: Herbert H. Werlin, "Elasticity of Control." Criticism of Werlin's view that New Development Administration cannot easily deal with centralization tendencies is found in: D. C. Korten, "The Community: Master or Client? A Reply," *Public Administration and Development*, IX, 5 (1989), pp. 569–75. Comparative analysis supporting Werlin is found in: Harry W. Blair, "Participation, Public Policy, Political Economy and Development in Rural Bangladesh 1958–85," *World Development*, XIII, 12 (1985), pp. 1231–47; David J. Kind, "Civil Service Policies in Indonesia: an Obstacle to Decentralization?" *Public Administration and Development*, VIII, 3 (1988), pp. 249–60; Henry Bienen, et al., "Decentralization in Nepal," *World Development*, XVIII, 1 (1990), pp. 61–75.

46. See: Samuel Huntington, *The Third Wave Democratization in the Late Twentieth Century* (Norman: University of Oklahoma Press, 1991).

47. For example: Robert H. Jackson and Carl G. Rosberg, *Personal Rule in Black Africa: Prince, Autocrat, Prophet, Tyrant* (Berkeley: University of California Press, 1982); Richard Sandbrook, *The Politics of Africa's Economic*

Stagnation (Cambridge: Cambridge University Press, 1985).

48. This point is well made in: Werlin, "Linking Decentralization and Centralization," pp. 223–35.

49. The roots of this literature are found in: Ostrom, Tiebout and Warren, "The Organization of Government in Metropolitan Areas;" Buchanan and Tullock, *The Calculus of Consent.* The application of this approach to development issues is illustrated by: C.S. Russell and N. K. Nicholson, eds., *Public Choice and Rural Development* (Washington, D.C.: Resources for the Future, 1981).

50. For a criticism of USAID's fascination with using public choice theory to assess decentralization during the 1980s, see: Rondinelli, McCullough, and Johnson, "Analyzing Decentralization Policies," pp. 73–93.

51. For example, public choice theory concerns have been adopted by Rondinelli and his colleagues: *Ibid.*, pp. 57–87.

52. Cohen, et al., "A Framework for Policy Analysis," p. 5.

53. This distinction was first elaborated in: Elliot Morss, et al., *Strategies for Small Farmer Development* (Boulder: Westview Press, 1976). It was expanded and popularized in: David C. Korten, "Community Organization and Rural Development: A Learning Process Approach," *Public Administration Review*, XL, 5 (1980), pp. 450–511. It has been extended, albeit weakly, to decentralization in: Dennis A. Rondinelli, *Development Projects as Policy Experiments: An Adaptive Approach to Development Administration* (New York: Methuen, 1983).

54. Among the major case studies that demonstrate that supposedly strong public sectors have serious managerial and financial incapacity are: Nora Hamilton, *The Limits of State Autonomy: Post-Revolutionary Mexico* (Princeton: Princeton University Press, 1982); Merilee S. Grindle, *Bureaucrats, Politicians, and Peasants in Mexico: A Case Study in Public Policy* (Berkeley: University of California Press, 1977); Francine R. Frankel, *India's Political Economy, 1947–1977: The Gradual Revolution* (Princeton: Princeton University Press, 1978).

55. Landau and Eagle, "On the Concept of Decentralization," p. 11.

56. Cohen, et al., "A Framework for Policy Analysis."

57. Ralston, Anderson, and Colson, *Voluntary Efforts in Decentralized Management*, p. 113.

58. Most notably by Conyers, "Decentralization: the Latest Fashion in Development Administration;" See also: Kochem and Deutsch, *Decentralization: Sketches Toward a Rational Theory*; Landau and Eagle, "On the Concept of Decentralization;" Cohen, et al., "A Framework."

59. This is the central argument in: Joel Migdal, "Strong States, Weak States:

Power and Accommodation," in Myron Weiner and Samuel P. Huntington, eds., *Understanding Political Development*, (Boston: Little, Brown and Co., 1987), pp. 391–434; and his *Strong States and Weak States: State-Society Relations and State Capabilities in the Third World* (Princeton: Princeton University Press, 1988).

60. Rondinelli, *Decentralizing Urban Development Programs*, p. 6.

61. A recent restatement of the literature on such coordination is found in: Esman, *Management Dimensions of Development* (West Hartford: Kumarian Press, 1991), pp. 74–135.

62. For example, Rondinelli notes a serious administrative problem in administrative decentralization is: "... difficulties in coordinating service delivery among national ministries and between central government agencies and local governments ..." *Decentralizing Urban Development Programmes*, p. 72.

63. K. Hanf and F. Scharpf, *Interorganizational Policy Making: Limits to Coordination and Central Control* (London: Sage, 1978); S. Davis and P. Lawrence, *Matrix* (Reading: Addison-Wesley, 1977); W. S. Wright, *Understanding Intergovernmental Relations* (North Scituate: Duxbury Press, 1978).

64. L. P. Jones and R. Moran, *Public Enterprise in Less Developed Countries* (Cambridge: Cambridge University Press, 1982); J. Heath, *Public Enterprise at the Crossroads* (London: Routledge, 1990).

65. John Nellis, *Contract Plans and Public Enterprise Performance* (Washington, D.C.: The World Bank, Discussion Paper No. 48, 1986).

66. For example: Jack H. Knott and Gary J. Miller, *Reforming Bureaucracy: The Politics of Institutional Choices* (Englewood Cliffs: Prentice-Hall, Inc., 1987); Gerald E. Caiden, *Administrative Reform Comes of Age* (Berlin: Walter de Gruyter, 1991); Frank R. Baumgartner and Bryan D. Jones, *Agendas and Instability in American Politics* (Chicago: University of Chicago Press, 1993); Merilee S. Grindle and John W. Thomas, *Public Choices and Policy Change: the Political Economy of Reform in Developing Countries* (Baltimore and London: The Johns Hopkins University Press, 1991).

Toward a New Theory
of Administrative Design

> It is not government's obligation to provide services but to see that
> they're provided.
>
> Mario Cuomo, Former Governor of New York State

TO DATE DEVELOPMENT professionals and academics have not formulated a theoretical framework that can pragmatically assist government
decision-makers in the design and implementation of administrative decentralization. This is the case despite four decades of effort and hundreds
of case studies of intervention experiences. To be sure, substantial progress
has been made in: (1) identifying and distinguishing the four *forms* of
decentralization; (2) defining and analyzing the three *types* of administrative decentralization; (3) specifying the major operational *tasks* central,
non-central, and private institutions and organizations need to carry out
the tasks they are responsible for; and (4) formulating matrices matching
types of administrative decentralization with functional objectives, result-
ing in the Type:Function Framework. This progress was reviewed in Chapter
2. However, as also pointed out in the last part of that chapter, a theoretical breakthrough beyond the structural and spatial limitations of the
Type:Function Framework is needed if governments and the aid agencies
that assist them are to more effectively address decentralization issues in
the 1990s and beyond.

Responding to political *pressures* to redefine the public sector, professionals and academics are currently making substantial progress in
identifying such alternatives. Much of their work is based on *principles*

found in the literature on organizations, public choice, fiscal federalism, and public finance, and largely focused on four *issues*: (1) economic growth; (2) financial incapacity of the state; (3) spatial concentration of development; and (4) bureaucratic reform.[1] The purpose of this chapter is to review these issues in order to outline the origins of the thinking that generates the framework proposed in Chapter 4.

REDEFINING THE PUBLIC SECTOR

Administrative strategies in the 1990s and beyond will of necessity be based on new definitions of the public sector and considerable rethinking about its role in producing and providing collective goods and services. In regard to decentralization, considerable progress has been made in rethinking the ways in which the state can ensure the execution of public sector tasks through increased devolution or delegation of the full range of task-related roles. This rethinking has led to the emergence of a new framework of administrative design that includes a mix of administrative strategies including centralization and decentralization. At the heart of this new approach are three approaches to administrative design: *Institutional Monopoly, Distributed Institutional Monopoly,* and *Institutional Pluralism.* Of these three types the most innovative is Institutional Pluralism.

1. Rethinking Economic Growth

In the late 1980s and early 1990s there was a reassessment of the process of economic development and the role of the state in that process.[2] Increasingly, tasks once considered to be the exclusive domain of the state are being privatized. This is because the "publicness" of tasks is consistently and creatively being redefined. The broader the range of tasks and the roles required to carry them out, the larger the array of private sector firms and organizations that can perform task-related roles or the tasks themselves.

The recent historical review of economic growth of the successful late developing countries, such as Asia's Tigers and Taiwan, suggests that the state's function is to provide infrastructure and promote human capital and financial markets. It is not to promote winners and losers in terms of preferential treatment of firms and organizations.[3] Maurice Scott argues that economic growth is caused by two factors: material investment and quality-adjusted employment, which includes investment in human capital.[4]

Scott's propositions on economic growth, which stress the importance of investment, highlight the need for the state to build competitive infrastructure rather than competitors and to promote human capital through health and education.

The state is viewed as a critical and essential partner in the development process. The state has to be as efficient as its country's firms. Public infrastructure is critical to an efficient market and firms will demand efficient operation of this infrastructure. An example of the demand for an efficient state is Singapore, which has the most modern and, arguably, efficient port in the world. For Singapore, its port is part of its comparative and competitive advantage.

2. Spatial Concentration of Development

In a persuasive address to a conference on decentralization, Columbia's Marino Henao argued that ". . . the geography of centralism is the geography of underdevelopment."[5] Using statistics on growth, he argued that by the end of the century the world's ten largest cities will all be in poor countries and their inhabitants will be poorly served by municipal authorities with inadequate administrative and fiscal capacities. Given the analysis in this study, it is unlikely that governments following either Institutional or Distributed Institutional Monopoly will be able to provide basic needs to burgeoning urban populations, much less support a productive infrastructure that can promote economic growth and social welfare. The crisis of centralized growth requires: (1) administratively decentralized development strategies that are more creative than currently can be formulated under the spatial and structural limitations of Distributed Institutional Monopoly strategies; and (2) Institutional Pluralism strategies that allow non-central and private sector institutions and firms to carry out task-related roles more accountably, effectively, and efficiently than governmental institutions holding monopolies over public sector tasks.

3. Financial Limitations of the State

Beyond the theories and recent experience of what the state should and should not do to promote growth, the primary factor driving the redefinition of the public sector most is the limited financial capacity of the state to provide public goods and services.[6] This is demonstrated by fiscal stress in the West, the virtual collapse of the public sector in the

Newly Independent States and Eastern Europe, and the near-bankruptcy of many countries in Africa, Latin America, the Middle East, and Asia. As a result of these and other financial pressures, de facto administrative decentralization to new actors is occurring, largely because the state has left the scene or simply cannot afford to contribute.

4. Bureaucratic Reform

The fourth source of pressure for Institutional Pluralism is the growing demand for public sector reform, which is increasingly a global chorus. Much of the debate focuses on how public bureaucracies perform or fail to perform. The debate on bureaucratic reform goes right to the heart of administrative design, for it questions whether the bureaucratic model or paradigm is appropriate. This is important, for limitations of that model have hampered efforts to promote decentralization over the past few decades.

Melvin Dubnick notes that there are three theories of bureaucratic reform vying to be the basis of bureaucratic reform in the United States and other developed countries: (1) deregulated government; (2) reinvented government; and (3) minimalist state.[7] These three approaches vary considerably in terms of their assumptions about change, their goals, and the extent to which they can be operationalized.

Deregulation is the most specific reform. It proposes the reduction of regulations that hamstring bureaucrats from being more productive.[8] As such, it is the least radical of the three approaches to reform, for it works within the dominant bureaucratic paradigm. In contrast, the minimalist and reinventing approaches are anti-bureaucratic. As the concept's label denotes, the minimalist approach seeks to reduce the scale of government because it assumes that government solutions are less efficient than market solutions. The third and latest addition to theories of bureaucratic reform is the "reinventing government" approach, which advocates entrepreneurial government.[9] The reinventors support entrepreneurial bureaucrats but they do not particularly or strongly support bureaucracy. The reinventors cite the former Governor of New York, Mario Cuomo, as succinctly making their argument: "It is not government's obligation to provide services but to see that they're provided."[10]

The reinvention perspective sees governments changing from doers to facilitators. Proponents of this argument envision government as being catalytic and involved in steering rather than rowing.[11] The reinvention perspective, however, does not advocate a simplistic minimalist role of the state where public tasks are simply privatized. Indeed, the reinvention perspective revitalizes the role of the state for it alone is able to facilitate critical investments in infrastructure and provide a regulatory environment that promotes a competitive economy.[12] The state is viewed as an active-smart partner in economic development that is able to use limited public resources to leverage private resources for public purposes. Public investments, in turn, multiply private resources, thus leading to a robust economy. Reinvention means transforming bureaucratic governments into entrepreneurial governments that "structure the marketplace to fulfill a public purpose."[13] The ten principles used by Osborne and Gaebler to define the reinvention perspective are:

Most entrepreneurial governments promote competition between service providers. They empower citizens by pushing control out of the bureaucracy, into the community. They measure the performance of their agencies, focusing not on inputs but on outcomes. They are driven by their goals—their missions—not by their rules and regulations. They redefine their clients as customers and offer them choices—between schools, between training programs, between housing options. They prevent problems before they emerge, rather than simply offering services afterward. They put their energies into earning money, not simply spending it. They decentralize authority, embracing participatory management. They prefer market mechanisms to bureaucratic mechanisms. And they focus not simply on providing public services, but on catalyzing all sectors—public, private, and voluntary—into action to solve their community's problems.[14]

Compared with the minimalist and deregulation approaches to bureaucratic reform, the reinventing approach is appealing to those seeking to design and implement improved decentralization reforms and programs. This is because it recognizes both the importance of public institutions and the need for those institutions to perform accountably, effectively, and efficiently. However, the work to date does not bridge the contradiction. The reinventors are long on anecdotes and platitudes but short on workable tactics.

Governments of late developing countries and the aid agencies that assist them are also trying to make public bureaucracies perform better. Specifically, the task is often viewed as one of assisting civil servants to behave less like administrators and more like managers. Management versus control is an enduring problem for all organizations, both public and private.[15] There are two dimensions to the problem: structure and behavior.

The bureaucratic reform approach to the problem assumes that the bureaucratic model has a structure that constrains the behavior of staff and prevents them from being productive. The deregulation approach assumes that the structure can be modified by reducing the web of regulations. The minimalist and reinvention schools argue for the market or a new entrepreneurial structure of public administration. However, proponents of the latter view provide little or no guidance on how to achieve entrepreneurial bureaucratic structures. While the reinvention literature provides a vision of what productive public agencies should look like, more is needed than simply a vision. What is needed are tactics for transforming existing administrative structures from a control orientation to a management orientation.

One problem with the reinvention approach to bureaucratic reform is that it was introduced in the 1990s at the same time fiscal stress was growing. Fiscal stress spawned the downsizing of government and reinvention has been associated more with downsizing and less with productivity increasing innovation.

While recognizing the faults and limitations of the bureaucratic model for designing public agencies, this study accepts the premise that the model is robust. To quote Elliot Jacques:

[Thirty-five] years of research have convinced me that the managerial hierarchy is the most efficient, the hardiest, and in fact, the most natural structure ever devised for large organizations. Properly structured, hierarchy can release energy and creativity, rationalize productivity, and actually improve morale. Moreover, I think most managers know this intuitively and have only lacked a workable structure and a decent intellectual justification for what they have always known could work and work well.[16]

The central issue, of course, is Jacques's point about "properly structuring" the bureaucracy to get productive behavior. The problem with bureaucracies in developing countries is that they are weak and poorly structured. Indeed, in Africa, Goran Hyden goes so far as to call them "pre-bureaucratic organizations,"[17] while David Leonard argues that they are "under-bureaucratized."[18] One of the most difficult yet intriguing questions in the field of comparative public administration is what to do with weak bureaucracies in developing countries. Stephen Peterson has argued that to strengthen bureaucracies in late developing countries the first step is to reinforce and fortify existing networks within the bureaucracy and the second step is to formalize these networks into hierarchies.[19] Clearly, this is a question that is directly related to efforts to promote administrative decentralization.

Instead of strengthening the existing albeit weak public agencies, a bureaucratic reform approach to a task requiring decentralization would, where appropriate, advocate simplifying through role differentiation or bypassing these structures. The heart of the problem is whether it is possible to give weak bureaucracies more discretion to be innovative and productive when there is so little accountability. Ironically, the very weakness of the bureaucratic culture may be an asset in embracing bureaucratic reform.[20] Dubnick rightly points out that: "the established cultural milieu and institutional setting [are] the greatest obstacles to the success of the debureaucratization movement."[21]

However, in those late developing countries where the administrative culture is not supportive of the legal-rational structure of bureaucracy, it is also not supportive of an alternative method of organization that would promote accountable, efficient, and effective use of resources.

In formulating the Administrative Design Framework, several assumptions are made about the model. First, it is assumed that the bureaucratic model is robust and, if properly structured, can perform well. Dubnick notes, "What many public managers have discovered is that it is often easier to reengineer than to reinvent,"[22] meaning it is easier to outsource public tasks than to change public organizations to do these tasks more efficiently. Second, it is assumed that the principal task in improving the bureaucratic model is to improve accountability which is achieved by monitoring from above by progressive political elites and monitoring from below by clients that demand efficient and equitable services. Third, it is assumed that extending the range of decentralization strategies by proposing deepened devolution and extensive delegation through the Institutional Pluralism strategy is not anti-bureaucratic. Rather, it is based on working through bureaucracies to formulate more flexible structural designs that promote accountability and also productivity.

Chapters 4 and 6 do not provide detailed guidelines for making public agencies and their employees perform more like managers and less like administrators. This issue requires a separate undertaking. This study does suggest a new way of thinking that leads to a decentralization strategy,

Institutional Pluralism, that can assist in maximizing the accountability of agencies and making them and their staff more productive.

A more systematic review of case studies of high performing public agencies is required. Still, it is possible to offer suggestions that should make public agencies more entrepreneurial at the central, non-central, and private sector levels. First, change the bureaucratic culture by encouraging a regular flow of private sector managers into the public sector (and even the reverse exchange). Second, develop institutes of management that combine both public and private sector training. Third, develop twinning arrangements for public sector posts. Fourth, strengthen the hierarchy by institutionalizing roles, not individuals. This lowers risk and make corruption by individuals far more difficult to sustain. But this is one of the most difficult factors to change. Fifth, establish performance contracts with line ministries and hold them accountable to an agreed level of performance. Sixth, change staff mobility and development. The public sector needs to improve its capacity to identify and bring talent up through the ranks quickly. To implement these strategies, it is necessary to change the culture of the organization and promote new images of the public servant. Such changes are difficult but not impossible.[23]

CAVEATS ABOUT REDEFINING THE PUBLIC SECTOR

While there are strong practical and theoretical reasons for rethinking which goods and services should be produced by the state and how best to provide them, there are two problems that need to be considered. First, while the state's role in the production of public goods may diminish as more creative market solutions are adopted, such as privatization of tax collection, the role of the state as the principal provider of goods and services will still continue. To a large extent, this is because public sector employment in many late developing countries is large and politically powerful. Reduction of the state's role in carrying out public sector tasks is viewed as a threat to civil servants holding jobs at both central and local levels of government. This is one of the major reasons why World Bank efforts to reduce the size of the public sector have made so little progress over the past decade.[24] In addition, because of ideological perspectives, many political leaders and their supporters distrust the private sector and NGO community. In this regard, the statist perspective, so dominant in the years after independence, is still very strong in many late developing countries, notwithstanding the momentous changes that have taken place in formerly state dominated command economies.

The second problem with redefining the public sector as exemplified in Silverman and this Chapter's analysis is the assumption that the task of providing goods and services, while not as administratively demanding as producing them, is still an administratively intensive task requiring management, financial, and technical resources that are difficult to build and sustain. One could argue that the role of providing resources is more susceptible to political manipulation compared to the production of goods and services, where the distribution issues are already settled. In such a situation, extensive oversight, if not control from the center, is required.

Finally, while the reinventing government perspective holds out a powerful entrepreneurial ideal for administrative agencies to aspire to, reaching that ideal through innovative reforms and programs is proving difficult. A recent review of the US Government's efforts to apply "reinventing" principles found considerable shortcomings. In a review of the program, one study found that reinventors made short-term tactical decisions to get quick wins that are not easily self-sustaining, largely because they come at the cost of building the foundation for lasting success.[25] One reason why the reinvention approach of the National Performance Review conducted by the US Federal Government faced stiff opposition was because it emphasized savings and thus staff reductions rather than performance.[26]

INCREASED ADMINISTRATIVE CAPACITY

In addition to redefining the public sector, the second force militating toward the consideration of administrative decentralization strategies based on Institutional Pluralism is the dramatic improvement in administrative capacity now made possible by new management techniques and the application of information technology. Because of these improvements, public agencies can now do much more with less.

Reengineering has arguably become the dominant management trend of the 1990s in advanced developing countries. It is being adopted by both the public and private sector.[27] Only in the past few years has the concept been discussed in late developing countries, and there are few cases describing its use in administrative decentralization.[28]

The reengineering approach seeks to reform organizations by strengthening those processes that promote performance and removing the maintenance of outdated organizational structures that waste resources and under-utilize staff. Reengineering seeks to counter the tendency of both public and private institutions and organizations to feather their nests and devote excessive amounts of scarce resources to maintaining the organization itself rather than delivering the goods and services.[29] The essence of reengineering is to determine the core public sector tasks of an institution and then creatively rethink how those tasks can be carried out using a mix of personnel, information technology, and revised organizational structures.[30] In this regard, a heavy emphasis is given to strengthening skill levels of personnel and supporting their productivity with generous investments in computer technology.

Reengineering emerged in the 1990s in advanced developing countries only after the role of information technology was reassessed and upgraded to a strategic level.[31] Governments in late developing countries and donor agencies that assist them have lacked vision as to what this revolutionary technology can do for administrative performance. Since the mid-1980s, however, there has been a growing recognition based on the hard won success of information technology-based reforms that this technology can dramatically increase the capacity of public sector bureaucracies to do things differently rather than simply accelerate the flow of work.[32]

There is growing evidence that information technology helps public institutions at both the center and non-center in late developing countries do more with less.[33] Recent studies of government and the private sector indicate that information technology can greatly reduce the hierarchy and thus the size of institutions and organizations.[34] Much of what middle-level managers do is to broker information from lower levels to higher levels. Information technology allows institutions and organizations to reduce those middle-level layers and improve the ability of remaining managers to better manage information flows. While information technology can reduce hierarchy, it may well not reduce costs. Information technology can, however, help government ministries and agencies avoid future costs for more work to be done with a relatively constant work force.[35]

Reengineering is in its infancy in many late developing countries because the strategic value of information technology has only recently been recognized.[36] However, the trend is clear. It is a trend that will allow public sector institutions to do more with less, which facilitates administrative downsizing. This results in the reduction in the number of personnel and the recurrent costs associated with their support. Since salaries, emoluments, and maintenance costs often consume a large share of most late developing government budgets, downsizing is a strategy to contain, if not reduce, costs. The word "contain" is used because it is not always the case that administrative downsizing leads to lower overall government costs. Administrative downsizing is often accompanied by organization reengineering that introduces information technology, which can actually increase a public sector institution's cost structure.[37]

Administrative downsizing of the state is most frequently carried out by governments because of structural adjustment agreements with aid agencies. But there are also cases where national political leaders and decision-makers have had the wisdom to seek efficiency gains. Pressures to move in this direction come from fiscal stress, which encourages the deficit-conscious governments to trim their payrolls through civil service reforms. Administrative downsizing can promote productivity and not just retrenchment if the state uses the reform opportunity to introduce measures promoting efficiency and effectiveness.

CAVEATS ABOUT INSTITUTIONAL PLURALISM

The growing move to redefine the role of the state from a producer to a provider of public goods and services reinforces the trend toward finding ways to use the administrative strategy of Institutional Pluralism. This is because it further focuses attention on the need to break the monopoly of central design. As the trend toward expanding the use of administrative decentralization continues to gain in strength, governments will increasingly be concerned more with the marketing, negotiation, management, and funding of contracts by private firms and non-governmental organizations than with the direct production of goods and services.

One must be realistic about the prospect of Institutional Pluralism. It is unlikely that the public sectors of late developing countries will easily reduce their role as a producer and simply become providers of public goods and services. Because of vested interests, established systems, and bureaucratic inertia, for the foreseeable future decentralization initiatives in late developing countries are likely to continue to be based on the strategy of Distributed Institutional Monopoly. Nevertheless, the financial realities of the 1990s and the pressures of aid agencies for expanded market solutions to government performance problems suggest that significant administrative downsizing, creative reengineering, deepened devolution, and increased delegation will occur in most late developing countries. Recent management innovations coupled with the growing use of information technology in the public sector should accelerate this trend and allow public sector administrative systems to perform more with less.

Beyond these contextual caveats, it is important to remember that Institutional Pluralism will be confined to the allocation objectives of the state and will have no relevance to the stabilization objective. Stabilization and most likely distribution objectives will still be performed through institutional monopolies, most likely at the center. Following the finding from the Berkeley Project on Managing Decentralization that a strong center is a precondition for meaningful decentralization initiatives, so too will a strategy of Institutional Pluralism hinge upon the effective delivery of stabilization and distribution policies from centralized institutions.

A developing country will most likely pursue all three administrative strategies simultaneously. The Musgravian framework suggests that states simultaneously pursue the three public purposes with stabilization being centralized, distribution centralized (though administratively decentralized approaches are emerging), and allocation administratively decentralized.

The reinventing government approach, with its emphasis on incentives, strengthens the role of central administration. To "structure the market for public purposes," as is advocated by the reinventing perspective, suggests an even greater role for government institutions at the center since such "structuring" should be done market-wide to avoid imperfections, while disparities from the incentives should be compensated through centrally delivered distribution policies. For example, changing the way urban centers could use land in Mexico, which was the heart of the 100 Cities reform program, was done by the center through a revision of the constitution. While local monitoring was needed to ensure that the change in the law was enforced, the decisive act was done at the center.

The comparative advantage of central institutions in mobilizing finance will continue and local-level governmental units will still remain dependent on them. A common theme in the decentralization literature is the advocacy of autonomy by local-level authorities.[38] Using the example of fiscal decentralization, Kenneth Davey sums up the error of this argument:

The choice is often between (a) a wide measure of functional responsibility combined with a heavy dependence upon central allocations, and (b) a narrow range of duties combined with a high degree of self-sufficiency. The quest for autonomy may really boil down to freedom to do very little.[39]

Decentralization reforms and programs provide the public objective of allocation. The administrative strategy of Institutional Pluralism involves a partnership with central institutions, especially in the early stages of implementation. Without this partnership, there is little capacity at the local level. The partnership will change over time, which is why Chapter 4 examines the roles of institutions and organizations needed to perform a public task in terms of the sequences of implementation.

While the trend toward Institutional Pluralism as a strategy of decentralizing public sector allocation tasks is discernible globally, this does not mean that the public sector in late developing countries is going to wither away. Changing, yes. Downsizing, yes. Withering away, no.[40]

CHAPTER 3
NOTES

1. A similar approach toward identifying such alternatives was taken by the USAID-funded Decentralization: Finance and Management Project, which was carried out between 1988 and 1994 by Associates in Rural Development, Inc., Syracuse University, and Indiana University. But there is little similarity between the framework and focus developed by this project and the one proposed in this Chapter. It gave particular attention to such administrative decentralization issues as transparency and accountability, local self-governance, and indigenous social capital. And its output was particularly focused on the administrative decentralization of public sector tasks related to rural infrastructure, social services, and natural resource management. The final report and documents produced by this project are available from: DFM Project, ARD, Inc., P.O. Box 1397, Burlington, VT, 05402.

2. Representative of this trend, the theme of the upcoming 51st Congress of the International Institute of Public Finance is "Reorganizing the Public Sector."

3. Robert Wade, *Governing the Market: Economic Theory and the Role of Government in East Asian Industrialization* (Princeton: Princeton University Press, 1990); David L. Lindauer and Michael Roemer, eds. *Africa and Asia: Legacies and Opportunities in Development* (San Francisco: ICS Press for Harvard Institute for International Development and the International Center for Economic Growth, 1994).

4. Interestingly, Scott rejects the argument about the importance of technical innovation in economic development (made most recently by Paul Romer). Scott argues that technical innovation has been erroneously deduced from national income accounts because relative prices have not been correctly determined. The residual in productivity is due to relative prices, not innovation. See Maurice F. G. Scott, *A New View of Economic Growth: Four Lectures* (Washington, D.C.: The World Bank, World Bank Discussion Paper No. 131, 1991), pp. vii–viii and Paul Romer, *Increasing Returns and New Developments in the Theory of Growth* (Washington, D.C.: National Bureau of Economic Research, Working Paper No. 3098, 1989).

5. Marino Henao goes further to argue that large municipal growth poles have outstripped their geographic division of labor and have not adopted a division of labor based on technology that would not necessitate aggregation in a few manageable growth poles. Henao presented his paper on "Regional Decentralization" to the Conference on Regional Decentralization hosted by the Center for the Study of Legislative Assistance of the Catholic University of Valpariso, held at Club Marbella, Chile, August

11–12, 1994. Many of the themes discussed in Henao's talk were published in *Transparencia: Una Estrategia Para Optimizar la Productividad Social de los Recursos Publicos*, The Final Report of the Presidential Commission on Public Reform in Colombia, May 1991.

6. Caiden, *Administrative Reform Comes of Age*, pp. 266–67.

7. Melvin J. Dubnick, "A Coup Against King Bureaucracy," in John J. Dilulio, Jr., ed., *Deregulating the Public Service: Can Government Be Improved?*, (Washington, D.C.: The Brookings Institution, 1994), p. 251.

8. Dilulio, *Deregulating the Public Service*.

9. The most popular statement of the "reinventing government" approach is: Osborne and Gaebler, *Reinventing Government*. See also: Barzelay, *Breaking Through Bureaucracy*.

10. Osborne and Gaebler, *Reinventing Government*, p. 30.

11. Osborne and Gaebler cite E.S. Savas, Chairman of the Department of Management, City University of New York, who states that "the word government is from a Greek word that means 'to steer.' The job of government is to steer, not to row the boat. Delivering services is rowing, and government is not very good at rowing." *Ibid.*, p. 25.

12. By providing basic infrastructure that encourages additional private investment and by investing in education, the state performs a major role in stimulating economic growth. The World Bank's most recent Development Report was devoted to the topic of infrastructure. Data suggest the magnitude of investment in infrastructure is substantial. World Bank, *World Development Report 1994: Infrastructure for Development* (New York: Oxford University Press, 1994), p. 1.

13. Osborne and Gaebler, *Reinventing Government*, p. 281.

14. *Ibid.*, pp. 19–20.

15. Russell Stout, Jr., *Management or Control: The Organizational Challenge* (Bloomington: University of Indiana Press, 1980); Martin Landau and Russell Stout, Jr., "To Manage is Not to Control: Or, the Folly of Type II Errors," *Public Administration Review*, XXXIX (March/April 1979), pp. 148–56.

16. Elliot Jacques, "In Praise of Hierarchy," *Harvard Business Review*, LXVIII (January–February 1990), p. 127.

17. Goran Hyden, *No Shortcuts to Progress: African Development Management in Perspective* (Berkeley: University of California Press, 1983), p. 144.

18. David K. Leonard, *African Successes: Four Public Managers of Kenyan Rural Development* (Berkeley: University of California Press, 1991), pp. 283–96.

19. Stephen B. Peterson, "Hierarchy vs. Networks: Alternative Strategies for

Building Organizational Capacity in Public Bureaucracies in Africa," in Merilee S. Grindle, ed., *Getting Good Government: Capacity Building in the Public Sectors of Developing Countries*, (Cambridge: Harvard University Press, 1997).

20. This is a major finding in the application of microcomputer technology in African bureaucracies. See: Stephen B. Peterson, "Saints, Demons, Wizards and Systems: Why Information Technology Reforms Fail or Underperform in Public Bureaucracies in Africa," *Public Administration and Development*, XVIII, I (1998), pp. 37–60.

21. Dubnick, "A Coup Against King Bureaucracy," p. 277.

22. *Ibid.*, p. 275.

23. *Ibid.*, pp. 277–78.

24. Louis de Merode, *Civil Service Pay and Employment in Africa: Selected Implementation Experiences* (Report Prepared for International Bank for Reconstruction and Development, Washington, D.C., 1991). An example of the difficulties is found in: John M. Cohen, "Importance of Public Service Reform: the Case of Kenya," *Journal of Modern African Studies*, XXXI, 3 (1993), pp. 449–76; Claudio Schuftan, John MacGregor, Stephen Peterson, "Downsizing the Civil Service in the Third World: The Golden Handshake Option Revisited," *Public Administration and Development*, XVIII, I (1998), pp. 61–76.

25. *Public Administration Times*, "NPR Under Scrutiny," XVII, 10, October 1, 1994, p. 1.

26. *Ibid.*

27. Michael Hammer and James Champy, *Reengineering the Corporation: A Manifesto for Business Revolution.* (New York: HarperBusiness, 1993); Thomas H. Davenport, *Process Innovation: Process Innovation Work through Information Technology* (Boston: Harvard Business School Press, 1993). The United States Government is adopting this strategy to redesign the Internal Revenue Service, which includes over 120,000 employees. The project is called Compliance 2000.

28. Peterson, "Hierarchy versus Networks."

29. Paul Strassmann notes that for most organizations, information is internally produced and internally used. In a typical private firm, 93 percent of all information flows internally. Further, he states: "It is a characteristic of unproductive organizational designs to foster passing information back and forth among the internal information workers while [client] inquiries remain ignored." *Information Payoff: The Transformation of Work in the Electronic Age* (New York: The Free Press, 1985), p. 27.

30. On reengineering see: Davenport, *Process Innovation.*

31. Peter G. W. Keen notes that up until the late 1980s, the application of information technology in organizations was limited because it was used principally for data, not document processing. *Shaping the Future: Business Design Through Information Technology* (Cambridge: Harvard Business School Press, 1991), p. 99. On reengineering with information technology see: Cheryl Currid, *Computing Strategies for Reengineering Your Organization* (Rocklin, California: Prima Publishing, 1994).

32. Note the distinction made above by Strassmann of the impact of information technology on increasing throughput (efficiency) versus changing "the way work is done" (effectiveness).

33. See: Mohan Kaul, Nitin R. Patel and Khalid Shams, *Searching for a Paddle: Trends in IT Applications in Asian Government Systems*, 2 vols. (Kuala Lumpur: Asian and Pacific Development Centre, 1987); Mukul Sanwal, *Microcomputers in Development Administration* (New Delhi: Tata McGraw-Hill Publishing Company Ltd., 1987).

34. On the role of information technology in reducing (or bypassing) the hierarchy in public bureaucracies see: Peterson, "Saints, Demons, and Wizards," p. 42. See also: Stephen B. Peterson, "Computerizing Personnel Information Systems in African Bureaucracies," *International Journal of Public Administration*, XX, 10 (1997), pp. 1865–89. On the role of information technology in reducing hierarchy in private firms, see: Michael S. Scott Morton, "Introduction." In Michael S. Scott Morton, ed., *The Corporation of the 1990s* (Oxford: Oxford University Press, 1991), pp. 3–26, and Thomas W. Malone, Joanne Yates, and Robert I. Benjamin, "Electronic Markets and Electronic Hierarchies." In Thomas J. Allen and Michael S. Scott Morton, eds., *Information Technology and the Corporation of the 1990s: Research Studies*, (Oxford: Oxford University Press, 1994), pp. 61–83.

35. Keen, *Shaping the Future*, p. 166. Experience from Kenya shows that information technology can allow for a greatly reduced work force, yet increase output. For example, computerization of the import licensing system in Kenya reduced the staff hours required from 640 to 80 hours and dramatically improved the output, for it promotes analysis and not just a processed output. See: Stephen B. Peterson, "From Processing to Analyzing: Intensifying the Use of Microcomputers in Developing Bureaucracies," *Public Administration and Development*, XI, 5 (1991), pp. 491–510.

36. For promising case studies, see: Stephen R. Roth and Charles K. Mann, *Microcomputers in Development: A Public Policy Perspective* (Boulder: Westview Press, 1987).

37. Peter Keen points out that information technology does not reduce current costs but allows an organization to avoid future costs. See: *Shaping the Future*, p. 166. For example, the United States Internal Revenue Service

has embarked on an ambitious program to reengineer income tax collection by extensively using information technology. Downsizing of staff is being achieved through attrition and the overall budget of the agency substantially increased in the short term. It is expected that the long-term gains of this reform will allow the agency to manage substantially more work more effectively and do this with a constant or slow growing personnel budget.

38. An example of the call for autonomy in decentralized systems is: Mushi, "Strengthening Local Government in Africa," p. 42. In fiscal decentralization, the capitalization and revenue models of local finance also advocate autonomy see: Davey, *Financing Regional Government*, pp. 164–70.

39. *Ibid.*, p. 168. Roy Bahl and Johannes Linn argue that municipal governments in developing countries are relatively self-financed. On average, 70 percent of their revenue is raised locally. They concede, however, that the remaining 30 percent, which comes from the center provides the bulk of investment capital. What these statistics do not reflect is the shortfall in total revenue needed to provide an adequate level of service and enough investment to promote growth. Roy Bahl and Johannes Linn, *Urban Public Finance in Developing Countries* (Oxford: Oxford University Press, 1992), pp. 32–41.

40. It is important to note that government can expand its provision of services without greatly expanding administrative costs. For example, for the thirty-year period between 1955 to 1985, programs of the United States Government grew by nearly a factor of three, even accounting for inflation, yet government employment increased by only 25 percent. Government can thus grow without government administration growing or growing only marginally. See: Donald F. Kettl, *Government by Proxy: Mismanaging Federal Programs* (Washington, D.C.: QC Press, 1988), p. 3. Wallace E. Oates concludes that: "... there is not enough clear support available to make a convincing case that decentralization in itself constrains government growth." see Oates, *Studies in Fiscal Federalism*, p. xviii.

Administrative Design Framework

To be effective in bringing concepts and knowledge to bear more effectively on policy analysis and program design, a framework for analysis is needed that focuses on alternatives for organizing and financing the (administrative decentralized delivery of goods and services).

Dennis A. Rondinelli,
Decentralizing Urban Development Programs, p. 19.

THIS CHAPTER INTRODUCES a framework for designing public sector administrative systems. The Administrative Design Framework goes beyond the categories of administrative centralization and decentralization, which were discussed in the first two chapters, and examines administrative design in terms of the concentration of organizational and institutional *roles* that implement *public sector tasks*. The central principle underlying this Framework is that providing allocative tasks through a pluralist, rather than a monopolist, administrative design promotes accountability, which in most late developing countries is the most important principal of administrative design. Breaking the "monopoly of central design" and expanding the options of administrative design is one of the major challenges facing administrators and development assistance agencies using decentralized strategies to promote accountable delivery of public goods and services.

Viewed from the perspective of roles, the framework identifies three administrative design strategies, which are defined by how concentrated roles are: (1) *Institutional Monopoly*, or centralization, is where roles are concentrated at the spatial center in an organization or institution; (2)

Distributed Institutional Monopoly, or administrative decentralization to lo-cal-level governmental institutions or private sector firms and organization through deconcentration, devolution, and/or delegation, but where roles are distributed spatially and concentrated in one organization or institu-tion; (3) *Institutional Pluralism*, or administrative decentralization through deconcentration, devolution, and/or delegation, but where roles are shared by two or more organizations or institutions, which can be at the spatial center, distributed, or a combination of both.

The Administrative Design Framework has three components: *principles* of administration, *purpose* of the public sector, and *properties* of design. The principles of design are the normative criteria by which to judge the performance of an administrative system. A hierarchy of three design principles is offered: *accountability, efficiency,* and *effectiveness.* Together these three principles optimize the *mobilization of public resources.* Briefly, ac-countability is holding public servants responsible for outcome, efficiency is the positive relationship of resource outputs to inputs, and effectiveness is a measure of the appropriateness of outputs. The most important prin-ciple of administrative design in most late developing countries is accountability.

The purpose of the public sector focuses on what is done. Public purpose has three levels, which are defined by the three objectives set out in the literature on public finance: stabilization, distribution, and alloca-tion.[1] These three objectives have usually implied an administrative design. For example, typically, stabilization and distribution are centralized and allocation is decentralized. The framework disaggregates these objectives into goals. For example stable exchange rates might be a goal for the stabilization objective. Goals are further disaggregated into tasks, such as money supply intervention. Tasks are the final level of public purpose and are the specific activities that organizations and institutions implement through roles.

The third and final component of the framework are the properties of administrative design, which center on the roles and sequence of roles that together define an administrative strategy. Roles are a key category of this framework for they are the specific actions (e.g., funding and moni-toring) that need to be implemented by an organization/institution or array of organizations/institutions to carry out a task. Role is a core con-cept in the framework because it disaggregates the actions needed to implement a task and allows mapping of responsibility for implementing tasks (and thus goals and purpose) from a single organization/institution to many. Roles can be shared by two or more organizations or institutions and they can be managed by one organization or institution. Role thus defines the administrative strategy as being one of either monopoly or pluralism.

One value of using roles rather than structure as the principal instrument of analysis is that it identifies, by task, which roles should not be distributed and should remain the monopoly of either central or non-central governmental units. A second value of using roles is that it gives important insight into the level of *accountability* a given administrative strategy can be expected to generate. As noted earlier, from the perspective of most late developing countries, accountability is the most important principle of administrative design. All things being equal, for tasks that should be administratively decentralized, such as allocation, a strategy of Institutional Pluralism, where tasks and roles are not monopolized but are shared between central and non-central public and private levels, is far more likely to promote accountability than strategies where roles are monopolized. Monopoly, be it public or private, delivers services at high costs, less efficiency, and less accountability.

The framework does not assume that Institutional Pluralism is a necessary and sufficient condition for democracy and civic participation in governance. For this reason, the book does not dwell on the utility of local planning groups, citizen advisory groups, town meetings, local ombudsmen, or quality commissions. However, this does not mean linkages between administrative decentralization and democracy are ignored by the framework. For example, the framework assumes Institutional Pluralism promotes administrative accountability through competition, which in turn can promote democratic processes to the extent that non-state institutions are involved in public service provision.

While this chapter reviews all three strategies of administrative design, it gives particular emphasis to elaborating the partnership of institutions and organizations that is found under the strategy of Institutional Pluralism. But this emphasis does not mean that the established strategies of Institutional Monopoly and Distributed Institutional Monopoly should not be promoted by governments. Quite the contrary.

The Administrative Design Framework's three strategies are grounded on the purposes of the public sector. A widely accepted systematic definition of these purposes is found in the writing of Richard A. Musgrave.[2]

Focusing on public finance, he identifies three *objectives* of the public sector: stabilization, distribution, and allocation. Stabilization concerns economic management (currency, balance of payments), distribution addresses the national imbalances, while allocation is the delivery of goods and services. *The Framework assumes that in most late developing countries two* of these objectives, *stabilization* and *distribution*, should continue to be centralized. The third objective, *allocation*, is a proper area for decentralization because goods and services should be tailored to local needs. Because of its grounding in public finance, Musgrave assumes away several obvious central objectives, such as national defense and foreign affairs. This is acceptable to the framework because in nearly all countries these activities are controlled by central governments.

For the foreseeable future, most late developing countries are going to continue to pursue the Distributed Institutional Monopoly strategy for administratively decentralizing public sector tasks. Given the control orientation of most political centers, the limited capacity of non-central institutions and organizations, and the centralization of revenue sources that characterize the task environments of most late developing countries, Distributed Institutional Monopoly in the form of deconcentration or devolution may be the only realistic approach most governments can follow when attempting to administratively decentralize public sector tasks. However, as the Kenyan (deconcentration) and Ethiopia (devolution) case studies presented in Chapter 5 demonstrate, that path is likely to continue to be as frustrating and unproductive as Chapter 1 suggests it has been over the past few decades.

It seems clear that the better strategy for achieving the objectives of administrative decentralization is that of Institutional Pluralism. The promise this approach offers is illustrated in Chapter 5's case study of Mexico's 100 Cities Program. It suggests that for the foreseeable future, the strategy of Institutional Pluralism will primarily be used in dealing with the production and provision of public sector goods and services in urban areas. There is little doubt that the strategy will eventually be extended to smaller towns. Whether it is a strategy suitable for providing goods and services in rural areas is unlikely to be tested for some time to come.

There are major similarities between the earlier discussed Type:Function Framework and the Administrative Design Framework proposed here. First, both frameworks can facilitate the analysis of the large number of case studies identified in Chapter 1. Second, both frameworks are based on the commonly agreed upon four forms of decentralization and three types of administrative decentralization. Third, both frameworks focus on institutional or organizational structures.

It is in regard to the third similarity that major differences between the two frameworks are found. The central issue for the Administrative Design Framework is not so much the spatial relationship of structures, as is the case with the Type:Function Framework, but the role of relationships among central governmental, non-central governmental, and private sector institutions and organizations relative to a given public sector task. For the Administrative Design Framework, the "de" in decentralization is about limiting the structural monopoly of roles and not the spatial distance between structures. The current Type:Function Framework focuses on the spatial dimensions of centralization and decentralization but does not address roles. The framework offered in this chapter augments this view with a focus on one role dimension: institutional concentration, which can range from monopoly to pluralism. While the spatial and the role dimensions are interrelated, the framework proposed here argues that focusing on roles leads to a more useful approach to understanding and promoting decentralization. Roles make administrative design both concrete and dynamic. It is concrete, for role directly relates task and the organization or institution. It is dynamic, because the role can change over time and be managed by different organizations/institutions or combinations of them.

Because of their differing perspectives, the two frameworks vary in regard to their capacity to offer options of administrative design. The reason for this is that reforms aimed at promoting extensive devolution and delegation involve increased sharing of roles. Yet, the Type:Function Framework has difficulties in dealing with roles. Its focus on structures and spatial relationships leads toward deconcentration and limited devolution. That is, the Type:Function Framework recognizes delegation as an administrative design option, but in practice the framework has largely been used to design and implement reforms and initiatives based on spatial deconcentration and some devolution to urban areas. As such, the framework has not been particularly good at providing governments and practitioners with administrative options to address the problems of limited administrative and financial capacity as well as low levels of accountability.

The first two strategies of the Administrative Design Framework (Institutional Monopoly and Distributed Institutional Monopoly) share some of these limitations because, to some extent, roles are allocated or held in monopolistic ways by specific institutions located in central or differing geographic locations. However, its third strategy allows for a mix of central, non-central, and private sector relationships for implementing a given public sector task. As such, it addresses major failings of past decentralization efforts and meets the new problems of the 1990s and beyond, which were presented in Chapter 1. It does this by: (1) identifying and focusing on the roles required to effectively and efficiently carry out a particular public sector task; (2) allocating those roles among an appropriate and changing mix of central, non-central, and private sector institutions and organizations so as to maximize the complementarities among these levels, in most cases increasing the amount of delegation and strengthening trends toward devolution; (3) recognizing that devolution, deconcentration, and delegation can occur at the center as well as in the periphery; and (4) raising the level of accountability through increasing the number of actors operating at similar and different levels and carrying out roles relative to the task. By focusing on roles as well as structures and spatial relationships, Institutional Pluralism avoids the major problems that are associated with the Type:Function Framework's tendency to have low accountability and static views of administrative end-states.

COMPONENTS OF ADMINISTRATIVE DESIGN FRAMEWORK

The Administrative Design Framework has three components: *principles* of administration, *purpose* of the public sector, and *properties* of design. The principles of design identify a normative set of measures by which to judge the performance of an administrative design. The purpose of the design addresses the question of what is to be done by focusing on objectives, goals, and tasks. As such it centers attention on the specification of public sector objectives and their goals as well as on the identification of specific tasks that must be performed to meet those objectives and goals. The properties of administrative design promote analysis of institutional and organizational roles that are required for tasks to be performed. As such it guides the formulation of administrative relationships required to allow central, non-central, and private sector institutions and organizations to sequence and carry out assigned roles. The following sections elaborate these points.

1. Principles of Administration

The design framework begins with three principles of administration: accountability, efficiency, and effectiveness. Of the three principles of administrative design, accountability is the most important. When achieved it promotes the efficient and effective mobilization and management of resources. One reason why administrative systems are so weak, and resource driven aid agency assistance strategies have not succeeded, is precisely because these three principles are weak or absent. Some studies have added *equity* to this list.[3] However, the framework assumes that equity emerges when all three principles are promoted and achieved by those designing and managing administrative systems.

A major reason why administrative systems in late developing countries frequently have inefficient management at headquarters and deconcentrated field-levels is because they do not have systems that promote accountability. Nor do they have political leaders or senior decision-makers who value accountability. Further, while administrative systems are often able to mobilize resources juridically, they frequently have little legitimacy to promote resource mobilization through the collection of user fees by deconcentrated field offices because of inefficient management. Devolved administrative systems face a different set of constraints. Either the center highly circumscribes local discretion and/or they have little or no resources to act upon the discretion. Accountability manages discretion and, as Robert Klitgaard has pointed out, discretion is the essence of administrative decentralization.[4]

2. Purpose of the Public Sector

The second component of the Administrative Design Framework, purpose, focuses on three descending levels of specification: objectives, goals, and tasks. Identifying the purpose of the public sector and carefully considering these levels is the key to determining which public activities should be administratively centralized or decentralized.

i. Objectives

In defining purpose, the Framework begins with the assignment of government *objectives*. As noted earlier these are drawn from the work of Richard A. Musgrave and Wallace E. Oates. Briefly these are (1) *stabilization* and maintenance of high levels of employment and output; (2) achievement of a desired *distribution* of wealth and income; and (3) efficient *allocation* of resources.[5] Musgrave termed these three objectives stabilization, distribution, and allocation. He concluded that:

The heart of fiscal federalism thus lies in the proposition that the policies of the Allocation Branch should be permitted to differ between states, depending on the preferences of their citizens. The objectives of the Distribution and Stabilization Branches, however, require primary responsibility at the central level.[6]

Musgravian orthodoxy holds, for example, that the stabilization and distribution objectives be centralized and the allocation objective be administratively decentralized. The stabilization objective should also remain centralized because most local-level governmental units lack the stabilization tool of monetary authority. As a result, they are not able to exercise deficit financing policies that compensate for lack of economic demand.[7] The distribution objective should properly remain centralized because the mobility of recipients and the potential tax base are high.[8] There are, however, benefits to administratively decentralizing the allocation objective, specifically to tailor the production and provision of public sector goods and services to the preferences of individuals.[9]

Musgrave's theory guards against the tendency to oversimplify administrative design and assume that all public sector tasks can be administratively decentralized. The literature of public finance demonstrates that there is no unilinear trend toward administrative decentralization or centralization. Rather, what is emerging is a complex structure of inter-governmental actors that are dependent, not autonomous. This complexity is described by Wallace E. Oates:

The perspective that emerges on the trends in inter-governmental structure is thus a complicated one. It does not point clearly to any simplistic thesis of increasing centralization or decentralization. Rather it suggests the evolution of a more complex system with a greater variety of both levels and types of governments. This does not imply a greater independence on the part of individual government units. On the contrary, the development of the public sector has moved toward a greater degree of shared responsibility in the provision of public services.[10]

Before turning to a critique of current decentralization interventions based on strategies of Distributed Institutional Monopoly, it is important to consider the two objectives that should be centralized: stabilization and distribution. The macroeconomic objective of stabilization is centralized at the national level. To an increasing degree, this is imposed by the growing requirements of the global economy. One insightful review of that economy argued that the requirements of worldwide competition are conformity in trade regulations and company law.[11] This standardization is proceeding rapidly and most developing countries willingly conform in order to participate in the trading order. The stabilization function is therefore centralized at the national level and increasingly standardized at the international level. There is little debate that the stabilization function is properly an institutional monopoly and the domain of centralized public institutions in the capital city.

While the stabilization objective is not problematic and accords with the Musgravian prescription of centralization, the argument for the distributive objective is more tenuous. The underlying economic argument is still valid for centralizing this objective. This is because experience shows that the poor will move to jurisdictions with more services. But the political rhetoric often determines the policy, and in recent years several countries have sought to administratively decentralize distribution.[12] A final objective of the state is allocation. Of the three objectives, allocation is the principal area for administrative decentralization. Specialists present the rationale for such action as follows:

[A] decentralized public sector possesses several economically desirable characteristics. First, it provides a means by which the levels of consumption of some public goods can be tailored to the preferences of subsets of the society. In this way economic efficiency is enhanced by providing an allocation of resources that is more responsive to the tastes of the consumers. Second, by promoting increased innovation over time and by providing competitive pressures to induce local governments to adopt the most efficient techniques of production, decentralization may increase both static and dynamic efficiency in the production of public goods. Third, a system of local government may provide an institutional setting that promotes better decision-making by compelling a more explicit recognition of the costs of the public programs.[13]

In terms of these three objectives of the state, administrative decentralization promotes accountability by tailoring services to the variations of local needs and it promotes efficient decision-making through competition.

There has recently been some criticism of the Musgravian categories and the theory of fiscal decentralization or fiscal federalism, as it is known in the public finance literature. If one accepts that the Musgravian categories provide the over-arching guidelines for designing administrative strategies, especially whether a particular task should be administratively centralized or decentralized, it is important to review these critiques.

One critique of fiscal federalism is that the theory is empirically based on the experience of developed countries and thus is not fully applicable to late developing countries.[14] An example of this argument on the risks involved in promoting administrative decentralization in late developing countries is found in a recent World Bank study titled "The Dangers of Decentralization."[15]

A more serious criticism, however, concerns administrative decentralization of the allocation objective.[16] Fiscal federalism contends that allocation tasks should be administratively decentralized to tailor the delivery of public goods and services to local preferences. Fiscal federalism supports administrative decentralization of allocation by assuming that labor is mobile, preferences are different and clear, and information is available on service provision in alternative locales. But critics question the applicability of these assumptions in late developing countries. In this regard their questions are based on two components: efficiency of demand and supply.[17]

The demand efficiency argument against administratively decentralizing the allocation objective for late developing countries is that, unlike more developed countries, preferences are uniform and labor is relatively immobile.[18] In developing countries, the critique goes: "... the problem is not to reveal the fine differences in preferences between jurisdictions but to satisfy the basic needs, which are, at least in principle, well known, and need not be revealed."[19]

In short, for critics such as the one cited, homogeneous demand coupled with immobility of recipients means that goods and services should be provided by administratively centralized, not decentralized, strategies.

The issue of labor mobility is very complicated. While the household in many late developing countries, especially in rural areas, may be rooted on the family plot and thus immobile, it is often quite common for household members to work at great distances from the household base. The household has migratory labor that is mobile and presumably migrates to areas that are most attractive in terms of employment and public goods and services even if the latter are limited.

The demand efficiency argument for centralizing provision of public goods and services is complex. It is true that in many poor developing countries, there are a standard set of services which are desired. For example, in most countries rural dwellers have a strong preference for water, health, and education services. These services may be standardized even though there will be variations in design. Income disparities, however, are often great, which differentiates access. It is possible to distinguish between those that can gain access (effective demand) and those that cannot (real demand). Demand does have preferences. Further, the Berkeley Project on Managing Decentralization found a decade ago that even for the standard inputs of agriculture, education, health, and public works there are program designs for these goods and services that are more or less vulnerable to local elite monopolization.[20] Thus, there is considerable scope for design within a "standardized" good or service and that scope creates preferences. Hence, the demand efficiency critique of decentralizing the allocation function can be questioned because there is mobility of labor and there are preferences within standardized public goods and services.

The argument that demand efficiency requires centralization of services is often coupled with an argument of supply efficiency. Here critics contend that centralization of public sector tasks, particularly the production and provision of goods and services, is preferred because local administrative capacity is too weak and local government is more corrupt than central government.[21]

The criticism that local-level institutions and organizations in late developing countries have little or no capacity is the most questionable supply efficiency argument against devolving or delegating public sector allocations tasks. The argument for centralization rather than decentralization is based on assumptions of scale economies of administration, greater technical capacity of the center, and the belief that local administration is more corrupt than the central administration and government.[22] It is true that when certain public sector tasks (such as highway construction) involve economies of scale, they should probably be centralized. However, centrally provided public goods and services, especially those related to health, education, agriculture, and public works, are often inappropriately designed and inequitable. For example, centralized design of health care often brings curative rather than preventative medicine and centralized design in agriculture tends to create agriculture extension strategies that are inappropriate to the administrative and technical capacity of both the center and the deconcentrated line ministry field offices charged with its implementation.

The most questionable supply efficiency argument against devolving or delegating public sector allocation tasks is that local-level institutions and organizations have little or no managerial and technical capacity. This limitation is often overstated because of the legacy of centrally designed development strategies that are overly complicated and factor intensive. It is also overstated due to experiences generated by insufficient transfers to local institutions of exogenous (aid agency) resources. And it tends to be overstated because insufficient attention has been given to simplifying programs to ensure that local institutions can more easily implement them.[23] Finally, physical isolation due to the poor transport and communication facilities common to many late developing countries argues for a decentralized rather than a centralized approach to the allocation of public goods and services.[24]

In late developing countries, the capacity of the center is often overstated while the capacity of alternative, non-central, and private sector institutions and organizations is both misunderstood and understated. The pathologies that beset most public bureaucracies in Africa, and to a lesser extent constrain central and non-central bureaucracies in Latin America, the newly independent states, and Asia, have been well described in the literature.[25] In Africa the problems are especially acute and are due to weak management and the lack of resources. A good example of this fiscal and managerial weakness is the inability of line ministries to sustain investments at the field-level because they lack recurrent cost support.[26]

Ironically, to critique the supply efficiency argument made against administratively decentralizing the allocation objective, one has to return to the theory of fiscal federalism. Two theories are applicable: the state as Leviathan and the "Flypaper Effect." The Leviathan theory contends that the state is a monolithic entity that seeks to maximize revenues from the economy without regard to the preferences of citizens.[27] The "Flypaper Effect" theory argues that money sticks where it lands because funds are siphoned off by the first institutions and organizations that receive them and local preferences are not considered in using these funds for programs and projects.[28] One can find considerable evidence in the late developing countries, and particularly in Sub-Saharan African countries, that support these two theories.[29] Couple the two tendencies with the critical role of exogenous aid agency funding, which channels resources through the center's ministries, and a situation emerges where resources are likely to be trapped at the center. The value of deconcentration and devolution is to disburse resource flows and break the trap. This is one example of the principle of breaking the monopoly of central design, a key principle underlying the Administrative Design Framework.

Critics argue that innovations seeking to administratively decentralize the allocation function have not adequately addressed the role of aid agency funding of development. For many late developing countries, and particularly African countries, such external funding is often the single largest source of development funding. In short, the critics have not considered the role of exogenous transfers, especially by aid agencies, and how they build and skew implementation capacity or otherwise shape the design of development strategies. The argument that there is little or no capacity in local-level institutions and organizations simply means that past transfers have built, if not over-built, capacity at the center. Capacity is needed at various levels, and it is essential that aid agency financing assist in building the partnership of administrative design and not overly focus on a particular level.[30]

A final argument made against administratively decentralizing the allocative function is that local institutions are more corrupt than those at the center.[31] There is no evidence to support this assertion. Indeed, in terms of absolute levels of corruption, the poverty of the locale relative to the affluence of the center would suggest that there is simply more to take at the center. It could also be argued that administrative decentralization facilitates the participation of citizen advisory committees that put a brake on corruption. The Berkeley Project on Managing Decentralization found that under conditions of corruption and in an environment that is not supportive of the poor, it is best to administratively decentralize to local-level institutions and organizations having little or no linkages to the center.[32]

ii. Goals

The framework disaggregates objectives into *goals*. Goals are often classified as economic, social, and security. However, under the framework goals are related to objectives: (1) major goals of the stabilization objective are *solvency, openness,* and *competitiveness*; (2) important goals of the distribution objective are *side payments, political support, economic growth,* and *equity*; and (3) central goals of the allocation objective are *adequate human, fiscal,* and *political resources.*

The goals of the stabilization objective are straightforward and concern macroeconomic management. Quite properly, most experts believe these should be centralized in such national institutions as ministries of finance, central banks, and planning ministries.

The distribution goal is less obvious and subject to conflicting views over whether it can be promoted by non-central governmental institutions or private sector firms and organizations. One distribution goal that is commonly pursued by late developing countries is side payments, which are defined as resource transfers to a narrow group of supporters who are typically members of the political and administrative elite. Side payments in this context are generally defined as bureaucratic rents or corruption. As a result, side payments are different than the second goal of distribution, which is political support. The goal of political support is broader than side payments. While it may involve resource transfers to favored individuals, the base for this goal is broader. Further, political support can be garnered through policies that do not provide direct transfers to individuals but can provide direct benefits they could enjoy. An example of this would be improved local services. A third distribution goal is economic growth, whereby the government targets resources to areas where economic multipliers are the highest. Finally, the fourth distribution goal is equity, which is the targeting of resources to areas and individuals to compensate them for inequities in factor and skill endowments.

Aside from equity, the goals of the allocation objective are closely related to the goals of the distribution objective. But for these goals to be operationalized it is essential for the public sector unit to have adequate human, financial, and political resources.

Assessing how the objectives relate to each other based on goals generates two important framework propositions. These focus on strategic changes needed to support the allocation objective and, thus, administrative decentralization initiatives. The allocation objective is best achieved when the goals of stabilization and distribution are supportive. Increasingly, the stabilization objective is not problematic because of the demands of a global economy, which require conformity for competition. Effective and standardized stabilization is supportive of the allocation objective and is not problematic in terms of administrative design. For this reason, it should be centralized.

What is problematic is the distributive objective, which in many late developing countries is defined as the goal of side payments. The framework makes the assumption that the effective delivery of the allocation objective using administrative decentralization requires the support of the center, at least initially. That is, without support and planning assistance from the center, autonomous local-level development can carry out few tasks or promote development. From these assumptions a conclusion is drawn that is central to the framework: effective administrative decentralization requires that all three Musgravian objectives be supportive and that distributive policies and their considerable resources be devoted to the distributive goal of economic development, not side payments. A strategic change needed to support administrative decentralization initiatives is the redirection of distributive policies from side payments to the goals of political support, economic growth, and/or equity. Such a change may occur if it is viewed as coincident with the goal of garnering political support and even equity.

In sum, the framework leads to two propositions: (1) effective administrative decentralization requires that all three Musgravian objectives be mutually supportive; and (2) distributive policies and their considerable resources must be devoted to the distributive goal of economic development rather than to side payments.

iii. Tasks

The framework makes it essential to specify the specific tasks that must be carried out for public sector objectives and goals to be performed. Tasks are extraordinarily numerous and need not be classified here, much less elaborated upon in detail. However, examples can be given that illustrate the relationship between objectives, goals, and tasks. For example, meeting stabilization objectives and goals requires the performance of such tasks as debt, currency, and fiscal management. Or to meet the distribution objective's goal of economic growth such tasks as building and maintaining feeder roads need to be executed. And carrying out allocation objectives and goals requires the performance of such tasks as managing clinics, operating cattle dipping stations, or collecting urban refuse. The significance of such tasks is that a major source of accountability, as noted earlier, is the degree of specificity characterizing a task.

3. Administrative Strategies to Achieve Public Sector Objectives

i. Monopolies of Administrative Design: Institutional Monopoly and Distributed Institutional Monopoly

The Musgravian objectives provide proven, useful, and robust guidelines for designing administrative strategies. From these three objectives, there are logically two *administrative strategies*: centralization and decentralization. A careful analysis of these two strategies reveals there is greater similarity than difference between them. The conventional view of both administratively centralized and decentralized strategies has been one of creating a *monopoly* that is either held by central institutions or legally distributed to non-central institutions, organizations, and firms. A major weakness of the theory on administrative decentralization, as argued in Chapter 2, has been its overemphasis on the spatial relationships of institutions, organizations, and firms rather than on how specific task-related roles are shared by them, regardless of their spatial relationship. *Institutional Monopoly*, be it held by a central governmental unit or distributed to non-central or private levels, is an administrative strategy that does not promote accountability.

Administrative decentralization does have a spatial dimension. This occurs when public sector tasks are moved geographically away from the administrative center. However, the *analytic* dimension of decentralization argues for breaking the monopoly of task-related roles held by a specific central or non-central governmental institution. For example, having two or more institutions or organizations share roles related to the financing, regulation, and implementation of primary education should increase administrative accountability. This role sharing may occur in the same geographic location so that there can be administrative decentralization of roles without spatial decentralization of organizational or institutional structures. Extending the example, a devolved municipality with jurisdiction over a country's capital city might be required under its charter to provide facilities, staffing, and materials for primary school students in its jurisdiction while the ministry of finance is responsible for funding the costs, the ministry of education for setting educational standards and rules, a local parent-teacher organization for advising schools and the government on education-related issues, and an external NGO for helping the financially pressed municipality to obtain textbooks and audio visual equipment. In this sense, the "*de*" in decentralization is first and foremost about breaking administrative monopolies over the range of roles required to carry out a specific public sector task.[33] The spatial relationships of the institutions and organizations performing those roles are a secondary concern.

The conventional approach to administrative decentralization in most late developing countries has been to create Distributed Institutional Monopolies. This approach has been largely unsuccessful.[34] The attempt to recreate administrative monopolies is often a crucial error in administrative design and a major reason why interventions centered on administrative decentralization often fail or under-perform. Interventions based on the strategy of Distributed Institutional Monopoly are typically faulted because they have neither the legal basis nor the technical capacity of the center to sustain a monopoly and extract resources. Nor do they have legitimacy to leverage local private resources for public goods and services. A Distributed Institutional Monopoly is at once both a dependent and a pariah institution, which limits its ability to mobilize resources from either the center or the locale. In terms of carrying out tasks related to the three Musgravian objectives, Distributed Institutional Monopoly is weak or fails on all three. In contrast, when there is an institutional monopoly the center is usually effective at resource mobilization, precisely because of its significant juridical and executive power. In sum, the major reasons given for the failure of Distributed Institutional Monopoly strategies are the lack of local-level technical and managerial capacity, limited resources, and elite cooptation.[35]

An additional explanation for the failure of Distributed Institutional Monopolies is that in effect they are still an Institutional Monopoly and an alternative source of administrative power to the center. This is especially the case if they have a monopoly over local-level revenues coupled with local political influence or control. Administrative autonomy and strength thus pose a potential political threat to the center.[36] Little wonder why the center limits the revenue-raising roles of such local-level administrative institutions and routinely starves them of funds from the center.[37] As a monopoly, decentralized administrative units have two major flaws. First, they can threaten the center. Second, they are less capable of responding to local needs and mobilizing local resources. The Tanzanian experience illustrates that such local-level administrative monopolies tend to serve themselves first, frequently at the expense of local resources and interests.[38]

ii. Pluralist Administrative Design: Institutional Pluralism

By focusing on how administrative systems assign and organize roles required to carry out public sector tasks, rather than on the structural and spatial assignment of such tasks and roles, it is possible to specify a third administrative strategy: *Institutional Pluralism.* This strategy is central to the framework's argument on the need to break the monopoly of central design. It does this in two ways. First, it offers an innovative way of thinking about administrative decentralization. This is because while it uses the types of administrative decentralization common to Distributed Institutional Monopoly, it avoids an excessive focus on spatial distribution and emphasizes the institutional and organizational distribution of *roles* required to carry out the task. Second, it departs from the conventional view of the public sector as that of *controlling* resources administered by public institutions monopolizing task-related roles to establish a new view of *leveraging* public resources with private resources that can be generated by promoting role pluralism among task-related actors.[39]

It is tempting to label this third administrative strategy "Institutional Partnership." This is because Institutional Pluralism does not view administrative decentralization as a zero-sum relationship. Rather it envisions a progressive network of central, non-central, and private organizations and institutions that share roles and tasks relative to the production and provision of public goods and services. Further, it implies a plurality of cooperative forms of networks that can provide such goods and services.

Instead of advocating a model of governmental monopoly, be it central or local, over a given public sector task's roles, Institutional Pluralism argues for using public institutions as *brokers* that network with an array of central, non-central, and (increasingly) private sector institutions and organizations performing roles required to carry out a given public sector task. By increasing the number and diversity of institutions and organizations involved in brokering, as well as providing services, accountability is increased, risk is reduced, and service delivery is better managed and tailored to local needs. Institutional Pluralism involves creating a market for the management and provision of public goods and services that includes but extends beyond the central and non-central public sector. In doing so, it breaks the monopoly of the delivery of public goods and services and promotes accountability. David Osborne and Ted Gaebler have won remarkable support for their argument that the goal of government should be to become an entrepreneur that can "structure the marketplace to fulfill a public purpose."[40] The thrust of their argument is correct, with one major change: the government is also an actor in the market.[41] While a given government's role may shift to increased brokering services, it will most likely retain the revenue role and provide some services that require economies of scale and are not suitable for a private firm to supply.

For indebted governments with moribund administrative systems, hard pressed to meet rapidly rising demands for local services, Institutional Pluralism may offer hope because it utilizes and promotes greater responsibility on the part of devolved local governments and delegated private sector's firms, civil organizations, or NGOs. Unlike the other two monopolistic-based administrative strategies, Institutional Pluralism promotes all three principles of administrative design, especially accountability. The Institutional Pluralism strategy may be the only administrative strategy by which late developing countries can bridge the fiscal gap and increase accountability.

In contrast with the other two administrative strategies, it allows designers and implementers of administrative decentralization reforms to break the monopoly of central design and promote a partnership of central governmental, non-central governmental, and private sector institutions and organizations forged to accountably and efficiently carry out public sector tasks. Institutional Pluralism is a strategy that allows public sector institutions, whether at the center or the non-center, to break up monopolies over task-related roles and serve as brokers for an array of private and non-governmental organizations in ways that allow public resources to leverage private sector resources for public objectives.

For several reasons, such as incapacity, insolvency, lack of accountability, and ethnic, religious, or regional-based factionalism, public sector institutions in late developing and some more developed countries are unable to meet the demand for public goods and services.[42] Ineffective public institutions disaffect citizens, who in turn withhold support and resources from the public sector. To break this cycle of ineffective management and uncertain or dwindling financial support of public sector tasks, some public institutions are introducing innovative, non-monopolistic approaches to leverage foreign and domestic private resources to produce and provide public sector goods and services. Innovative central or non-central public agencies are using incentives and providing seed capital to partner with private and non-governmental firms and organizations to deliver public goods and services. Here, the objective is to urge both central and local public sectors to become entrepreneurs and structure the marketplace and civil society to fulfill a public purpose.

The distinctive feature of this third administrative strategy is, of course, *pluralism* rather than monopoly as the principle of administrative design. A pluralist administrative strategy has a higher probability of promoting accountability than does a strategy based on monopoly. This is because it can promote efficiency by using private firms, NGOs, and community associations to carry out roles related to the delivery of specific public goods and services, wherever it makes sense. But it is essential that firms, NGOs, and civil associations are able to carry out their assigned roles. It is more likely that they will be able to play these roles if they have direct contact with individual users and their communities. Accountability is promoted by this strategy through the empowerment of local citizen groups to more directly participate in central and non-central governmental operations. That is, the more the state's monopoly on task-related roles can be reduced, the higher the likelihood of increased accountability and efficiency in the production and provision of public sector tasks. This is because it is assumed that citizens will consume more goods and services when they are more efficiently delivered, a finding that is empirically supported.[43]

Institutional Pluralism is rooted in a conception of the public sector and grounded on the allocation of task-related roles. As such, it is a strategy that is not analytically generated by the Type:Function Framework.

The traditional conception of the public sector was that of *control* of resources administered by monopolistic central or non-central public institutions. The new conception that is the basis of Institutional Pluralism is "*leveraging* public sector resources with private sector resources through central or non-central government institutions that broker an array of private and non-governmental firms and organizations."

While this strategy of government playing an entrepreneurial role may require less staff and smaller physical facilities than under a strategy based on a monopolistic role, it is a far more complex and challenging strategy than the traditional bureaucratic approach of administering resources wholly controlled by central or non-central bureaucracies. Though the physical scale of public institutions may decrease, the impact of government institutions can dramatically increase because of the multiple resources they can influence through a strategy of leveraged development as distinct from the earlier strategy of controlled development. Economic historians have long argued that the state will play a greater, but different role in late capitalist development.[44] Institutional Pluralism personifies both a greater and a different role for the state as it seeks to broadly influence economic development by brokering rather than controlling resources. In sum, the administrative strategy of Institutional Pluralism indicates that the role of the public sector in countries marked by low economic development should be greater and more sophisticated. The state should manage the process of delivering goods and services but not be as involved in their direct provision.

Based on historical evidence about the role of unitary or federal states in promoting successful growth while maintaining a realistic assessment of their limited fiscal capacity, a new view of the public sector's role in development is emerging. Under this view, central or non-central governmental institutions should perform a critical but sharply limited set of roles in the carrying out of tasks essential to public sector allocation objectives. This view is based largely on the grounds of financial constraints. Under this administrative strategy, governmental institutions do less and facilitate more, by structuring the market with incentives and targeted but limited allocations of seed capital that induce private firms and non-governmental organizations to become involved in the production and provision of public sector goods and services.

This emerging view of public sector institutions as either delegating all aspects of specific tasks or playing a reduced range of roles in regard to their execution has been especially endorsed by neo-classical economists in such aid agencies as the World Bank and the International Monetary Fund. The thrust of their position is that the objectives of the public sector should be transformed from producing and providing all aspects of collective goods and services to more limited objectives such as: (1) carrying out only the most essential public sector tasks; (2) leveraging private sector firms and organizations to carry out role components of non-essential tasks; and (3) protecting the public by monitoring the performance by private sector firms and organizations charged with carrying out all aspects of a particular public sector task or particular roles related to a given task. In poorer developing countries this prescription is increasingly being given teeth through conditions in structural adjustment programs.[45]

Interest in this prescription is also increasing in countries where demands for regional autonomy are reaching a level where pluralism, rather than monopoly, is the only answer.

An example of this thinking is found in the 1992 World Bank-funded study on administrative decentralization.[46] It makes a useful distinction between the *production* and *provision* of public goods and services.[47] "Production" is the creation of goods and services, ranging from bridges and piped water systems to solid-waste plants and health clinics, while "provision" is the planning, budgeting, revenue raising, contracting, and administrative and technical management required for the delivery and utilization of such goods and services.

This analysis contends that the state should be moving away from the administratively intensive obligation of being a producer of most public goods and services to a more limited responsibility for providing only essential goods and services.[48] Service provision can require varying levels of administrative action, the least being to structure the enabling environment for service provision. For the World Bank, conventional administrative decentralization to local-level governmental institutions failed largely because it burdened non-central administrative units with production roles for which they lacked the requisite managerial, technical, or financial competence to carry out. This was particularly the case with regard to domestic and aid agency-assisted development projects and programs. The evolution of the state to that of provider of essential goods and services and facilitator or leverager of others, through the devolution or delegation of specific tasks or role components of given tasks, helps overcome those obstacles and spatial decentralization thus becomes feasible. In this regard, the World Bank report notes:

The current literature suggests that many of the reasons, both technical and political, given as justification for decentralization relate to the provision function while much of the criticism relates to the lack of capacity to perform what are, essentially, production functions. Removing the responsibility for production from local governments reduces the need for many types of technical capacity at local government levels.[49]

Evidence of the trend toward Institutional Pluralism is beginning to emerge. One example is found in Mexico's 100 Cities Program, which is presented as a case study in Chapter 5. In this innovative program the objective is to "incentivize a city" to entice private participation in tasks and roles related to urban renewal.[50] Another example is found in Nepal. A recent study of this example states that the objective of the country's decentralization reforms are to expand the array of institutions and organizations to increase choice, though the report conflates political and administrative decentralization:

> Decentralization is also more than just a process of simply replacing the center with local politicians; rather, it must include a desire to go beyond government to create a competitive environment where government, community organizations and private sector operate to provide a range of choices for the people.[51]

In other countries there is considerable innovation in defining the delivery agent and involving the clients in assisting the agent and holding it accountable. Bolivia, for example, established a Social Emergency Fund as a temporary institution outside of the bureaucracy charged with delivering poverty alleviating projects in partnership with local communities.[52] Further, the Guatemalan government established the Fundacion del Centavo as a private sector organization and then delegated it responsibility for delivering credit to poor farmers, a task it has done successfully despite the fact that previous efforts by public sector agencies had failed.[53] In Africa contracting the procurement process has been used in road construction and road maintenance.[54] Finally, in Mexico tax administration is being privatized to overcome the inertia and corruption of the central bureaucracy.[55]

The two principal forces shaping this emerging strategy of Institutional Pluralism are: (1) a redefinition of the public sector; and (2) increased capacity of the public sector through advances in management theory and information technology. As a result, it is essential to consider the issues involved in redefining the public sector. These forces were discussed at length in Chapter 3.

4. Guidelines in Administrative Design

The final component of the framework is the properties of administrative design. These properties guide those charged with designing administrative systems. The most important properties are: *roles* and the *sequence of roles*.

So far this chapter has made two arguments. First, the Musgravian categories are robust and can provide government decision-makers and aid agency personnel guidance in allocating tasks to central, non-central, and private sector institutions. Second, of the three administrative strategies (Institutional Monopoly, Distributed Institutional Monopoly, and Institutional Pluralism) the latter appears to offer great promise for dealing with the constraints that have hampered administrative decentralization initiatives over the past few decades and addressing the tough economic and political demands of the 1990s and beyond. The next step in elaborating upon the Administrative Design Framework is to explain how these three administrative strategies can be used singly or in combination.

The primary administrative design principle related to administrative decentralization of a particular public sector task is to establish the appropriate *level of accountability* required. A major objective for doing this is to promote greater effective and efficient execution, recognizing that accountable systems are not always efficient. Accountability manages discretion and discretion is defined as the latitude allowed in the exercise of authority, and administrative decentralization involves delegating such authority.

Absent or limited accountability has been one of the principal constraints hampering the implementation of administrative decentralization reforms and programs over the past few decades. Additional constraints found at both the center and local-level are limited fiscal resources and skilled personnel, and managerial and technical capacity to deliver specific goods and services. Adequately designated and supported accountability would greatly help in assisting to remove such constraints. The proposed administrative strategy of Institutional Pluralism has a greater probability of ensuring adequate levels of accountability than the widely used administrative decentralization strategy based on Distributed Institutional Monopoly.

As such, the central issue that should determine the selection of an administrative strategy is accountability. Figure 2 sets forth a matrix that can guide designers of administrative systems in selecting strategies that promote accountability. The matrix is based on the relationship between two variables, both of which affect the capacity of the public sector to generate and sustain accountability: (1) *task specificity*; and (2) *level of resources* in society. For example, in Cell I, where task specificity and the resources of the task environment are both high, a high level of accountability exists. This allows designers to use a less accountable administrative strategy, such as Institutional Monopoly. In contrast, where both task specificity and environment resources are low (Cell IV), accountability is low. When this is the case, designers should consider the strategy of Institutional Pluralism, because it is the one that promotes administrative accountability through sharing multiple actors and roles.

The *specificity of the task* affects the degree of accountability.[56] As the specificity of a given task decreases, the need for accountability increases. Significantly, this suggests that more means and actors are required if accountability is to be achieved. Many of the most important tasks performed by public sector institutions in late developing countries are not specific. Examples of generalized tasks include the construction and maintenance of basic infrastructure, the provision of basic education programs, and the provision of primary health care facilities. These tasks demand high levels of accountability to ensure adequate delivery, and hence major investments in means and actors.[57] The task environment in many late developing countries is characterized by inadequate fiscal resources and limited capacity in terms of means and actors. As such, it is extremely difficult to design a decentralization intervention for government that can achieve the desired accountability. Under such conditions, the Administrative Design Framework, summarized in Figure 2, suggests that Institutional Pluralism is a better strategy than the more traditional approach

RESOURCES

	HIGH		LOW
		I | II	
HIGH	Institutional Monopoly (high accountability)		Distributed Institutional Monopoly
TASK SPECIFICITY		II | IV	
LOW	Institutional Pluralism		Institutional Pluralism (low accountability)

FIGURE 2: Task Environment Resources (Actors and Means) and Task Specificity Relative to Level of Accountability and Type of Administrative Strategy

of Distributed Institutional Monopoly. This is because it offers the greatest probability of maximizing the means and the actors required to promote the accountability needed for the production and provision of selected public sector tasks.

The four most important *resources* of promoting accountability in administrative systems are political oversight, laws, competition, and administrative mechanisms.[58] Among the most important *administrative mechanisms* are: professionalism, incentives, and monitoring systems.

In sum, the level of accountability required is a major factor in determining whether the administrative strategy selected will be based on monopoly, pluralism, or a combination of the two. The level of accountability is determined by: (1) the degree of specificity of the task; and (2) the level of resources, in terms of means, that characterize the task environment. In terms of administrative decentralization, these variables determine whether the design should be based on Distributed Institutional Monopoly or Institutional Pluralism.

i. Promoting Accountability: Task Environment

As noted earlier, accountability is promoted by the task environment resources in terms of means. The key means for promoting accountability are: political and legal oversight, institutional competition, and administrative mechanisms.[59] Significantly, these means vary in robustness. The most robust and important sources of accountability are external, particularly political oversight and laws. Effective administrative systems, whether administratively centralized or decentralized, require capable and committed political leadership. Likewise they require enabling legislation and regulatory law that make clear the tasks to be carried out and requirements and rules that implementers must meet and operate under.

Institutional competition is less robust than political and legal oversight but more robust than administrative mechanisms. This is because it is not a management intensive means and it does not require the kinds of training, communication, information, and supervision investments that the administrative mechanism requires.

Administrative mechanisms include monitoring systems, incentives, and professionalism. They are the least robust means of promoting accountability. This is because they are relatively complex and managerial intensive.[60] Meeting such criteria and dealing with such complexity is often difficult for central and non-central government institutions in late developing countries. Incentive systems are also management intensive and require extensive information as well as evaluation criteria. Again, limited administrative and financial resources make it difficult for many late developing country governments to establish and maintain effective incentive systems.

Such governments also have substantial difficulty building professionalism among their public servants, which involves the internalization of standards. Professionalism can be particularly important to implementing administratively decentralized activities in remote areas with poor communication, where it is difficult to supervise field staff. The drawback with this means of accountability is that it requires considerable public investment in building an elite administrative cadre that is committed to reinforcing professionalism. In sum, the principal drawbacks of administrative means of promoting accountability are that they are management intensive.

The principal-agent-client model is useful in explaining the array of actors involved in an administrative strategy. This model can be visualized spatially as the principal being an administrative agency at the center, which delegates to a local-level governmental or private sector institution or organization (the agent) the authority to deliver health care to the citizen beneficiaries (client). However, as the administrative strategy of Institutional Pluralism clearly demonstrates, it should not be assumed that these actors are spatially distributed. It is common for the principal, agent, and client to all reside in the same geographic location. For example, a ministry of health (principal) may, through devolution and budgetary allocations, transfer responsibility for providing primary health services to a municipality (agent) in the capital city, with citizens (clients) paying user fees to the municipal health department (agent), which transfers them to the ministry of finance (principal) and provides services according to standards and rules set by the ministry of health (principal).

Principals, agents, and clients provide accountability in two major ways. First, and most obviously, they implement the means outlined above for promoting accountability. For example, principals and clients can make agents accountable through such administrative mechanisms as compliance with service rules, professionalism, or competition. The second way accountability tends to be promoted is through a multiplicity of actors, an approach which increases the redundancy of means. For example, agents providing goods or services can be monitored by both the principal and the clients. Or agents can monitor each other by such simultaneous means as competition and the administrative mechanisms of regulation and beneficiary voting. A municipality operating under a devolved charter can sell off its wholly owned bus system and delegate the provision of bus transport in its jurisdiction to one or more licensed companies, which must comply with public safety regulations and tariffs set by municipal government officials and which compete among themselves for riders through the provision of reliable service.

If the objective of administrative decentralization is to increase accountability, then this can be done by both increasing the number of means and of actors that promote accountability. In this regard, the strategy of Institutional Pluralism is especially attractive because it increases the actors and means involved.

Under the Institutional Monopoly strategy there are only two actors: principal and clients. Here one actor, the agent, is automatically eliminated from providing accountability. The other actor, the clients, have very limited information with which to hold the principal accountable and few incentives to offer. The principal also has very few incentives to critically evaluate its performance. In short, Institutional Monopoly or centralization offers few sources of accountability. Administrative mechanisms, such as information and incentives, are weak to non-existent and competition is not available. The principal sources of accountability are the specificity of the task and the professionalism of the staff.

The Distributed Institutional Monopoly strategy increases the level of accountability over Institutional Monopolies by introducing another actor: the agent. In effect, agents can be monitored by principals and clients, thereby providing an administrative mechanism for promoting accountability through increased information and incentives. Under this strategy, task specificity becomes especially important because it facilitates the use of administrative mechanisms. However, when the expansion in numbers of the civil service cadre is coupled with the distance from the center, which is very common in regard to deconcentrated field agents and chartered municipalities and towns, it becomes more difficult to rely on professionalism as a means of promoting accountability.

The strategy of Institutional Pluralism significantly raises the level of accountability over that of the Distributed Institutional Monopoly strategy. This is because it involves all three actors in monitoring tasks and a range of different means of accountability: administrative, professional, and competitive. As a result, public sector tasks that have low specificity and promote little accountability have some probability of being carried out more accountability, efficiently, and effectively (assuming adequate resources) under this strategy. What distinguishes Institutional Pluralism from the other two strategies and makes it a better way of promoting the accountability required is that it relies on more robust means, such as competition, rather than more tenuous administrative mechanisms.

ii. Promoting Accountability: Task Specificity

Arturo Israel's work on institutional performance has led to a simple, elegant, and useful argument for improving the performance of institutions and organizations implementing development tasks in developing countries.[61] He argues that the specificity of the task limits discretion and creates effects that generate positive and negative incentives that promote performance.[62] Using the example of jet engine maintenance by technicians employed by a national airline as a highly specific task, he points out that specificity will limit discretion and the effects of poor performance will be intense, immediate, identifiable and focused.[63] Specific effects induce high performance. Diffuse tasks, in contrast, such as the promotion of rural primary education and provision of agricultural extension will not limit discretion and will have diffuse effects that limit, if not eliminate, incentives. In terms of the Administrative Design Framework, the degree of specificity of the task promotes accountability. The more specific the task, the more specific the role, and the easier it is to define determine performance.

iii. Level of Accountability and Administrative Strategy

Based on the above elaboration of task environment resources and task specificity, Figure 2 can facilitate analytical efforts to link the level of accountability required to one of the three administrative strategies. In Cell I of the matrix, task specificity is high and the level of accountability in the task environment is very high. This level of accountability suggests two possible administrative strategies: (1) a centralization strategy based on Institutional Monopoly; or (2) an administrative decentralization based on Distributed Institutional Monopoly. Under conditions of high accountability, it is inefficient to have a variety of actors competing for the provision of public services. In most late developing countries, the conditions prevailing in Cell I are the rare exception rather than the rule. An example of a task with high specificity and accountability would be one where a technician in a ministry of transport is charged with setting weight limits on lorries being licensed by owners paying for the evaluation services provided.

Cell II presents a situation where specificity is high but the number of actors that can help carry out the task are limited and the financial resources of these few actors is heavily constrained. In this situation, accountability is likely to be low and a strategy of Distributed Institutional Monopoly based on standard deconcentration or devolution makes sense. An example of this situation is where the collection of specific income and sales taxes in provincial capitals and small towns is low because central ministry of finance personnel lack the information, field agents, and mobility required to prevent tax evasion by local businessmen. The deconcentration of responsibility for such collection to district officers of the ministry of interior or field agents of the ministry of finance is likely to be a more effective strategy. So too, the devolution of tax collection responsibility to administrators employed by chartered urban centers as agents might also raise collection levels.

Cells III and IV detail many difficult strategy issues related to administrative decentralization in the 1990s and beyond. A key issue is that most development tasks are highly generalized and typical task environments lack the resources (actors and means) to promote the accountability required for accountable and efficient administration. For example, it is exceedingly difficult to promote "improved rural health care" in countries marked by weak health ministries, few trained doctors and nurses in the field, inadequate recurrent budget resources for transport and medical supplies, and passive, frequently poor and unempowered rural and urban populations. Under such adverse conditions, government decision-makers and aid agency professionals should consider the administrative strategy of Institutional Pluralism, largely because it provides innovative ways to maximize the actors and means required to generate accountability.

5. Properties of Design

Role is a central concept in the Administrative Design Framework. The Framework focuses on roles connected to the performance of public sector tasks and their appropriate sequencing. Actors in assigned roles are essential to carrying out required tasks. Several roles and relationships between them may be involved in performing a particular task. Some of the most generic of such roles are leadership, planning, policy innovation, financial management, resource mobilization, operational management, regulation, and oversight. In the course of an administrative reform, these roles may be located in the central and non-central public sector, the private sector, and even foreign institutions and organizations. Again, focusing on roles lies at the heart of the three strategies proposed under the Administrative Design Framework.

Implementation of each public sector task generated by the three public objectives and their goals requires that a range of *roles* be performed by actors, be they in government institutions or private sector firms and organizations. General administrative theory identifies three types of relationships among these actors: principal, agent, and client. When analyzing roles and tasks it is essential to be specific about the relationships among actors.

The Administrative Design Framework is concerned with two types of roles: (1) macro-level roles carried out by governments designing and implementing an overall strategy of administrative design in general and in regard to administrative decentralization in particular; and (2) task-related roles required to effectively carry out a public sector task that is being wholly or partially administratively decentralized through deconcentration, devolution, or delegation. However, from the perspective of conceptual clarity and terminological specification, both types of roles should have the same labels: leadership, strategy and policy formulation, planning, oversight, financial mobilization and auditing, need identification and planning, operational implementation and management, brokerage, evaluation and revision, and so on.

It is the Administrative Design Framework's emphasis on identifying, assigning, and sequencing such *roles* rather than on *functions* performed by institutions, that more than any other characteristic distinguishes it from the Type:Function Framework.

Institutional and Distributed Institutional Monopolies retain all roles in central or non-central governmental institutions. Under Institutional Pluralism, it is likely that macro design roles should be oriented toward reinforcing the difficult transition from monopoly to pluralism, while public sector task-related roles are likely to be shared among governmental institutions and private sector firms and organizations.

Identifying, assigning, and sequencing design and task-related roles to

institutions and organizations are some of the most difficult issues addressed by designers of administrative systems. The Administrative Design
Framework provides guidance for resolving these tough design issues. In
particular, guidance is provided by giving careful attention to: (1) the
means for achieving accountability and efficiency; (2) analysis of issues
related to task specificity and task environment resources; and (3) how
characteristics of a particular task affect role identification, assignment,
and sequencing.

The framework emphasizes the concept of *sequences* of roles. Over
time, roles may be performed by different institutions and organizations.
The three role sequences described are: *initiation, expansion*, and *maturity*.
With the concepts of task, role, and sequence, designers of administrative
systems can formulate and map an appropriate administrative strategy. They
can also avoid the Type:Function Framework's tendency to focus on rigid
end-states that cannot respond well to the dynamic processes and implementation stages that mark administrative decentralization reforms and
programs.

Roles related to an administrative design strategy or a particular public sector task can be assigned to different institutions or organizations
over time as experience is gained, expansion required, maturity achieved,
and innovation tested. This is particularly the case for allocative tasks. Under
Institutional Monopoly strategies, all roles related to a particular task are
held by central agencies. As a government administratively decentralizes
under the strategy of Distributed Institutional Monopoly, some of these
roles are transferred, either through deconcentration or devolution, to
local-level institutions. They may also be delegated to private sector firms
or organizations. If a strategy of Institutional Pluralism is pursued, a given
task's roles are distributed among governmental institutions and possibly
shared with private sector firms and organizations in constantly changing
patterns, depending on the stage of experience relative to the task, the
patterns of actor and means resources that mark the task environment,
and the overall strategy of the government.

A typical example of the gradual shifting of roles would be where the
ministry of public works retains financing responsibility for ensuring that
solid waste disposal is carried out in large urban areas until such time that
it can devolve responsibility for refuse collection to chartered municipalities, which may delegate the task to private sector firms. In most cases, the
center plays a greater role in financing the costs of carrying out a public

sector task in the early stages of a decentralization reform compared to the later stages. Eventually, the costs of refuse pick-up and disposal may be administratively decentralized from the ministry of finance to users who pay fees to either a department in the municipality or to the firm itself.

There are three stages in the evaluation of a task-related role: initiation, expansion, and maturity. Over time different roles related to a specific task will pass through these stages at different rates. Roles that should be centralized throughout, such as regulation and oversight, may be expanded and become well established. However, they are unlikely to be administratively decentralized. On the other hand, operational management and resource mobilization roles may well be centralized in the early stage but eventually decentralized as administrative systems are established, tested, and strengthened. In turn, they can be deconcentrated to field agents of the initiating ministry, devolved to local-level governmental units, or delegated to private sector firms and organizations. For example, a ministry of health may initiate a family planning program, test its methodology and contraception technology through its field offices at the local-level, and eventually delegate operational responsibility for carrying out the program at the grassroots level to NGOs. Meanwhile it can continue to fund the contraceptive devices being provided to the public and monitor the performance of the NGOs.

CAVEATS ABOUT ADMINISTRATIVE DESIGN

The Administrative Design Framework has now been described. There are five caveats that should be observed in applying it. First, it must be remembered that *monopoly is not always bad and should not be rejected by government decision-makers and aid agency professionals in favor of Institutional Pluralism.* As described in this chapter, there are a range of means and actors options available to those designing administrative strategies.[64] Clearly, there are some tasks that must be centralized because to administratively decentralize them would introduce inefficiencies in their delivery. For example, there are a number of technical reasons why the collection of particular types of taxes should be centralized.[65] Reform requires resources. While it is important that the local-level governmental units mobilize resources as much as possible, it is clear that for the foreseeable future, the center will have access to the most robust revenue sources. Ensuring that the center's revenue base is productive is critical to any reform strategy.

Further, many central ministries and agencies are weak and greater benefit may well be had from strengthening them rather than distributing scarce resources through an under-funded administrative decentralization strategy. The importance of this point is reinforced by research that shows why effective administrative decentralization requires a strengthening of the principal as well as the agents and clients.[66] In this regard, Harold Wolman cautions that: "... while administratively decentralized structures promote innovation, centralized structures are more likely to promote adoption."[67]

The second caveat is that *Institutional Pluralism is not always efficient and should not be promoted because it resonates with many of the current proposed solutions to inadequate public sector performance in late developing countries*. Cells I and II in Figure 2 illustrate that there are conditions where the strategy of Institutional Pluralism is not as desirable as Institutional Monopoly or Distributed Institutional Monopoly. For example, when accountability is high, especially due to task specificity, administrative monopolies can be more efficient and thus socially optimal. This view is reinforced by Richard Nelson and Sidney Winter, who believe that one should: "emphasize the role of rules, norms and culture in organizational change and explicitly disavow the view that market competition ensures the selection of efficient organizational structures and processes."[68]

A third caveat is that *administrative design is eclectic and the administration of some public sector tasks may well involve a mix of all three administrative strategies as well as all three types of administrative decentralization*. As the first two caveats suggest, there are cases for Institutional Monopoly even in countries committed to administrative decentralization of important governmental tasks. Designing an overall administrative strategy for a country should first focus on an assessment of tasks, giving particular attention to the specificity required and the level of accountability available. Such analysis will lead to different approaches for different tasks. A country's administrative system may well include all three strategies and its national design will be a complex and ambiguous process.[69] Indeed, this is common, as pointed out in Chapter 2's discussion of variability and the need to avoid linear assumptions. One problem with the literature on administrative decentralization are the assumptions that it is a linear process aimed at decentralizing as many functions as possible and that decentralization is an all or nothing process. Figure 2 helps guide government decision-makers and aid agency professionals against such thinking.

The fourth caveat cautions against *neglecting the complexity of existing institutions and cultural norms during the design phase*. Most task environments of late developing countries are characterized by a number of different administratively centralized and decentralized administrative systems. Just as important, the central, non-central, or private sector institutions and organizations carrying out such interventions are deeply attuned to cultural values and norms particular to the country or its regions. Culture often constrains central and non-central governmental institutions and may be the principal obstacle to implementing any given administrative design. As noted earlier, in these environments Western public administration principles are questionable, and it is essential to consider cultural values and views.[70] In Latin America for example, where there is a strong heritage of centralism and corporatism, it may be very difficult for even the most committed governments to pursue administrative strategies of Institutional Pluralism.

The fact that *unconventional administrative creativity is required in designing administrative arrangements* comprises the fifth caveat. Unconventional approaches to administrative change are essential in many late developing countries characterized by moribund structures that stifle initiative. Under some conditions the first step toward modernizing pre-bureaucratic monoliths is to simply bypass public sector institutions, building alternative but effective networks. For example, research on building information systems in Kenya's line ministries has shown that unconventional networks can be established and nurtured among effective members of staff that bypass ineffective staff and bureaucratic procedures and promote productivity.[71] In this sense, establishing networks of committed individuals within and between organizations may be an appropriate strategy for building decentralized administrative systems.[72]

From the perspective of this caveat, it may be useful to treat administrative reform as a two-speed process involving intensive and extensive reforms.[73] An intensive approach to rapid reform would involve linking productive individuals and bypassing, as much as possible, unproductive civil servants and bureaucratic structures. Further, it should be pursued for the functions critical to economic development such as revenue collection, national statistics, and expenditure management. The intensive reform approach would be complemented by one that is extensive, but slower and broader. Civil service reform is an example of an extensive reform.

STRATEGIES, CAPACITIES, AUTHORITY, AND LINKAGES

Chapter 2 concluded with a lengthy discussion of four problems that are not well addressed by the Type:Function Framework of decentralization. Briefly these were: (1) over concentration on end states and inadequate attention to transition strategies; (2) inattention to accountability, legitimacy, and political commitment; (3) limited attention to levels of human and financial resources; and (4) failure to sufficiently consider coordination and linkage problems arising during a transition from monopoly to pluralism. These problems need not be fully revisited here. On the other hand, it is useful to consider how the Administrative Design Framework addresses some of them.

The framework recognizes that the administrative end-state will be an ever-changing mix of centralized and decentralized institutions and organizations carrying out the production and provision of collective goods and services. It acknowledges that in most countries all three administrative strategies are being attempted at any given time and that strategies for specific tasks shift from time to time as situations change. Indeed, it acknowledges that under certain specific conditions centralization is more efficient and effective than decentralization. As such, the framework explicitly recognizes that administrative systems have to evolve and are typically in transition.

The Administrative Design Framework's focus on roles, actors, means, and task specificity requires that careful attention be given to administrative and financial capacities. Here, accountability is the essence of capacity. Close attention to capacity is important to efforts aimed at analyzing strategies for addressing administrative decentralization issues, such as breaking the monopoly of central design, downsizing the public sector, reengineering government, and turning to private sector firms and organizations when possible. Further, it helps ensure that reforms and programs seeking to transfer tasks to quasi-public institutions, NGOs, and private firms calculate the administrative, professional, technical, and financial capacities of the transferee to carry out specified tasks, as well as the competence of public sector role players to ensure execution through oversight and support.

The Administrative Design Framework explicitly recognizes that in the late 1990s and beyond the objective of administrative decentralization is to expand the array of public, quasi-public, and private institutions and organizations providing collective goods and services at the lowest possible cost and risk. As a result, it demands that in designing and implementing interventions, attention be given to the fact that expansion creates a number of intra- and inter-organization coordination and linkage problems that must be addressed. In making this explicit, the framework incorporates a principal lesson of the Berkeley Decentralization Project: strengthening the center should be an integral part of any administrative decentralization intervention.[74]

Finally, this chapter offers a framework that is dynamic. Embedded in the Administrative Design Framework is the notion that choice in the strategy of administrative design is a function of the level of accountability relative to a given task. This framework is not trapped in static categories, as is the case with the Type:Function Framework. In Chapter 5, the framework is applied to analyze three case studies that illustrate the types of administrative design strategies.

REGIME TYPE, ADMINISTRATIVE DESIGN, AND ADMINISTRATIVE DECENTRALIZATION OPTIONS

Governments tend to rely heavily on a particular type of administrative design strategy for carrying out most public sector tasks. The strategy that predominates plays a powerful role in determining the forms of decentralization and types of administrative decentralization that can be effectively introduced. That is, it affects the probability that a given country can successfully: (1) carry out political, market, or administrative decentralization initiatives; or (2) design and implement the range of available administrative design strategies.

There are strong arguments for the center to be responsible for the objectives of stabilization and distribution. Nearly all developing countries, whatever their regime type, do this. But the implementation of allocative objectives can be administratively decentralized if governments favor doing so. Some governments do not consider this. This is particularly likely for insecure governments.

Highly centralized states find it difficult to do more than pursue carefully controlled and centrally dominated deconcentration. For this reason, Distributive Institutional Monopoly is the dominant strategy found in most developing countries for allocative public sector tasks. Deconcentration aimed at maintaining law, order, and tax collection occurs in all such states, frequently accompanied by line ministry control down to the field-level. For example, a government will authorize its ministry

105

of interior to supervise lower-level governmental activities related to maintenance of law and order and collection of taxes and grant sectoral ministries extensive supervisory powers over field-level units carrying out technical and operational roles.

Devolution is not common in the developing world. It occurs primarily in urban areas, where chartered municipalities and towns exist. This devolution is often closely controlled. For example, after devolving responsibility for education to selected municipalities, a control-oriented centralized state might issue a decree that limits municipal responsibility to primary education only. The decree might require that the central public service commission regulate pay, hiring, and promotion through a national scheme of service for teachers, allow the ministry of education to set curriculum standards, place responsibility for allocating budgetary resources required by municipalities in the ministry of finance (usually on a line item basis), and direct the ministry of interior's governors or commissioners to ensure that municipality administrators carry out their education management roles and settle administrative disputes. The remaining roles, however limited, are left to the municipality's department of education and the principals of primary schools within its jurisdiction.

On the other hand, stronger governments marked by both political commitment to administratively decentralized interventions and the resources to back up that commitment can look beyond Institutional Monopoly toward more extensive experimentation with approaches based on the principles of Distributed Institutional Monopoly, particularly devolution. This appears to be the trend in such countries as the Philippines, Chile, and Indonesia. Further, governments meeting these conditions tend to have the capacity to stimulate and support expanded delegation of public task roles to community and market-based organizations and firms.

Most countries maintain substantial central control over administratively decentralized tasks and do not transfer adequate human and financial resources to non-central government units. As a result, countries whose administrative decentralization strategy are based on Distributed Institutional Monopoly, whether deconcentrated or devolved, find that the public sector task and roles they administratively decentralized are inadequately carried out, consequently slowing down efforts to promote national economic and social development.

Administrative strategies that promote monopolies may not always work for control-oriented states. This is most likely to be the case where multi-party democracy is being promoted and parties have regional bases. It also occurs when states are threatened by regions struggling for greater autonomy or secession, such as is the case with the Kurds in Iraq and the Tamils in Sri Lanka. Today, it appears that politically based ethnic, religious, or nationalist demands may undermine strategies of Institutional Monopoly, forcing political leaders to consider extensive administrative decentralization reforms. Under such conditions, the leaders of countries so threatened may find the strategy of devolution through Distributed Institutional Monopoly useful for meeting the demands of groups or regions seeking to build political power through increased local control or, in an increasing number of countries, to break free of the unitary state and its monopolies of control. This appears to be the case in Ethiopia, where more than forty years of centralization and deconcentration have rapidly given way to an attempt at ethnic federalism under principles of devolution, a strategy likely to be followed by other countries.[75]

Currently, few developing countries use the design principles of Institutional Pluralism, and hence have little capacity to extensively experiment with delegation.

Aside from state-owned enterprises, which are not reviewed in this study, delegation by governments is not common. However, selected delegation does occur in a number of ways. For example, a locally chartered municipality may contract with a private company to carry out solid waste disposal, a ministry of local government might delegate responsibility for maintaining urban water systems to a public works ministry, a finance ministry might contract with a local government authority to collect taxes when it lacks adequate numbers of capable field agents, or a government unit might delegate responsibility for maintaining its vehicles to a parastatal.

Despite this range of possibilities, when countries experiment with Institutional Pluralism it is usually in regard to urban settings. The reason is urban centers, especially large agglomerations in late developing countries have over-taxed governmental sectors. The failure to provide services in such cities can, given population densities, lead to political instability. Such conditions are particularly common in Asia and Latin America where governments are administratively decentralizing urban infrastructure tasks to private firms and organizations. Mexico has a highly centralized state but is experimenting with a pluralist strategy in its 100 Cities Program. This experiment is discussed at length in Chapter 5. Elements of the strategy are only beginning to appear in advanced developing countries, most notably in the United States federal government's efforts to redefine the public sector and reengineer government.[76]

Perversely, when fragmentation is extensive in countries currently on the edge of political collapse, such as Liberia, Somalia, and Afghanistan, far reaching de facto political and administrative decentralization rapidly emerges. Such countries are often marked by political enclaves operating independently from the center and private sector operations carrying out tasks the public sector cannot provide, through entrepreneurial firms, aid agency-assisted NGOs, and community self-help activities. But these situations are temporary and aberrant and should not be considered as examples of Institutional Pluralism.

Nor is it Institutional Pluralism when resource-limited governments look the other way and allow NGOs and community-based associations take over public sector tasks that are not being performed. This is the case with Kenya's famed Harambee activities.[77] It was also the case in North Yemen in the 1970s, when Local Development Associations led by local elites, using contributions drawn on high remittance earnings of Yemeni workers in the Arabian Gulf, built roads, schools, and health clinics without government involvement.[78]

In sum, there are no governments of late developing countries whose overall administrative design strategy is that of Institutional Pluralism. But it is clear that the time for this strategy has come. A gradual move toward Institutional Pluralism is occurring in secure and progressive states. It will also happen in countries where political leaders are committed to strong central presence and the administrative design strategies of Institutional Monopoly and deconcentration.

CONCLUSION

Four points need to be made about the three administrative decentralization strategies generated by the Administrative Design Framework. First, today most late developing countries are highly centralized, following the strategy of Institutional Monopoly in regard to most public sector tasks. Most also have some minimal level of administrative decentralization, through the strategy of Distributed Institutional Monopoly. This is largely characterized by mixed patterns of extensive line ministry deconcentration and limited local-level devolution, most typically to a few chartered municipalities. Delegation is minimal in systems dominated by Institutional Monopoly and Distributed Institutional Monopoly.

Second, it is increasingly clear that whatever the political, managerial, and financial constraints, administrative decentralization in the 1990s and beyond requires a move toward more extensive devolution and delegation, through the strategy of Distributed Institutional Monopoly, coupled with increased experimentation with the strategies of Institutional Pluralism. This is because the combined strategy of central control and deconcentrated administrative decentralization have failed or under-performed in most situations. As a result, experimentation with a greater mix of all three strategies of administrative design and the strategy of Institutional Pluralism is called for.

Third, the strategy of Institutional Pluralism is based on expanding the *array* of local-level government and private sector institutional and organizational role players to which the center can divest some of its responsibilities for the production and provision of a particular public sector task. But this is not the same as delegation, because it seeks to expand the number of institutions and organizations providing the goods and services. As such, it is a different perspective than that found in aid agency arguments for delegation to private firms and organizations, the neo-classic economic notion of downsizing the state through extensive privatization, or naive "power to the people" strategies. Rather, it is a strategy that starts from the notion of breaking the monopoly of central design and focuses on expanding an array of institutional and organizational role players required to carry out a specific public sector task. The logic of the Institutional Pluralism strategy is not only to increase accountability by promoting multiple actors, but to progressively transfer public tasks to the private sector. In sum, Institutional Pluralism is an evolving strategy of redefining the boundaries of the public and private sectors.

Institutional Pluralism gives developing countries more choices in designing administrative systems. But the expansion of choice raises problems. Increasingly, the key question may be more one of how to select from the wider range of choices and generate support from them rather than one of following guidelines to achieve an end-state that is largely public in character. The reason for this is that for some task-related roles, Institutional Monopoly or Distributed Institutional Monopoly may make more sense. For other task-related roles, it may be better for the government to divest them through a strategy based on Institutional Pluralism. If choice is widened in this manner, countries willing to consider breaking the monopoly of central design may well be marked by a much larger mix of administrative strategies than is currently found, thereby developing hybrid systems.

Fourth, it is recognized that the transition toward Institutional Pluralism is going to be a gradual process. Many central ministries will not willingly support downsizing through extensive devolution to highly autonomous local-level units with their own employees or delegation of task-related roles to the private sector. To a large extent this is because public sector employment is so important in late developing countries. It is also important to recognize national-level politicians tend to be control-oriented. Such resistance will continue, even in the face of pressures for public sector reform and arguments that the new orthodoxy of the 1990s and beyond is to transfer part or all of some public sector tasks to private sector institutions and organizations in order to achieve greater efficiencies and sustainability.[79] Nevertheless, this process has begun and will accelerate over the coming years.

CHAPTER 4
NOTES

1. Musgrave, *The Theory of Public Finance.*

2. *Ibid.*

3. This is essentially the argument made by the USAID-funded study of decentralization carried out by the University of California at Berkeley: Leonard and Marshall, *Institutions of Rural Development for the Poor.*

4. Robert Klitgaard argues that discretion, "the heart of the problem of decentralization," is managed through information and incentives. Klitgaard, *Adjusting to Reality*, pp. 141–142.

5. Musgrave, *The Theory of Public Finance*; Wallace E. Oates, "The Theory of Public Finance in a Federal System," *Canadian Journal of Economics*, I (February 1968), pp. 37–547.

6. Musgrave, *Theory of Public Finance*, pp. 181–182, cited in Oates, *Studies in Fiscal Federalism*, p. xii. Fiscal federalism is the term used in public finance for fiscal decentralization. See: Oates, *Fiscal Federalism.*

7. *Ibid.*, pp. 38–44.

8. Oates, "The Theory of Public Finance in a Federal System," p. 45.

9. The classic argument for decentralization to meet local preferences was presented by Charles Tiebout, "A Pure Theory of Local Expenditures," *Journal of Political Economy*, LXIV, (October, 1956), pp. 416–24. See also: John Joseph Wallis and Wallace E. Oates, "Decentralization in the Public Sector: An Empirical Study of State and Local Government," in: Oates, ed., *Studies in Fiscal Federalism*, p. 107.

10. Wallace E. Oates, "The Changing Structure of Intergovernmental Fiscal Relations," in H. Recketenwald, ed., *Secular Trends of the Public Sector*, (Paris: Editions Cujas, 1978), p. 159. This argument was updated in Wallace E. Oates, "Decentralization of the Public Sector: An Overview," in R. Bennett, ed., *Decentralization, Local Governments, and Markets* (Oxford: Oxford University Press, 1990), pp. 43–58. See also: Hubert J.B. Allen, "Enhancing Administrative and Management Capacity in the Area of Local Government," In *Seminar on Decentralization in African Countries: Banjul Gambia, 27–31 July 1992*, New York: United Nations Department of Economic and Social Development and African Association for Public Administration and Management, 1993, p. 107.

11. Jeffrey Sachs, "The State of Economic Reforms in the Developing Countries: A Comparative Perspective" (Paper presented to the Harvard Institute for International Development, Harvard University, Cambridge, October 17, 1994).

12. The most notable case in recent years of decentralizing the redistribution objective is the New Federalism of the Reagan Administration. See: Charles C. Brown and Wallace E. Oates, "Assistance to the Poor in a Federal System," *Journal of Public Economics*, XXXII, (1987), pp. 307–30; Wallace E. Oates, "The New Federalism: An Economist's View," *Cato Journal*, II, 2 (1982), pp. 473–488.

13. Oates, *Fiscal Federalism*, p. 2.

14. Recent examples of the critique of decentralization are: Rémy Prud'homme, *On the Dangers of Decentralization* (Washington, D.C.: The World Bank, Transportation, Water, and Urban Development Department, Policy Research Working Paper No. 1252, 1994); Paul Smoke, *Is Local Public Finance Theory Relevant for Developing Countries?*, (Cambridge: Harvard Institute for International Development, Development Discussion Paper No. 316, November, 1989). It should be noted that fiscal federalism is not based solely on inter-governmental transfers in federal systems (of which there are few in the world) and while the empirical work tends to be dominated by cases from more developed countries, there has been considerable cross-national work. Examples of cross-national work on fiscal federalism are: Oates, *Fiscal Federalism*, and Wallace E. Oates, "Searching for Leviathan: An Empirical Study," *American Economic Review*, LXXV (March 1985), pp. 748–57.

15. Prud'homme, *On the Dangers of Decentralization*.

16. The critique of the stabilization and redistribution functions will not be addressed because there is little debate that these functions should be centralized.

17. Prud'homme, *On the Dangers of Decentralization*, p. 7.

18. Prud'homme, *On The Dangers of Decentralization*, p. 7; Smoke, *Is Local Public Finance Theory Relevant*, pp. 6, 17–18.

19. Prud'homme, *On The Dangers of Decentralization*, p. 7.

20. David K. Leonard, "Analyzing the Organizational Requirements for Serving the Rural Poor," in D. K. Leonard and D. R. Marshall, eds., *Institutions of Rural Development for the Poor: Decentralization and Organizational Linkages*, (Berkeley: Institute for International Studies, University of California, 1982), pp. 8–15.

21. *Ibid.*, pp. 9–10.

22. Prud'homme, *On The Dangers of Decentralization*, pp. 8–11.

23. David K. Leonard, "Choosing Among Forms of Decentralization and Linkage," in D. K. Leonard and D. R. Marshall, eds., *Institutions of Rural Development for the Poor: Decentralization and Linkages*, (Berkeley: Institute for International Studies, University of California, 1982), p. 213.

24. Smoke, *Is Local Public Finance Theory Relevant*, p. 20.

25. The most enduring of these studies is: Jon Moris, "The Transferability of Western Management Concepts and Programs: An East African Perspective," in W. D. Stifel, J. E. Black, and J. S. Coleman, eds., *Education and Training for Public Sector Management in Developing Countries* (New York: The Rockefeller Foundation, 1977), pp. 73–83.

26. Stephen B. Peterson, "The Recurrent Cost Crisis in Development Bureaucracies," in N. Caiden, ed., *Public Budgeting and Financial Administration in Developing Countries* (Greenwich: JAI Press, 1996), pp. 175–203.

27. Geoffrey Brennan and James Buchanan, *The Power to Tax: Analytical Foundations of a Fiscal Constitution* (Cambridge: Cambridge University Press, 1980), p. 184.

28. Edward M. Gramlich, "Intergovernmental Grants: A Review of the Empirical Literature," in W. E. Oates, ed., *The Political Economy of Fiscal Federalism*, (Lexington, Mass: Heath-Lexington, 1975), pp. 219–40.

29. It should be noted that there is mixed empirical evidence for the leviathan thesis from more developed countries, see: Jeffrey S. Zax, "Is there a Leviathan in Your Neighborhood?," *American Economic Review*, LXXIX (June 1989), pp. 560–67 and Wallace E. Oates, "Searching for Leviathan: A Reply and Some Further Reflections," *American Economic Review*, LXXIX (June 1989), pp. 578–83. Despite the mixed empirical testing of the argument from developing countries, there is intuitive support for the leviathan thesis from the behavior of African governments. There is also evidence to support the "flypaper effect" of funding central governments in terms of how investment allocations are politicized in line ministry public investment programs and budgets and reflect narrow interests. See: Stephen B. Peterson, "Financial Reform in Kenya: Implementing a Public Investment Program in Line Ministries," in N. Caiden, ed., *Public Budgeting and Financial Administration in Developing Countries* (Greenwich: JAI Press, 1996), pp. 115–40; and his "Budgeting in Kenya: Practice and Prescription," *Public Budgeting and Finance*, XIV, 3 (1994), pp. 55–76.

30. The experience of poverty grant programs in the United States shows that limited local capacity can be compensated for in the short run and long run capacity can be created. See: Dale Rogers Marshall, "Lessons from the Implementation of Poverty Programs in the United States," in D. K. Leonard and D. R. Marshall, eds., *Institutions of Rural Development for the Poor: Decentralization and Organizational Linkages* (Berkeley: Institute for International Studies, 1982), pp. 40–72.

31. Prud'homme, *On The Dangers of Decentralization*, pp. 10–11. In making this assertion, Prud'homme cites his own 1992 study but cautions that while he measured local corruption, he did not measure corruption at

the center. Without this comparison, it is difficult to determine how Prud'homme concludes that local institutions are more corrupt. See: Remy Prud'homme, "Informal Local Taxation in Developing Countries," *Environment and Planning C, Government and Policy*, X (1992), pp. 1–17. See also: Robert Klitgaard, *Controlling Corruption* (Berkeley: University of California Press, 1988).

32. Leonard, "Choosing Among Forms of Decentralization and Linkage," p. 202; Stephen B. Peterson, "Alternative Local Organizations Supporting the Agricultural Development of the Poor," in *Institutions of Rural Development for the Poor*, pp. 125–50; Stephen B. Peterson, "Government, Cooperatives, and the Private Sector in Peasant Agriculture," in *Institutions of Rural Development for the Poor*, pp. 73–124.

33. The Oxford English Dictionary defines "de" as the act of undoing and thus decentralization is "to undo centralization." Undoing centralization is thus an analytic dimension but need not have a spatial dimension. See: *Oxford English Dictionary* (Oxford: Clarendon Press, 1978), pp. 55, 92. Similarly, in their popular treatise, Osborne and Gaebler discuss "uncentralization," in *Reinventing Government*, p. 281.

34. Dele Olowu, "The Failure of Current Decentralization Programs in Africa," in J. S. Wunsch and D. Olowu, eds., *The Future of the Centralized State: Institutions and Self-Governance in Africa*, (Boulder: Westview Press, 1990), pp. 74–90. Klitgaard, *Adjusting to Reality*, p. 142.

35. Allen, "Enhancing Administrative and Management Capacity," pp. 99, 106.

36. A participant in a United Nations-sponsored senior policy seminar on decentralization summed up the problem of trust by charging the seminar participants to explain "why there is such a widespread lack of confidence in decentralization."

37. On central-regional financial relations in developing countries see: Davey, *Financing Regional Government*, pp. 163–79.

38. Olowu, "The Failure of Current Decentralization Programs in Africa," pp. 79–80.

39. Even the World Bank's 1992 elaboration of combinations of Distributed Institutional Monopolies, which is sensitive to but not explicit about the need to break the monopoly of central design through transferring task-related roles private sector firms and organizations, does not deal with the opportunities offered by Institutional Pluralism. Silverman, *Public Sector Decentralization*.

40. Osborne and Gaebler, *Reinventing Government*, p. 281.

41. The concept of "market" must not be too narrowly construed. It appears narrow because is drawn from the economics literature. An expanded

view is held here. On debates related to this point see: Paul Smoke, "Local Government Fiscal Reforms in Developing Countries: Lessons From Kenya," *World Development*, XXI, 6 (1993), pp. 901–23; and his *Is Local Public Finance Theory Relevant for Developing Countries?*.

42. The withdrawal of citizenry support is best measured as compliance with tax laws is a growing problem not only in developing countries but also in developed countries. In the past decade compliance with the United States income tax has declined from 94 percent to less than 83 percent. "Auditing the IRS," *Barrons* (December 23, 1996), p. 35.

43. Evidence that entrepreneurial government creates greater demand is evidenced in the United States and in Mexico. See: Osborne and Gaebler, *Reinventing Government*, pp. 25–48; SEDESOL, "The 100 Cities Program: A Concerted and Sustainable Regional Urban Development Strategy," (Project paper prepared for SEDESOL, 1994, translated from Spanish by Dale Johnson, October 1994).

44. Alexander Gerschenkron, *Economic Backwardness in Historical Perspective* (Belknap Press: Cambridge, Massachusetts, 1962), pp. 26–30.

45. A good example of public sector reform sponsored by structural adjustment is the Second Agricultural Adjustment Operation (ASAO II) implemented in Kenya. This World Bank-sponsored structural adjustment operation offered a $70 million balance-of-payments support loan in exchange for the following reforms: liberalization of the cereals market, liberalization of fertilizer, analysis of staffing needs, and financial reform of the sector.

46. Silverman, *Public Sector Decentralization*.

47. *Ibid.*, p. 11.

48. Samuel Mushi also argues that the "role of local authorities is likely to change from direct action or intervention in development and service delivery functions to a preoccupation with the coordination efforts of others." Mushi, "Strengthening Local Government in Africa," p. 41.

49. Silverman, *Public Sector Decentralization*, p. 11. Note that Silverman is not specifying administrative or political decentralization with his term local government.

50. SEDESOL, "The 100 Cities Program," p. 4.

51. From the Nepal case study on decentralization presented to: United Nations Development Program, *Workshop on the Decentralization Process*, p. 24.

52. Klitgaard, Adjusting to Reality, pp. 146–52.

53. William H. Rusch, Fred L. Mann and Eugene Brausn, "Rural Cooperatives in Guatemala: A Study of their Development and Evaluation of AID Programs in Their Support (Report prepared for USAID, Washington,

D.C., 1976); Peterson, "Alternative Local Organizations," p. 131.

54. On recent attempts in Africa to use this approach, see: Jean-Marie Lantran, "Managing Small Contracts: (Contracting Out of Road Maintenance Activities: Vol IV) Practical Guidance on How to Streamline and Manage Small Contracts for Public Works and Services." (Paper prepared for The World Bank, April 1993).

55. Stephen Peterson, "A Second Path: Mexico's Second Customs Inspection," paper presented to the Symposium on Innovations in Trade Administration: Customs in the 21st Century convened by the Harvard Institute for International Development and the International Tax Program, Harvard Law School, Harvard University, Cambridge, Massachusetts, November 14–15, 1996. For an insightful view of how Mexico is privatizing its tax administration, see: Francisco Gil Diaz, "Reforming Mexico's Tax Administration," in Glenn Jenkins, ed., Information Technology and Innovation in Tax Administration (The Hague: Kluwer Law International, 1996), pp. 27–35. See also: Luis Fernando Ramierz Acuna, "Privatization of Tax Administration," in Richard M. Bird and Milka Casanegra de Jantscher, eds., *Improving Tax Administration in Developing Countries*, (Washington, D.C.: International Monetary Fund, 1992).

56. Arturo Israel, *Institutional Development: Incentives to Performance* (Baltimore: The Johns Hopkins University Press, 1987), pp. 47–64.

57. Israel even provides an index of specificity for a range of development tasks. *Ibid.*, pp. 70–71.

58. Herbert Kaufman, "Administrative Decentralization and Political Power," *Public Administration Review*, XXIX (January–February 1969), pp. 3–15. For Kaufman, "efficiency" means "hierarchy."

59. Arturo Israel contends that competition and competition surrogates also promote accountability and institutional performance. *Ibid.*, pp. 89–107.

60. Klitgaard stresses that the monitoring system of Bolivia's Social Emergency Fund was effective not because it was modern and computerized, but because it was constantly verified by frequent field inspections. Klitgaard, *Adjusting to Reality*, p. 150.

61. Israel, *Institutional Development*.

62. For Israel, task specificity has four components: objectives, time, methods and control. *Ibid.*, pp. 52–56. The objective is the desired outcome of the task. Maintaining a jet engine is more specific than delivering quality primary education. The time factor concerns how long the objective can be sustained. Israel notes that "in high-specificity activities a higher proportion of actors can undertake similar tasks for a longer period of time than in low-specificity ones (p. 53)." Methods concern the level of standardization that is possible. "Among low-specificity activities, methods

are less universal, lack generally accepted standards, and are applicable without changes for a shorter time (pp. 54–55)." Control is the fourth component of specificity and is the "ability to control achievement (p. 55)."

63. *Ibid.*, pp. 47–73.

64. Harold Wolman, "Decentralization: What It Is and Why We Should Care," in Robert J. Bennett, ed., *Decentralization, Local Governments, and Markets: Towards a Post-Welfare Agenda*, (Clarendon Press: Oxford, 1991), p. 34.

65. Davey illustrates the need to centralize the administration of complex taxes with the case of Indonesia where experiments to allow regional authorities to administer export taxes lead to disruption in trade. *Financing Regional Government*, p. 167.

66. Leonard and Marshall, *Institutions of Rural Development for the Poor*, p. x.

67. Wolman, "Decentralization," p. 34.

68. Richard Nelson and Sidney Winter, *An Evolutionary Theory of Economic Change* (Cambridge: Harvard University Press, 1982). Israel notes that introducing competition in "societies where collaboration and avoidance of conflict are paramount, ... could be counterproductive." Israel, *Institutional Development*, p. 97.

69. In their innovative work, Paul J. DiMaggio and Walter W. Powell note that "the creation and implementation of institutional arrangements are rife with conflict, contradiction, and ambiguity." "Introduction," in Walter W. Powell and Paul J. DiMaggio, eds., *The New Institutionalism in Organizational Analysis* (Chicago: University of Chicago Press, 1991), p. 28.

70. Moris, "The Transferability of Western Management Concepts," pp. 73–83.

71. Peterson, "Saints, Demons, Wizards and Systems," and his "Making IT Work: Implementing Effective Financial Information Systems in Bureaucracies of Developing Countries," in Glenn Jenkins, ed., *Information Technology and Innovation in Tax Administration* (The Hague: Kluwer Law International, 1996), pp. 177–94.

72. An influential statement of networking is Jessica P. Lipnack and Jeffrey S. Stamps, *The Team Net Factor: Bringing the Power of Boundary-Crossing Into the Heart of your Business* (Essex Junction, Vermont: Oliver Wight Publications, Inc., 1993). See also: Peterson, "Hierarchy versus Networks."

73. Peterson, "Saints, Demons, Wizards," p. 3.

74. See endnote 3.

75. Huntington, "The Clash of Civilizations?"; Kaplan, "The Coming Anarchy;" Gottlieb, "Nations Without States;" Colburn, *The Vogue of Revolution*

in Poor Countries.

76. For example, see: Osborne and Gaebler, *Reinventing Government*.

77. See: Philip Mbithi and Ramus Rasmussion, *Self-Reliance in Kenya: The Case of Harambee* (Uppsala: Scandinavian Institute of African Studies, 1977); Barbara P. Thomas, *Politics, Participation and Poverty: Development Through Self-Help in Kenya* (Boulder: Westview Press, 1985).

78. John M. Cohen and David B. Lewis, "Development from Below: Local Development Associations in the Yemen Arab Republic," *World Development*, IX, 11/12 (1981), pp. 1039–91.

79. A good example of such resistance is found in the recent World Bank study by Dillinger, *Decentralization and Its Implications for Urban Service-Delivery*, which finds that instead of functioning as a carefully designed sequence of reforms, decentralization has become a disorderly series of reluctant concessions by central governments attempting to maintain political stability.

Administrative Design Framework in Practice

What is needed is not power for either central government or local
organizations but complementary strength in both.

David K. Leonard,
Institutions of Rural Development for the Poor, p. 193.

THIS CHAPTER PRESENTS case studies that illustrate the Administrative Design Framework's strategies and concepts in action. In addition,
it seeks to demonstrate why governments should seek opportunities to
break the monopoly of central design and begin a transition away from
deconcentrated forms of Distributed Institutional Monopoly toward increased devolution, delegation, and participation through adoption of the
principles associated with the strategy of Institutional Pluralism.

The Kenya case study focuses on that country's 1983 District Focus
initiative. This administrative reform, which is still evolving, is based on a
deconcentrated strategy of Distributed Institutional Monopoly that seeks
to maintain central control over allocation while increasing the efficiency
of line ministry field offices and promoting the politically useful illusion
of local participation in governmental decision-making. Kenya is an ideal
case because many developing countries currently follow the same strategy for the same reasons.

The second case study describes the attempt of the post-1991 Ethiopian Government to implement a devolved type of Distributed Institutional
Monopoly. Its efforts to introduce a federal system represents a strategy of
administrative design that a number of countries, such as Somalia, Rwanda,
Sudan, and Sri Lanka, are likely to turn to as they seek to respond to

growing demands by ethnic, religious, and other movements for greater regional autonomy. The administrative difficulties faced by Ethiopia's new federal system raise important questions about the application of this strategy in countries with limited financial and human resources, particularly at the non-central levels. The case study also underlines the importance of giving close attention during the reform design stage to the complex sets of goals, tasks, roles, and role sequences.

The promise of Institutional Pluralism is illustrated by the case study of Mexico's new and innovative 100 Cities Program, which seeks to strengthen selected municipalities so they can decide upon and manage the development of local infrastructure. As such, the case study describes a strategy some governments should consider as they seek to find ways to downsize the central government while ensuring that key collective goods and services are provided in metropolitan regions. In this regard, the case study illustrates the common practice of governments to follow more than one strategy of administrative decentralization, a practice that allows for gradual experimentation and reform. No case study is presented of a country actively pursuing a strategy of Institutional Monopoly where roles are concentrated at the spatial center's institutions and organizations. This is because the focus of this book is on strategies for breaking the monopoly of central control. Nevertheless it is important to note that there are countries, such as Indonesia, Malaysia, and Thailand, that for decades have successfully used a centralization strategy to promote economic growth and to carry out governmental objectives with accountability, efficiency, and effectiveness. Leaders of these countries pursuing such an administrative strategy argue that centralization is essential for economic development and must come before decentralization. They also argue that it is possible to avoid sharing power while enlisting the participation of local-level institutions and organization in the provision of public goods and services. While no case is provided of such countries, Kenya does come close to it, for as will be shown, it recentralized after independence and then commenced in the 1970s to promote a strongly controlled deconcentration dressed up as devolution. As such, Kenya does, to some extent, represent this fourth model.

Throughout their history, Kenya, Ethiopia, and Mexico have had strong central governments that have followed the strategy of Institutional Monopoly while carefully pursuing limited innovations based on the Distributed Institutional Monopoly. All three case studies describe such

experimentation, illustrating the point made in Chapter 1 that administrative decentralization is not a linear process and that most states are
marked by substantial variability due to overlapping past and emerging
strategies.

Today, however, the administrative design strategies in all three countries are in transition. Whether these countries will succeed with their
described strategies remains to be seen. Currently, unfolding political dynamics in Kenya raise questions as to how long the government will
continue to dominate urban and rural areas through its strategy of tightly
controlled deconcentration and limited devolution.[1] Ethiopia's experiment with federalism is instructive precisely because many experts think
it unlikely that successful devolution will occur.[2] Mexico, too, has severe
local limitations to the full transfer of administrative and fiscal resources
to the local governments. While the 100 Cities Project appears to have
strong supporters, past administrative reform efforts have proved to be
more rhetoric than reality, a tendency likely to be reinforced by the effects of the 1994–95 financial crisis.[3]

DISTRIBUTED INSTITUTIONAL MONOPOLY: KENYA'S DECONCENTRATED DISTRICT FOCUS STRATEGY

Kenya is a unitary state that is marked by both devolved and
deconcentrated types of decentralization. While the country inherited a
vibrant devolved system of municipalities and county councils from the
British, which still function, albeit as shadows of their former colonial
role, government policies since independence have largely sought to
strengthen central ministry control over the country through a
deconcentrated form of Distributed Institutional Monopoly. As such, Kenya
is representative of the administrative decentralization strategy followed
by most late developing countries. Kenya was selected as a case because
since 1983 its government has followed a well-defined strategy that illustrates the opportunities and constraints deconcentration generates for states
seeking to promote administrative principles of accountability, management efficiency, effective resource mobilization, and, ultimately, equity.

1. Recentralization and Institutional Monopoly

Kenya's historical experience with administrative decentralization par-
allels the trends discussed in Chapter 1. Briefly, toward the end of the

colonial period the British strengthened the local authorities by increasing their tasks and transferring, through devolved forms of Distributed Institutional Monopoly, access to revenue sources and financial tasks and roles. After independence, President Jomo Kenyatta undermined this inherited pattern of Commonwealth-style local authority and forged a powerful centralized state.[4] He quickly moved the country toward Institutional Monopoly by taking some tasks, roles, and resources away from the local authorities inherited from British rule and transferring them to line ministries. Then he reinforced this monopoly by strengthening the administrative and supervisory tasks and roles of the President's appointed Provincial and District Commissioners over field agents of line ministries, departments, and agencies. To a large extent, this was because he preferred strong rule. By recentralizing control over the allocative objective, he also gained the power to advance the political and economic interests of his home region and ethnic group through such practices as allocating substantial Government resources to areas dominated by them, employing them at all levels of the civil service, and advancing their private sector opportunities.

During the 1970s, Kenyatta's administration came under pressure from aid agencies to distribute some centrally monopolized tasks and roles to the districts and local authorities. As pointed out in Chapter 1, this was done largely because aid agencies believed a strategy of Distributed Institutional Monopoly would lead to more local involvement and hence improved implementation success in projects and programs they were funding. The limited response of his monopoly-oriented government was to introduce a district planning system based on District Development Committees (DDCs) charged with preparing five-year plans for the Ministry of Planning and National Development (MPND) with the assistance of District Development Officers (DDOs) seconded by and accountable to the Office of the President (OOP) and the MPND.[5] This planning system emerged out of several innovative programs and administrative reforms that sought to create special rural development centers and build local-level planning capacities.[6] This intervention transferred some roles related to planning tasks to local development committees, comprised almost entirely of field agents of central ministries. This innovation did not change the fact that at Kenyatta's death in 1977, Kenya was strongly dominated by the strategy of Institutional Monopoly coupled with a Distributed Institutional Monopoly strategy based on strong central control, weak devolved local authorities, and limited, involuntary pluralistic delegation to ethnic associations and self-help organizations that carried out activities line ministries and local authorities ignored or lacked the resources to provide.

2. The District Focus Strategy

Shortly after President Daniel arap Moi's succession to the Presidency in 1978, the government indicated a renewed and increased interest in making the country's districts the operational centers for rural development planning and project and program implementation. Eventually, he launched an administrative reform superficially aimed at responding to, if not complying with, aid agency demands of the late 1970s for increased administrative decentralization and local-level participation. He did this through a deconcentrated form of Distributed Institutional Monopoly labeled the "District Focus Strategy." In this September 1982 directive, President Moi called for districts to become centers for the development of rural areas by mid-1983 and outlined the basic legal provisions for the Strategy.[7]

Importantly, unlike the Ethiopia's transitional government, Moi's administration gave extensive attention to the properties of administrative design: task-related roles, sequences of roles, and relationships between actors. It also gave specific attention to role players and resources. The documents issued under the District Focus Strategy demonstrate the extent to which senior decision-makers gave attention to specifying the principles and patterns of their administrative design. They also make it clear that this reform was intended to strengthen central control while claiming to be granting devolved tasks and roles to local-level governmental units. While speeches announcing the reform were clothed in the rhetoric of devolution and delegation, District Focus: (1) extended and consolidated the Moi Government's political control over all governmental levels; and (2) allowed his Government to redistribute budget allocations, public sector employment benefits, and private sector advantages to his own region and ethnic group or to other regions led by his major political supporters.

The District Focus Strategy was based on Kenyatta's earlier reform that introduced district five year plans written by field agents of the MPND.[8] In announcing the reform, President Moi implied it was to constitute an extensive "decentralization" initiative, a term which was never defined, that he implied would move the country's strategy for carrying out selected public sector tasks related to the allocative objective from central control to strengthened district level institutions operating under the strategy of Distributed Institutional Monopoly. He further implied to aid agencies and the public that this would lead to more meaningful devolution and expanded local-level participation.

The District Focus Strategy has not required any significant change in the established pattern of deconcentrated administration or limited devolved urban local government. It has, however, transferred some technical and administrative responsibility from central personnel at ministerial and provincial headquarters to central personnel stationed in field offices at provincial, district, and divisional levels. At best, this change has led to some marginal improvements in managerial efficiency. But it has made little contribution to achieving greater accountability or promoting resource mobilization and effectiveness. Indeed, because of the monopoly implicit in the District Focus Strategy's design, district accountability has declined and corruption has increased.

The Strategy does not create new resources for districts, though its draftsmen hoped to use its theme of decentralization to attract aid agency funding. Rather, the Strategy was used for political reasons to redistribute centrally controlled resources away from Kenyatta's key districts to the districts of the supporters of Moi.

Importantly, and unlike Ethiopia, the central government has clearly spelled out the details of its administrative design. This is done is a series of "Blue Books" published between 1983 and 1990 that give specific attention to tasks, roles, and relationships among actors. These were the product of a high-level district focus committee located in the Office of the President. Its members represented major administrative decision-makers and gave great attention to principles of administrative design. They also coordinated the implementation of the District Focus Strategy and provided technical guidance for district planners. Under the Strategy, the Ministry of Finance (MOF) is responsible for revenue collection and budget allocations. Finally, most line ministries have posted appropriate staff to act as their representatives at the district level, together with supporting and administrative staff. In sum, the center controls.

3. Tasks and Roles

The administrative tasks and roles at the district level that are required to support the District Focus Strategy are now well established. Nearly all task-related roles are performed by central ministry actors. The District Development Committee (DDC) forms the foundation of the decentralized development strategy. The District Focus Strategy requires the DDC to meet four times per year to: (1) review ongoing progress to ensure that current projects are rapidly implemented and that completed projects and existing infrastructure are effectively operated and maintained; (2) consider new proposals submitted by Division Development Committees (DvDCs); (3) establish priorities for future projects in the five-year District Development Plans (DDP); (4) endorse the district's annual submission of project proposals prepared by Department Heads of line ministry field offices; and (5) review and endorse all project proposals of local authorities, parastatals, regional development authorities, and NGOs operating in the district.

Because of its emasculation of the formerly powerful provincial system, the District Focus Strategy brings more budgetary allocations directly to district departments of line ministries. But because of central monopoly, decisions about those funds are controlled at the center. Authority to expend money is held by either the District Commissioner (DC), which enhances the power of the President, or the headquarters Department or Division Heads of the line ministries. In order to facilitate payments for the increasing volume of expenditures at the district level, the MOF's District Treasuries have been strengthened and the levels of district cash floats, or imprest, have been raised. Further, District Supply Offices have been established and staffed in each district to handle the procurement needs and District Tender Boards have been established to process procurement for district development activities.[9] Yet, despite all this improvement in allocation processes, corruption has increased at the district level. The Administrative Design Framework's principles predict this, for monopoly reduces accountability.

Although established separately under the Local Government Act, local authorities are obliged to pass their development proposals and activities through the DDC for review and endorsement. Towards this end, under guidance from the Ministry of Local Government (MLG), local authorities now prepare Local Authority Development Programs (LADP). These are capital expenditure plans which outline long-term investment programs. The LADPs must pass through the DDC before being submitted to the MLG for approval. The exact relationship between the DDC and local authorities is not particularly well defined and there is often a degree of tension between them. Clearly, more attention to task and role specificity is needed in regard to financing of local authorities.

The deconcentration form of Distributed Institutional Monopoly allows for a shift in management structures and responsibilities to field staff, providing them with some level of discretion in the planning and implementation of central policy directives to better suit local conditions. It may also allow a two-way flow of information between the center and its field offices but does not create autonomy, revenue generation powers, or the transference of full authority for decision-making. It is within this context that remarks concerning the DDC's strengths and weaknesses must be framed.

The DDC has several strengths. First, it provides the focal institution for the District Focus Strategy, bringing together all the major "actors" immediately concerned with development at the local-level. As such it draws together representatives of central government, local authorities, state corporations, non-government organizations and other interested local development groups (Harambee).

Second, the DDC provides a forum for discussion among national and local politicians, the Party, administrators and technical officers. The DDC is thus able to make decisions and set priorities that reflect a broad spectrum of opinion and a balance between technical and political considerations. Third, through the system of sub-DDC committees, it provides a conduit for passing the views and aspirations of the local people to decision-makers at both the district and national levels.

Fourth, the DDC facilitates cross-sectoral coordination and enables an integrated approach to the planning and implementation of rural development. A central aspect of this is coordination between governmental and non-governmental institutions. The DDC also has an essential role in the monitoring and management of programs and projects that enables remedial action to be instigated more quickly and effectively than would be possible from the center. Finally, projects discussed by and receiving inputs from DDC members are more likely to meet the needs of local people and be sensitive to local conditions than projects designed in Nairobi.

As presently operating, the DDC has several weaknesses. Although it has a major role in the planning and implementation of rural development, it has only a very limited role in the budgetary process that allocates funding for that development. The system of District Plans and annual budgetary annexes and the procedures laid down for drawing up both annual estimates and the forward budget are all designed to enable districts to play a major part in the allocation of development funds. In practice, this seldom happens and funding allocations continue to be dominated by ministry headquarters. This nullifies the DDC's ability to set local priorities and coordinate across sectors.

DDCs do not have access to sufficient discretionary funds to counteract the failure described above. Aside from two aid agency projects that provide funds directly for districts, the Scandinavian Rural Development Fund and the EEC Micro-projects Program, DDCs have no discretion over resources and priorities. These remain under the control of the President's DC and the District Head, who, as noted earlier, is controlled by the centralizing pressures of the country's unintegrated prefectoral system.

Further, although the increase in technical manpower resources at the district-level since the introduction of the District Focus Strategy has been impressive, there remains a gap between the responsibilities assigned to the districts and their capacity to undertake them. And, in order for the DDC to fully undertake its responsibilities, further training of all its members is essential. This should include inducing a better understanding of the strategy, planning and managing development projects, setting priorities, and so forth. For Departmental Officers, further technical training is also required. The Ministry of Planning and National Development and the Office of the President, have produced a detailed training document, which is to be expected given the attention to specificity that has marked the implementation of the District Focus Strategy.[10] Yet little can be invested in such training because of limited central budget resources.

4. Missed Opportunity and Failed Development Impact

The Kenya case demonstrates how a deconcentrated form of the Distributed Institutional Monopoly strategy, when implemented by a monopolist-oriented central government, can block improved accountability, management efficiency, and resource mobilization. The case is important because Kenya's administrative decentralization strategy is found in many late developing countries. In this regard, the Kenya case supports the Administrative Design Framework argument that monopoly weakens the capacity of a government to produce and provide public goods and services in all regions of the country.

The District Focus Strategy devolved no real power over public sector tasks and roles to districts. Rather, it reinforced the centralized control of lower-levels of government and increased the center's penetration of the rural and urban areas. At its heart, it strengthened the deconcentrated administrative design that was already in place.

To a large extent, this is because the major impetus behind the implementation of the Strategy was to strengthen the center's control over the use of domestic resources in a task environment marked by high population growth rates, rising expectations by rural and urban people for increased and equitable provision of public sector goods and services, declining growth rates, reduced levels of Government revenues, and aid agency limitations on budget deficits. The argument in support of this decentralization reform came from the 1982 report by the "Working Party on Government Expenditures."[11] It argued that the established district planning system carried out by MPND field officers could be expanded to promote coordination of development in rural areas that had become too complex to be well managed entirely from the center. This forthright report was critical of the highly centralized system built up during the Kenyatta era, arguing it was a major obstacle to effective decentralization.[12]

Beneath this financial and administrative rationale for decentralization were two significant political objectives: (1) greater political control for an insecure President whose major supporters came from poorly developed and neglected districts; and (2) enhanced power to transfer development resources away from the former President's region to his own region and those of his supporters. In this sense, what appeared as a move toward devolvement and participation was at its core a deception.

Because the District Focus Strategy gives DDCs the task of specifying district development priorities, Members of Parliament (MPs) need to participate in DDC meetings. They can no longer simply deliver projects they favor through lobbying with Cabinet ministers and manipulating clientalist relations with powerful central provincial civil servants. As a result, MPs became more involved in district level politics, which made them more vulnerable and weaker, a clear objective of President Moi's administration.

The District Focus initiative gave little thought to urban development and the problems of the devolved local authority system that had survived in crippled form since Kenyatta's dismantling efforts and recentralization. This was to be expected, given the fact that no cabinet ministers from urban areas have served under Moi's rural-focused Government. While a deconcentrated form of decentralization, the District Focus Strategy has potential to allow some progress toward the advantages identified by proponents of devolution and delegation strategies. But this new Strategy was a long way from extensive and meaningful devolution and delegation. In the words of two long-term observers: "...decentralization to the district level and the empowerment of the rural population are not the same, not least because the former has resulted more in deconcentration than in devolution."[13]

The District Focus Strategy illustrates the difficulties of promoting decentralization through an administrative strategy that is long on central monopoly and short on pluralism.[14] Field agents of line ministries have few financial and operational resources to promote development projects and programs or provide collective goods and services. This is the result of low economic growth, scarce government revenues, limited budgetary resources for allocation to central line ministries charged with carrying out public sector tasks, aid agency restrictions on the size of budget deficits, and the channeling of aid agency funds through central ministry budgets. With regard to devolution, the Ministry of Local Government lacks the funds to provide either grants or loans to local authorities that can compensate for the revenue sources that were stripped away in 1969. What financial resources are available are inadequate to carry out the limited public tasks that were left in the hands of local authorities.

Local self-help groups and NGOs have shown themselves capable of taking on tasks and performing roles that central agents are unable to carry out. Yet, instead of encouraging them and pursuing Institutional Pluralism through delegation strategies, those controlling the central government seek whenever possible to control and shape their activities. The result of this Kenyan approach to Distributed Institutional Monopoly is the inadequate execution of public sector tasks, a failure which adds to the large number of other constraints that are currently blocking economic and social development in Kenya.

DISTRIBUTED INSTITUTIONAL MONOPOLY: REGIONAL DEVOLUTION IN ETHIOPIA

A number of political leaders, aid agency professionals, and academics are currently examining the utility of administrative decentralization reforms as a strategy for dealing with ethnic, religious, and regional separatists. Their discussion of federal, confederal, and devolved unitary models of administrative decentralization is plagued by two problems. First, there are few developing countries that have adopted federal or confederal approaches to governance and their experience is generally not relevant to the current problems of such countries as Ethiopia, Somalia, Rwanda, Sudan, and Sri Lanka.[15] Second, there are few case studies explicitly focused on the design and implementation issues faced by fragmented states seeking to use administrative decentralization as a foundation for reconstruction.[16] Using the principles, purposes, and properties of the Administrative Design Framework, this case addresses both problems. It does this by documenting the complex implementation problems faced by the Federal Democratic Republic of Ethiopia (FDRE) as it seeks to reconstruct a post-imperial state based on ethnic federalism through reforms grounded on a strategy of devolving public sector powers and tasks to regions dominated by the country's major ethnic groups.[17] In doing so it highlights the complex implementation problems faced by governments adopting devolved forms of Distributed Institutional Monopoly.

Since taking control of the government in 1991, the leadership of the FDRE have been strongly committed to an administrative strategy aimed at transforming Ethiopia from a highly centralized unitary state, which for decades administered its rural and urban areas through tightly controlled administrative deconcentration, into a federal government based on substantial devolution to ethnically defined jurisdictions.[18]

The FDRE's administrative decentralization reforms merit close attention. In Ethiopia, like most of these fragmented countries, the central Government has very limited human and financial resources. As such, the Ethiopian experiment challenges one of the central propositions that has emerged out four decades of research on administrative decentralization: namely, its effective implementation requires strong, confident states backed by adequate financial and manpower capacity.

Further, the FDRE's experience reflects on the advice of Western specialists who argue that devolution is the only strategy that can: improve government effectiveness in the delivery of public goods and services, promote revenue collection, and facilitate civil society, popular participation, and democratisation. Ethiopia's efforts help one evaluate the arguments by seasoned professionals that devolution based on ethnicity is a not a viable strategy for reconstructing politically fragmented states, arguments based in part on the fact that only Switzerland and Canada have ever succeeded in building a federal state based on ethnic identifications.[19] In sum, a case study of the FDRE experience has much to offer senior decision-makers in troubled states and aid agency professionals seeking to assist them.

1. Emergence of a New Government

The Tigrayan People's Liberation Front (TPLF) seized power from the military government of Mengistu Haile Mariam in May 1991.[20] A July 1991 National Conference attended by most political groups led to a charter that established the Transitional Government of Ethiopia (TGE) and set forth guidelines for drafting a new constitution, promoting economic and social development, establishing a system of devolved regional decentralization, holding democratic elections, ensuring basic human rights, and protecting cultural heritages.[21] Of all these initiatives, the most difficult was the one aimed at clarifying legal relationships between central government ministries and agencies and administratively decentralized regions.

The major objectives for this top-down initiative were to: (1) reduce the inter-ethnic conflict that has divided Ethiopian society for centuries; (2) address the effects of military dictatorship, civil war, failed agrarian socialism, and famine; (3) build a polity based on democratic principles; (4) promote equitable material conditions for all of the country's fifty-five million people, the majority of whom are subsistence farmers and peri-urban unemployed; and (5) improve the efficiency and effectiveness of project and program implementation. The TGE's leaders argued that they could use devolution to promote these objectives without threatening other important objectives such as economic growth and political stability.

2. Implementation of Devolution Reforms Prior to Ratification of the Constitution

Prior to the drafting and ratification of the Constitution, the TGE began the process by formulating regulations and systems that outlined the relationships between central ministries and devolved local-level governments. The march toward this objective began in early 1992 when the TGE issued Proclamation No. 7, which aimed at establishing a provisional "federal" system of regions based on ethnic-linguistic identities and two urban regions that were too diverse to be subdivided by ethnic identity.[22] By mid-1994 there were ten regions, because five regions voluntarily decided to coalesce into the single Southern Nations Nationalities People's Regional Government.

The next step was to divide the regions into zones and *weredas*.[23] The boundaries of these districts and subdistricts have historical roots in the deconcentrated system of the Emperor and the military government that followed him. The boundaries of these units were reviewed and in some cases altered. The process of boundary demarcation was not without difficulty, particularly in regard to weredas located along the borders of regions. As of mid-1995, some boundaries were still contested and not all zonal boundaries had been specified. But ethnic-based boundary disputes were anticipated by the 1992 proclamation, which provided that the TGE continue to revise boundaries as the "details of geographical borders of each nation, nationality and people are specifically laid down." The emerging draft Constitution contained similar provisions for dealing with boundary disputes and revisions.

The structure, tasks, and roles of the system of administrative decentralization established between 1992 and 1994 are only briefly reviewed here. This is because the 1994 Constitution does not adequately describe these structures, tasks, and roles. It is also because the new Constitution authorizes regions to draft their own constitutions and establish their own administrative hierarchy, legal structures, and organizational patterns. It should be noted that to date, those regions that have drafted and adopted their own constitutions have largely repeated the language in the federal Constitution.

Because not all regions had zones during the 1991–94 period, only the *wereda* need be considered here. This local-level unit has jurisdiction over rural and urban divisions, called *kebeles*.[24] *Wereda* government is supposed to consist of a directly elected council having responsibility for tasks necessary to prepare, determine, and implement within its jurisdiction plans concerning social services and economic development, as well as to implement laws, policies, directives, and programs of the national and regional governments.

Interestingly, this legislation fails to address the status of municipalities. Ethiopia, like Kenya, was until the TGE a unitary state that ruled through deconcentration and limited devolution to municipalities. In 1973 there were more than 150 municipalities that were overseen by the Municipalities Department of the Ministry of Interior. This Ministry was abolished. Yet, these municipalities continue to elect mayors and councils, collect specified taxes, and carry out public tasks spelled out in pre-1974 legislation. Clearly the government has to give attention to the future of municipalities and build that future into the emerging federal system.

An attempt at clarifying the activities, responsibilities, and resources of different governmental levels in this emerging system of devolved administrative decentralization is found in three additional proclamations. Proclamations No. 26 and No. 33 of 1992 attempted to define how revenue would be shared between the central Government and regional, zonal, and *wereda* "self-governments."[25] Proclamation No. 41 of 1993 sought to define the tasks and roles of the Central and Regional Executive Organs of the Transitional Government.[26] Despite these three additional proclamations, disputes over federal and regional structures, roles, and resources continue.

The FDRE has given a great deal of attention to the spatial and structural components of its emerging administrative decentralization reforms. Difficult jurisdictional boundary tasks have been addressed and the levels and structures of central and local-level government units have been defined.

3. Federalism and Governance Under the New Constitution

The 1994 Constitution established the Federal Democratic Republic of Ethiopia (FDRE), comprised of nine ethnically based regions: Tigray, Amhara, Benshangul-Gumaz, Afar, Somali, Oromia, Harar, Southern Ethiopia People's, and Gambela.[27] In addition, there are two ethnically mixed urban areas: Addis Ababa and Dire Dawa. Most of these regions, such as Tigray, Amhara, Oromia, and Somali, are dominated by one ethnic group. Others are more diverse, such as Southern Ethiopia People's, which is composed of at least forty-five ethnic groups.

Ethnicity was the key criteria used in drawing boundaries. Indeed, Ethiopians are to be registered according to their ethnic group. Identification of ethnicity is not precisely spelled out in Ethiopian law, but the major factor for defining groups appears to be linguistic.[28] So, while under the new constitution the official language of the country is Amharic, all Ethiopian languages are to enjoy equal recognition, with each region having the right to determine its respective official language.

The Constitution offers little guidance on managing federal-regional powers and tasks. In most federal systems this is done by the courts, however, legal experts on Ethiopia do not believe the judiciary, as currently organized, can carry out this role. Further, unlike successful federal systems where the constitution is the product of a contract entered into by sub-units to form a federal government, in Ethiopia the federal system was created by the center, poising the potential that at some future date the center could declare a return to a unitary state. Finally, most legal scholars hold that federal systems should not allow a right to secession.

The apparently clear identification of respective federal-regional tax powers is qualified by the fact that additional articles of the constitution allow federal and regional governments to jointly levy and collect employment, income, and sales taxes from public enterprises that are jointly established by the federal government and a region, dividends private firms issue to shareholders, and the income on large mining, petroleum, and gas operations. What appears to be missing from the Constitution and previous proclamations is any attention to the power of regions to tax individuals working in the private sector.

Relative to administrative decentralization, the Constitution provides little specificity about federal and regional objectives and tasks. The 1992–94 proclamations and political statements that preceded the Constitution are also not very specific. Aside from the obvious implementation problems this lack of clarity will generate, the Administrative Design Framework suggests the absence of task specificity will make it difficult for the new administrative strategy to achieve accountability, management efficiency, and effectiveness. This suggests the Government will also have trouble achieving equity, a central requirement if its system of ethnic federalism is to gain popular support and achieve stability.

The federal government has yet to begin to design a monitoring mechanism that can track the capacity of devolved local government units to collect revenue, budget effectively, accountably expend allocations, or effectively administer the implementation of public sector programs and projects.

4. Devolution Constraints

The government's attempt to promote devolution is full of risks. Foremost among these is that devolution to large regions reinforces the demands of some ethnic groups for regional secession or partition.[29] A further risk is that the promotion of devolved ethnic governments hampers central government efforts to build a democratic system, for the emerging region-based ethnic parties have frequently disagreed with the governance systems and electoral rules being formulated at the center. Finally, regional-based ethnicity is a development risk because it limits population movements required to take advantage of economic opportunities, and creates entitlements that can block development.[30] In this regard, it threatens to disenfranchise a number of Ethiopians who, over the past few decades, have moved into regions dominated by other ethnic groups, most notably northern farmers who were resettled in the south during the Mengistu era.

Initial bureaucratic opposition to devolution and confusion over emerging inter-governmental tasks, roles, and relations delayed and complicated the implementation of the government's reforms. Government failed to anticipate, much less specify, the complex tasks, roles, and relationships required to translate the devolutionary strategy they promised into a functioning reality. Further, they did not clearly articulate the assignment of responsibility for policy, regulatory, personnel, service provision, revenue, and budgetary activities. By 1996 there was evidence that senior officials were making progress in addressing these difficulties, progress that supported the goal of meaningful devolution to regions.

Nevertheless, the new Constitution did little to clarify these complexities, demarcate the tasks and role responsibilities of the different levels or units of governance, and formulate clear procedures and systems governing the relationships between the federal and regional governments.

There is, as yet, no extant comparative review of current organizational structure, institutional and personnel capacity, and procedural processes of the newly devolved governmental units. On paper the proposed system of administrative decentralization appears to be radically different from the previous system. But given the absence of task specificity and attention to roles and relationships, the transition to devolution will be marked for some time by an opaque, de facto combination of shifting deconcentrated and devolved forms of Distributed Institutional Monopoly. This combination is likely to have great variability by region.

The implementation of the government's strategy of administrative decentralization has been slowed in some regions by human resource constraints. Demand for managerial, professional, and technical manpower is generated by the fact that regional bureaus, and to a lesser extent *wereda* bureaus, mirror central ministries. But regions and *weredas* lack the personnel to staff these bureaucratic units. This is particularly the case in the more remote region and *wereda* capitals.

Regions whose capitals were developed in the imperial and military eras seem to be progressing in their ability to take on highly generalized tasks. To some extent, this is because their major towns are more attractive for posting, there are better infrastructure linkages between them and Addis Ababa, and because they have more adequate offices, facilities, vehicles, and supplies. Remote regions lack these advantages and have trouble attracting and retaining competent public servants. But the problem of capacity is far deeper than skilled personnel and infrastructure. It lies in weak resource bases and inadequate financial allocations.

At the heart of the coming struggle between the federal government and the regions for definition of structure, organization, tasks, and roles will be the revenue and budget system. Substantial debate and accommodation has to take place over how revenue will be shared and grants-in-aid will be formulated.

In terms of revenue the center is in the dominant position. Its control over regional budget allocations is declining, though it is currently possible for the political party in power to ensure that central government priorities are followed at the regional level. Central control is needed and beneficial for a major strategy of the EPRDF is to address inter-ethnic inequality and the righting of past wrongs through federal allocations. Government also acknowledges that it will be a long time before devolved units can increase their revenues and that central domination of budgetary resources will continue well into the future. But officials argue that the federal government intends to give regions considerable control over their budget priorities and expenditures, even to the extent of reallocation among sectors. This appears to be happening. Developing a growth-oriented and equitable revenue and budget allocation system for a country as ecologically diverse and economically imbalanced as Ethiopia will be much more difficult than current statements by the Government suggest.

There are marked inter-regional disparities that affect the capacity of various regions to raise revenues, staff governmental units with capable personnel, and administer or implement federal and regional policies, plans, programs, and projects. Given the range of inter-regional disparities, the federal government will have to give serious attention to formulating its allocation objective goals. Perhaps the most important goal that must be specified relates to the government's often stated hope that it can reallocate resources from richer to poorer areas. But to date, little thought has been given to this goal or to the implications of related allocation goals for widespread economic growth and political stability. This poses a problem, because current regional disparities are sure to affect the coming debate over how to shape and implement the Constitution's directives for administrative decentralization.

It can be argued that the new Constitution and the government's proclamations create a de facto hybrid pattern of administrative decentralization, one that is still part deconcentrated and part devolved. If Ethiopia is really following a hybrid strategy of administrative decentralization, the question arises of how long will it take for it to make the transition to meaningful devolution. Aid agency professionals closest to the situation have concluded that it will take a considerable period of time, particularly because tasks, roles, role sequences, and relationships are not well defined.

Finally, it should be noted that efforts to specify objectives, goals, tasks, roles, and relations will not be easy because the bureaucracies, political parties, NGOs, and civic associations involved in debating how to implement ethnic federalism differ in several ways: (1) in their expectations about the possibilities and difficulties of empowering local populations; (2) in their experience in managing large-scale institutions other than military units; (3) in their understanding of the difficulties of formulating policies essential to development and implementing such policies through the preparation of regulations, the provision of basic goods and services to urban and rural populations, and the identification, design, and implementation of sustainable development oriented projects and programs; and (4) in their appreciation of the complexities of public sector planning processes, revenue generation, budgeting, expenditure, and accounting procedures in line ministries and agencies. Debates among these parties and associations will greatly effect efforts to better define the structures of government, formulate clear objectives and goals, specify and sequence roles, establish relationship patterns, and address problems related to the level and distribution of human and financial resources.

5. Grounds for Optimism?

This case is one of a government and an administrative decentralization reform still in flux. It is a case which illustrates that the political and economic objectives of devolution can be in conflict. If regions are granted extensive responsibility over such tasks as determining development priorities, establishing economic and social policies, and controlling revenue and budget allocations, then devolution can possibly undermine the national economic objectives and reforms while serving as an effective tool of conflict resolution through regional self-governance. On the other hand, if the federal government retains substantial policy, revenue, and budgetary control while limiting the capacity of devolved governmental levels to determine and finance their own priorities, then the political effectiveness of ethnic federalism as a strategy of peaceful reconstruction may be undermined. Finding the balance between these two objectives will take a good deal of the attention of political leaders and senior decision-makers over the next few years.

The elaboration of federal-regional tasks, roles, and relations will take time. It is also going to occur unevenly, for there is great variability between the regions in terms of economic potential, administrative and financial capacity. Given the perseverance of the TGE and the FDRE in promoting devolutionary reforms over the past four years, there is some hope that a viable federal system will emerge within the next decade. Central to this prediction is that the country will experience substantial economic growth and that useful aid agency funding will be available to support the devolution reforms. But whatever the outcome, the Ethiopian experience is going to generate insights into the complexity and potential for fragmented regions to use the Distributed Institutional Monopoly strategy of devolution as an effective approach for dealing with demands for greater autonomy from region-based ethnic, religious, and nationalist groups.

INSTITUTIONAL PLURALISM: DELEGATION IN MEXICO'S 100 CITIES PROGRAM

This case study describes and analyzes Mexico's new and innovative 100 Cities Program. This exercise in administrative decentralization provides an excellent illustration of the principles of Institutional Pluralism. The program seeks to strengthen selected urban governments so that they can decide upon and manage the development of local infrastructure. The delegation of tasks and roles that is occurring under the program illustrates a strategy some governments should consider as they seek to find ways to down-size the central government while ensuring that key collective goods and services are provided in metropolitan regions. At present, few developing countries are attempting to follow an administrative design strategy based on Institutional Pluralism. But, as argued in earlier chapters, there is a solid rationale for delegation of public sector tasks and roles to private sector firms and organizations. Hence, it is likely that Mexico's approach will, over the coming years, be increasingly adopted by late developing countries.

The Administrative Design Framework presented in Chapter 4 gives specific attention to pluralist strategies. Unlike the Kenyan and Ethiopian cases, the Mexico case is one of a partial transition from institutional monopoly to institutional pluralism. For this reason, it utilizes the principles the framework more than the other two cases, demonstrating with greater effect the guidelines suggested by the framework.

1. Administrative Organization

Mexico is a federal republic comprised of thirty-one states and a federal district, Mexico City, governed under a constitution adopted in 1917. It is one of the few developing countries classified as having a federal system, though it operates in practice more like a centralized Institutional Monopoly.[31] Each state has its own constitution, governor, and legislative chamber. The federal district is administered by a regent governor appointed by the President and is divided into sixteen delegations.

The states are divided into municipios. In Mexico, as in most Latin American countries, a *municipio* can have jurisdiction over a rural area, a mixed rural and urban area, or an urban area. Indeed, it is not uncommon to find a large urban area divided into two or more *municipios*. Municipios are in essence a district.

Despite this pattern of decentralized governance, Mexico is controlled and guided by a highly centralized administrative, political, and economic system. At the head of the system is the President, who is directly elected for a single six-year term. For all of Mexico's post-revolutionary period, presidential candidates have been hand-picked by their predecessors and expected to lead the powerful, and until recently, completely dominant organization: the Institutional Revolutionary Party (PRI). The President rules through powerful central ministries. Real power is held by the President who selects all of the top personnel in the strong central ministries. This gives him enormous political, administrative, and fiscal power. Federal ministries control most of the country's governmental resources and administer the country. Because of the limited deconcentration and devolution to the states and municipios, in the early 1980s Mexico could best be described as a state based on the administrative design of Institutional Monopoly pursuing a tightly controlled and limited form of Distributed Monopoly in regard to its federal states and their lower-level governmental municipios.

2. Historical Centralism and Recent Transition Toward Decentralization

There are historical reasons for Mexico's highly centralized and monopolistic administrative systems and the current transition toward more meaningful forms of political, market, and administrative decentralization. In response to the dislocation of the revolutionary period, both political and military leaders viewed centralization as a means of linking the divided country together.[32] It was hoped that a centralized state would be a source of social stability and economic development into which regional leaders could be integrated through political and economic enticements. This process of centralization was aided by the development of strong clientalist networks created by the PRI, which has ruled the country since 1929.

In the 1980s, three events occurred which revealed fundamental weaknesses in the centralized socio-political system and created opportunities for advocates of economic liberalization and administrative decentralization to make some headway into reforming the government. The first was the debt crisis, which forced a reevaluation of the dominant role the central government had played in economic and administrative affairs. Second, the 1985 earthquake revealed weaknesses in the ability of the central Government to respond to domestic crisis. And third, the 1988 election, which was widely believed to have been less than fair, sent shock waves through the political establishment which had ruled the country continuously for almost sixty years. These and other events widened the debate about the need for decentralization and created a political opening for considering new roles for the states and *municipios* in Mexico.

A program for decentralizing the federal public administration was planned in the late 1970s. However, after the debt crisis in 1982, the centralized administrative and political system found that the dwindling financial resources forced the flow of direct patronage to the regions to be cut back; other means of placating the local party bosses needed to be developed.[33] The government of Miguel de la Madrid which came to power in 1982, addressed this crisis of power and political legitimacy by modifying Article 115 of the Constitution the following year to provide more political and financial autonomy to the *municipios*. The program also called for the transfer of health and education services to state and local governments and included both personnel shifts and financial grants from the central administration. Under the direction of the Ministry of Programming and Budget, regional parastatal organizations were to be transferred to the states, development plans were to be made at the state level, and administrative tasks and roles were to be moved out of Mexico City. Additionally, a system of fixed transfers to *municipios* was proposed to replace the old local financing system, which relied on political contacts and personal power to gain access to resources. The hope was that these measures would create more local-level administrative autonomy by granting the municipal governments more responsibilities and creating more reliable, less politically dependent local sources of financing for those programs.

As the administrative decentralization program got underway in 1985, a major earthquake struck Mexico City. The physical destruction of many central government offices, and the subsequent problems the federal government had in continuing to implement public sector tasks throughout the country, provided a powerful symbol of the dangers of excessive centralized Institutional Monopoly over public sector tasks. The federal government's efforts to manage the crisis in an open manner encouraged the participation of more local and regional institutions in the decision-making process. This reinforced the decentralization already underway in some ministries.

Eventually, the implementation of the administrative decentralization program was threatened by central power brokers who were committed to the historical strategy of Institutional Monopoly and the benefits of control that it generated. Central ministries resisted the transfer of public sector personnel, tasks, and roles to the state and local governments. Unions, historically one of the largest beneficiaries of centrally controlled political patronage, feared the diffusion of their membership and the accompanying loss of power. And local politicians in the *municipios,* accustomed more to distributing favors than to managing health and education programs, were ill-equipped to handle these new responsibilities. Further, the proposed decentralization reform, which established a system of stable financial transfers to the municipios, were undermined by state governments that either failed to enact the necessary enabling legislation or didn't cooperate fully in the program. The result was a shadow structure of municipios highly dependent on the central government for their funding and generally unable to implement the social service programs with which they had been entrusted with. The limited administrative and economic impact of de la Madrid's attempt at administrative decentralization left the central Government vulnerable to a third major shock to Mexican's centralized socio-political system. This occurred in 1988 when the PRI support sank to historically low levels, winning a national election with only 51 percent of the vote. Upon taking office, Mexico's new president, Carlos Salinas, found himself confronted with a hostile populace, economic instability, and political uncertainty both in the PRI and the population at large. In response, he developed a new program intended to stimulate economic activity, reinforce the PRI's political base, and help *municipios* develop economically and strengthen their administrative resources. The program, known as SOLIDARIDAD, is a poverty alleviation initiative that directly funds locally planned and implemented projects. These grants provide tangible aid to rural and urban populations, which are being hurt by the economic reforms underway in Mexico. Four years later, the 100 Cities Program was developed to aid urban areas. This program is focused on assisting the selected *municipios* in identifying strategic needs and generating significant local resources to meet these needs.

In spite of the fact that the SOLIDARIDAD program spent billions of dollars during the Salinas administration, the uprisings in Chiapas State in January 1994 highlighted the fact that half the country's ninety-two million people are mired in poverty. The uprising also signaled the strong desire among the southern states for meaningful local-level empowerment and greater role in the process of national economic development. The events in Chiapas affected both the PRI and the 1994 presidential election. The winner of that election and current president of Mexico, Ernesto Zedillo, publicly stated during the campaign and his inaugural speech that the Government was now firmly committed to increased devolution of public sector tasks to *municipios* and to increased delegation of particular roles related to those tasks to private sector firms and organizations. Many state and *municipio* governments now have found themselves struggling financially to pay off past debts and are without funds to follow through with their development plans. Therefore, it remains to be seen if the rhetoric on administrative decentralization can be effectively translated into action in this time of economic and fiscal crisis created by the rapid devaluation of the peso.

3. Overview of the 100 Cities Program

In less than two years, the Mexican Government launched its 100 Cities Program, which is an ambitious strategy for improving the development of 116 cities containing 207 *municipios*.[34] All of the newly targeted *municipios* are located outside of the four major urban clusters. The program is of interest in its own right because of its bold strategy for economic development, but it is also of interest to this study because it illustrates an attempt to apply the administrative strategy of Institutional Pluralism. The objective of the program is, in the words of the Mexican Government, to use the public sector to "incentivize the city" and promote private investment through a range of legal, planning, and investment mechanisms. Like the "reinventing government" school, the program seeks to structure the market for public purpose. This public purpose is the economic development of the targeted cities.

The 100 Cities Program is based on an evaluation of current patterns and development trends in Mexico. As such, the program is set in a larger context of policy change and reform. Instead of continuing a centralized development strategy of import-substitution that has led to concentrated but congested expansion of a handful of urban clusters, the program is based upon, and embodies, the principles of a new form of market-oriented decentralization that emphasizes export-led growth and broad-based development in the urban municipios outside the country's four urban clusters: Mexico City, Guadalajara, Monterrey, and Puebla.[35] The development strategy hinges on the belief that these 116 selected urban centers are potential economic growth poles that can: (1) facilitate the growth of historically underdeveloped municipio areas serving as sources of economic activity; (2) promote more balanced regional growth; (3) serve as the principal nodes in expanded international trade, especially under the

North American Free Trade Agreement (NAFTA); and (4) attract the rural migrants who have historically gone to the four large urban agglomerations in search of economic opportunities.[36] Preliminary economic surveys and some detailed studies of economic strategies suggest that there is reason to be optimistic and expect some of the targeted cities to become growth poles and promote these four development objectives.

The program is primarily intended to support the development of municipal areas outside of the four largest urban clusters. The targets, known as municipios, are administrative areas that include both urban and rural lands. The first step, and the cornerstone of the decentralization strategy, was to liberalize the land market in the *municipios* around the urban areas to facilitate investment and promote growth. This liberalization process was accomplished by improved land use planning intended to successfully incorporate that land into urban areas controlled by local municipal administrations. The second step now underway is to strengthen *municipio* administration and reorient it from traditional administration to proactive planning that "incentivizes the city." The third step is to build infrastructure in the *municipio* that will facilitate economic growth. The program gives priority to the public sector tasks of sewerage and solid waste disposal, environmental improvement, and road provision. It does this while pursuing a strategy of delegating responsibility to private sector firms for investing, building, and maintaining this infrastructure.

The 100 Cities Program is guided by four principles: participation, sustainability, equity, and environmentally sound development. The program's design tightly interconnects these four principles. Perhaps most significant is the participatory nature of the strategy's design. As a working principle, the program requires local participation in the planning process, local funding for a portion of the projects, and local implementation and maintenance oversight. The program requires the *municipios* to establish citizen advisory groups that participate in the elaboration, oversight, and evaluation of the plan in an ongoing process. Once the plan is developed, it becomes a public document available to both the advisory groups and other interested parties.

Because the program's development strategy is initially focused on revising land use, and because land-related issues are culturally sensitive, active participation is critical to facilitate reforms that promote the equitable and efficient use of land as well as limit abuse of reform initiatives. Like the macro-development strategy it is based on, the program seeks to avoid imbalanced development by increasing participation. Participation facilitates the achievement of the commitment that the interests of land-holders, business organizations, unions, agricultural associations, environmentalists, and other groups will be considered. Towards this end, the municipios are required to make efforts to coordinate the participation of these parties assuring their input into the formulation and implementation of land-related initiatives.

There are five components of the program: (1) land use regulation and urban management; (2) urban land and territorial reserves; (3) highways and transportation; (4) environmental objectives; and (5) renovation of the urban centers. These components are carried out through a number of tasks, the roles for which are made the responsibility of central, non-central, and private sector institutions and organizations. The components, and their mix of tasks and roles, will be briefly described, with particular attention being given to how the program matches the model of the Institutional Pluralism strategy.

Under the first component of the Program, land use regulation and urban management, the central ministry responsible for initiating the program, SEDESOL (the Ministry of Social Development), is assisting municipios in preparing land use plans. To improve the tax base of local government, SEDESOL is also assisting municipios in updating their cadastral records to increase local revenue generation, principally through expanding the tax base rather than increasing the tax rates. Aside from strengthening the planning and land registration capacity of the municipios, SEDESOL is also assisting them to strengthen their capacity to manage urban development.

The second component of the program involves the management of urban land and territorial reserves. The principal action here was the reform of Article 27 of the Constitution, which freed up the land from the *ejido* structure of land tenure.[37] With the liberalization of the land market, the areas around the urban *municipios* have also been opened up to new development. One use that the government has promoted for this land is the creation of more low cost housing. To date, over 50,000 low-income dwellings have been built in less than two years, for approximately one billion dollars. The funding for that housing development has been divided into thirds, with the central government, *municipios,* and private funders each paying an equal share.

The third component of the program is building transportation infrastructure. Because it is in an early stage of development, much of the work to date has been studies on the transport needs and training on transport management. Once these studies are completed, it is anticipated that a mix of deconcentrated, devolved, and delegated governmental and private funding and implementation will be used to improve roads in the targeted municipios.

The fourth component of the program is environmental protection through planning and infrastructure investment that protects water and manages sewage and solid waste. Recognizing the limited financial resources of the *municipios,* the program has adopted a strategy of delegating responsibility to private sector firms for carrying out public sector tasks related to this component. The fifth component of the program is the renovation of the urban centers of 116 cities. This part of the program is an explicit recognition that a plan for a given *municipio's* growth should not just involve expanding the edges of the city, but should also revitalize the core of the city. The core not only gives a city its character, but, because of its link to a cultural heritage, gives a city its dynamism. Urban renovation needs to preserve the balance of a city's core and the program is considering preserving and developing the low income housing in the urban core, again through a mix of public and private involvement in the roles related to this component.

To achieve the program's ambitious goals, the administrative mechanism is fourfold: (1) to build capacity at the local municipio level; (2) to coordinate federal, state, and local government (*municipios*); (3) to introduce local participation in planning and implementation at the *municipio* level; and (4) to delegate selected public sector tasks and roles to private sector firms and organizations. The ultimate objective is to create a partnership between the public and private sectors to provide investment that, in turn, promotes job creation.[38] As such, the administrative strategy of the program closely approximates the Institutional Pluralism strategy outlined in Chapter 4. Instead of operating on the basis of the Distributed Institutional Monopoly strategy and controlling tasks and resources, the municipios are trying to use public seed capital and their planning resources to reveal to private firms growth opportunities that lead to delegated task-related responsibilities. Further, as expected by the Administrative Design Framework, by opening up the planning process to public scrutiny through urban development advisory councils and citizen consultation forums, the program increases the accountability of *municipios.*[39] In short, the program is attempting to redirect *municipio* administration to serve a brokerage role—to leverage public resources to shape the market to serve public purposes.

The 100 Cities Program is ambitious, both because its *development strategy* promotes an intervention that connects investors with *municipios* and because its *administrative strategy* seeks to transform the *municipio* into a broker that increases the participation of private sector firms and organizations in the execution of public sector tasks. The program is of interest to students of decentralization precisely because it provides a model of how to begin a transition process that moves the design of decentralization strategies relating to public sector tasks and roles from monopoly to pluralism. To understand the significance of this transition in Mexico, it is essential to understand the political and economic heritage that underpins the current day administrative culture of the country's *municipios*. It is also important to understand how the recent evolution of Mexico's political economy and development strategies make a move toward pluralism possible.

4. Roles and Sequencing of Roles

At the time of this writing, the 100 Cities Program has been in operation for less than two years. Given this short time span, it is difficult to draw definitive conclusions about the role of Institutional Pluralism in this administrative systems reform. Still, it is possible to make some tentative observations about the Program reform in terms of the roles played by different administrative levels and the private sector. There are three roles which the center has exclusively exercised and three roles that have been jointly performed by the central Government and the municipios.

Changing the inertia in the administrative system at both the center and local levels required a strong *leadership* role from the center. President Salinas initially provided that leadership, as demonstrated by the reform of Article 27 of the Constitution, which completed changes in the land tenure system. Implementing this constitutional reform was not an easy task, for there was strong political opposition to any change in a land policy initially forged out of the Revolution.[40] Another indicator of Presidential commitment was the scrapping of the previous planning ministry, called the Secretariat of Programming and Budget. Many of the planning and budgeting tasks were transferred to the Ministry of Finance and a new Ministry of Social Development (SEDESOL) was created. This new ministry was charged with developing and implementing the social policies that had been a part of the President's office before the reorganization. The 100 Cities Program was then added to SEDESOL in an effort to promote administrative decentralization and new economic development.

A second role that the center performed was as a *strategist*. A strategy is more than a plan. It is both an ambitious vision and a pragmatic approach for achieving that vision. A third and critical role that the center provided was that of *regulator*. SEDESOL regulates a broad process of consultation, cooperation, and coordination among many actors, both public and private.

While the roles that the central government performs are important, what is critical to the success of local-level administration is the sharing of roles. As discussed in Chapters 3 and 4, role sharing promotes accountability, which in turn should increase the efficiency of service delivery. Breaking the monopoly of central design in *municipio* government is a major objective of the program. Three roles are shared between the *municipio* and the central ministries in implementing this Program: financial, oversight, and planning.

The *financial* role is critical and it often determines the balance of administrative authority. From the very beginning, the central planning ministry implementing this program, SEDESOL, made it clear that funding from the center would be limited and that it would decline over time. The success of the program depends upon the entrepreneurship of the *municipio* to mobilize both public funds through taxes and private capital through the delegation of some role tasks to firms. To date, the program's prescription for participatory financing of development has succeeded. The program's initial tranche of fifty thousand low-cost homes was financed in roughly equal shares by SEDESOL, the municipios and private capital. Whether such financial support can continue given 1995 economic crisis in Mexico remains to be seen.[41] But clearly, with adequate resources this initiative appears extremely promising.

Sharing the financial role is an achievement in decentralization because it provides non-central government institutions like the municipio with both a stake in the program and some leverage with the central government ministries. Control over and use of local funds also strengthens the second shared role, which is *oversight*. With local funds involved as well as private capital, there is a strong incentive on the part of local citizens to ensure that the capital is spent appropriately. Toward this end, since 1993 the Program has established fifty-four urban development advisory councils, with thirty more in the process of being installed. Oversight from the center comes in the form of the planning process. Those plans serve as guides to the programming of investments, though the entire decision process is controlled at the local level.

A third shared role is *planning*. The heart of the administrative reform being implemented through the 100 Cities Program is to increase the capacity of *municipios* to plan local economic development that aggressively promotes growth and employment, while being mindful of the need for environmental balance. SEDESOL has helped promote these two objectives by funding training programs for municipio staff and by funding consulting studies for activities that are beyond the technical capacity of most municipios.

It is possible to make some observations about the sequencing of reform. Clearly, the preliminary key to this reform is the uncompromising and firm leadership of the President. Commitment from the center is critical to break the inertia of entrenched bureaucratic interests and change the center's relationship with non-central governmental and private sector institutions and organizations. As a result, the center has developed an ambitious strategy that makes sense both in terms of promoting economic growth and garnering political support. As was noted in Chapters 3 and 4, decentralization strategies that serve the allocation objective can be successful if they promote both economic growth and political support. Political commitment to decentralization is essential for success, but in return decentralization must have political payoffs.

Another factor that was critical to launching this program was the financial position of the central government. Far reaching economic and administrative reforms require substantial resources. The center has to be willing and able to bankroll the reform until its results begin to bear fruit in terms of new and growing local-level revenue sources. Prior to the introduction of the 100 Cities Program, the central government embarked on a privatization program and a tax reform effort that provided both money to pay off some of Mexico's debt and the means to finance both the 100 Cities and the SOLIDARIDAD components of the reform.[42] The political pact for reform is based, in part, on the effective use of those funds, a portion of which are spent on social development programs. In the 100 Cities Program, those federal funds are intended to be seed capital to start the local processes called for in the program. To date, for every new peso the federal government has invested, an additional 1.38 new pesos have been raised from local sources and private investment. The experience of Mexico's 100 Cities Program appears to affirm the conclusions of the Berkeley Decentralization Project that the most successful route to introducing a decentralization reform is to strengthen the center first, a critical part of which involves increasing the revenue sources of the center.

5. Preliminary Assessment of the 100 Cities Program

While it is too soon to thoroughly assess this program, it is possible to offer some tentative observations about the potential of Institutional Pluralism for meeting the allocation needs of late developing countries. These observations are central to this study, as the 100 Cities Program is being held up as an example of the Institutional Pluralism strategy.

Brokering Role: The principal feature of the administrative strategy of Institutional Pluralism is that the state brokers public and private resources to achieve public purposes. The reinventing government literature calls this brokerage role "entrepreneurial government." This literature emerged in the United States and is principally concerned with the state (especially local governments) harnessing the market to provide services usually provided by the state. What is different about the 100 Cities Program and the application of the Institutional Pluralism strategy to developing countries is that some of these countries want to not only broker the market to provide public goods and services (a first phase of development), they want to harness the market to promote rapid growth, especially employment. Put another way, the state does not confine itself to simply providing the "enabling environment" for development by brokering resources that will provide the basic infrastructure for growth. The state also seeks a more active role because there is a need to deliver development rapidly for economic and political reasons. In the case of the 100 Cities Program, the term used in project design documents is to "connect the investor to the city."[43] Through strategic planning that highlights the comparative advantage of the various cities, the object is to demonstrate to private firms where they should invest in response to specific public sector tasks and roles that the state is willing to delegate.

The attempt by governments in developing countries to steer the market is fraught with problems. The state can do many things: it can provide infrastructure to make cities and rural areas competitive arenas for private investment, it can harness the market to provide that public infrastructure, and it can provide baseline information services to assist businesses in making investment decisions. What the state should not do is determine, at the level of the firm, who should be winners and losers.

There are limits to what government can do in brokering private resources for public means. In the case of the 100 Cities Program, the principal intervention is one of planning and regulation of land use. This is why the focus has been on strengthening local management capabilities in the areas of urban planning and administration to help them start up the process. While the goal for the 100 Cities Program, like the goals of many state-sponsored development programs, is to promote economic development, the reality is that this goal can be planned but not managed. Harnessing the private sector for public purposes does not mean managing the private sector. The organizational cultures of government and private industry are very different and always should be. Whereas private firms have to manage the risk-return relationship, public organizations have to manage a no-risk-acceptable relationship. Private firms must have room for upside gain and downside loss. Public organizations must confine performance within a politically varying zone of acceptance. In short, there are limits to what the state can and should do to promote development.

In some ways the selection of a city to participate in the 100 Cities Program allows the central government ministries to determine winners and losers amongst cities. However, there is no redistributive objective explicit in the program's agenda, though this may occur. The selection of twenty-seven northern cities that border the United States and would serve as conduits of the NAFTA reflects the belief that those cities might serve as mechanisms for the others to gain access to new markets. Overall, the 116 cities are seen as complementary in the sense that exports to the north will generate economic activity in other regions as well. The development strategy of the program makes economic sense and illustrates that the redistribution objective can promote economic development and not simply equity.

Finally, a key to successfully playing the brokerage role is the relative balance of power. Institutional Pluralism can, through its emphasis on delegation of some public sector tasks and task-related roles, increase private sector involvement in the provision of public goods and services. While the intent is for the public sector to broker the process, in situations where economic power is highly concentrated, such as in Mexico, the brokerage process can work in reverse. In this case, the private sector brokers the public for private ends. Instead of incentivizing the city to promote public goods, the relationship is reversed such that the state becomes incentivized for the benefit of the firm. This is a major problem that can be created through the Institutional Pluralism strategy, and it is a concern against which the 100 Cities Program should guard.

Oversight Role: Another issue of concern is that of oversight. While the creation of citizen advisory groups is a laudable measure, designers and implementation managers must ask what prevents such institutions from becoming simply window dressing for the reform. Mexico has a highly concentrated economy and a tradition of patronage in which participation can be bought. Hence, it may be difficult to regulate the influence of large firms with such local oversight bodies.

Procurement Role: Given the economic concentration that prevails in Mexico, designers and implementators of Institutional Pluralism initiatives must ask two questions. How can it be assured that the procurement of public goods and services is done fairly and competitively? Despite all the good intentions of the Program and the structures that are in place to promote oversight, will procurement be done correctly?

Financial Role: From the very beginning, the Program has attempted to create a balance of financing with the center playing a minority and declining role. This approach is appropriate and appears to be working. However, one question that is increasingly being raised in other late developing countries is whether debt financing is more appropriate than local tax revenues or transfers from the center for financing local infrastructure. Would debt financing of local infrastructure make sense and provide more control over the development process by local-level governments and citizen oversight committees?

Program Complementarities: This case study has not been able to review the relationship between the 100 Cities Program, which supports the development of the urban component of the municipios, and the SOLIDARIDAD program, which supports the rural component of the municipios. While separate activities, one assumes that municipio planning should include facilitating linkages between the rural and urban sectors. Given that the SOLIDARIDAD program is funded by grant transfers, a sustainable development strategy should consider alternative means of financing development in the rural areas.

6. Summary

The 100 Cities Program provides a valuable sketch of the Institutional Pluralism strategy of administrative design and how it can be used to deepen devolution and stimulate delegation. Through planning and seed capital, it seeks to harness the market to provide critical infrastructure that will lead to growth. It has an ambitious agenda because the country demands rapid growth, which its political leadership must deliver. While rapid economic development is often accompanied by excesses and abuses, there are also repercussions if development is not aggressively promoted. The key issue for Mexico is whether a rapid pace of economic development can be sustained while preserving the decentralization principles underlying the design of the 100 Cities Program: equity, participation, sustainability, and environmental soundness. Previous attempts to decentralize the Mexican bureaucracy, such as the program attempted in 1984, failed. Hence, it is important to ask what is different in the current political economic environment, as well as the design of the 100 Cities Program, that will ensure sustainable success.

CHAPTER 5

NOTES

1. The most current overview of Kenya's political situation is: Jennifer A. Widner, *The Rise of a Party-State in Kenya: From "Harambee!" to "Nyayo!"* (Berkeley: University of California Press, 1992).

2. The problems currently faced by the transitional Government are summarized in: John M. Cohen, "Ethnic Federalism in Ethiopia," *Northeast African Studies*, II, 2 (New Series) (1996), pp. 157–88.

3. "Economic Crisis Hits Mexico's States, With Some Nearly Broke," *The New York Times* (May 10, 1995), p. A13.

4. An overview of constitutional and government changes between 1964 and 1975 is provided by: Irving Kaplan, et al., *Area Handbook for Kenya* (Washington, D.C.: U.S. Government Printing Office, 1976), pp. 187–211.

5. This initiative is summarized in: John M. Cohen and Richard M. Hook, "Decentralized Planning in Kenya," *Public Administration and Development*, VII, 1 (1987), pp. 77–93.

6. This is specifically the case with the Special Rural Development Projects. On these see: Walter O. Oyugi, *Rural Development Administration: A Kenyan Experience* (New Deli: Vikas Publishing House, 1981).

7. Republic of Kenya, Office of the President, *District Focus for Rural Development* (Nairobi: Government Printer, June 1983).

8. The planning basis of the reform, as well as the historical background and content, is presented in: Cohen and Hook, "Decentralized Planning in Kenya," pp. 77–93.

9. The Tender Board is chaired by the District Commissioner (DC) and tender values over approximately $30,000 have to be recommended to the Central Tender Board in Nairobi for adjudication.

10. Republic of Kenya, Office of the President, *National Training Strategy for District Focus* (Nairobi: Government Printer, 1985).

11. Republic of Kenya, *Economic Management for Renewed Growth: Sessional Paper No. 1* (Nairobi: Government Printer, 1982). For a view of this new initiative when it was first presented, based on 1981–82 field experience, see: Joseph Makokha, *The District Focus: Conceptual and Management Problems* (Nairobi: Africa Press Research Bureau, 1985).

12. Republic of Kenya, *Economic Management for Renewed Growth*, p. 52.

13. Joel D. Barkan and Michael Chege, "Decentralizing the State: District Focus and Politics of Reallocation in Kenya," *Journal of Modern African Studies*, XXVII, 3 (1989), p. 446.

14. It may be a step toward devolution and delegation. Diana Conyers notes that this sort Moi's type of administrative decentralization tends to precede the introduction of true devolution-directed reforms: "Decentralization: the Latest Fashion in Development Administration," p. 104.

15. Daniel J. Elazar lists twenty-two countries that are federations, confederations, unions, and regions with constitutional protection: *Federal Systems of the World*. Profiles of fragmented states in this book are useful. An example of a rare case study is: E. B. Richmond, "Senegambia."

16. This point is well illustrated, generally, by the case studies in: Zartman, *Collapsed States*.

17. Ethiopia contains approximately ninety distinct cultural-linguistic groups, of which the principle ones are: Amhara (38%), Oromo (35%), Tigrinya (9%), Gurage (3%), and Sidamo, Afar, and Somali with 2% each. The Oromo argue that this data, from the 1984 Census, understates their numbers and overstates those of the Amhara.

18. It is likely that the EPRDF position was influenced by a Nationalities Commission, which was created in the final years of the Mengistu period and charged with identifying administrative strategies for supporting ethnic- or territorial-based claims for greater self-determination.

19. For example, after recent field work in Ethiopia Samuel P. Huntington concluded: "Drawing regional boundaries on ethnic lines ... supplements what is unavoidable with what is undesirable ... the combination of ethnic territorial units and ethnic parties cumulative cleavages and can have a disastrous effect on national unity and political stability." Samuel P. Huntington, "Political Development in Ethiopia: A Peasant-Based Dominant-Party Democracy? (Report prepared for USAID Ethiopia, Addis Ababa, May 17, 1993), pp. 14–16. Ali Mazuri has argued that Ethiopia disintegrated when ethnic groups demanded self-determination, leaving Ethiopia a limited option to adopt a form of federation similar Russia's Confederation of Independent States. "Planned Governance and the Liberal Revival in Africa: the Paradox of Anticipation," *Cornell International Law Journal*, XV (1992), pp. 541–42.

20. The social aspects of the fall of Haile Selassie's Government, the unfolding revolution, and the Marxist disaster the country suffered are best described in: Christopher Clapham, *Transformation and Continuity in Revolutionary Ethiopia* (New York: Cambridge University Press, 1988); John W. Harbeson, *The Ethiopian Transformation: The Quest for the Post-Imperial State* (Boulder: Westview Press, 1988). Basic materials on the overthrow of the Mengistu Government and the current transformation process are reviewed in: Cohen, *Transition Toward Democracy and Governance in Post*

Mengistu Ethiopia.

21. The legal basis of the TGE was established by Charter July 22, 1991. "Transitional Period Charter of Ethiopia," Charter No. 1 of 1991, *Negarit Gazeta*, 50th Year, No. 1, July 22, 1991. The previous constitution, issued by Mengistu's government in 1987 showed little sensitivity towards ethnic devolution, though the drafts reviewed arguments for greater ethnic self-determination prepared by the Institute for the Study of Ethiopian Nationalities.

22. "Proclamation to Provide for the Establishment of National/Regional Self-Government," Proclamation No. 7 of 1992, *Negarit Gazeta*, 51st Year, No. 2 (January 14, 1992).

23. It should be noted that during the 1991–94 period the TGE and the CC identified local-level units by the terms "regions," "zones," and "*weredas*," which represented the provinces or administrative regions, districts (*awrajas*), and subdistricts (*weredas*) of Haile Selassie and Mengistu's deconcentrated system of administrative decentralization. The 1994 Constitution uses the term "state" rather than "region" and "zone" rather than "*awraja*," while retaining the term "*wereda*" for subdistricts.

24. These local-level governmental units were established as part of the 1995 land reforms and efforts by the military Government to establish peasant and urban dweller associations that facilitated increased political penetration. See: John M. Cohen and Peter H. Koehn, "Rural and Urban Land Reform in Ethiopia," *African Law Studies*, No. 14 (1977), pp. 3–62.

25. "1984 E.C. Budget Proclamation," Proclamation No. 26 of 1992; "Proclamation to Define the Sharing of Revenue Between the Central Government and the National/Regional Self-Governments," Proclamation No. 33 of 1992.

26. "Proclamation to Define the Powers and Duties of the Central and Regional Executive Organs of the Transition Government of Ethiopia," Proclamation No. 41 of 1993, *Negarit Gazeta*, 52nd Year, No. 26 (January 20, 1993).

27. Southern Ethiopia Peoples' is a short title for the "Southern Nations, Nationalities, Peoples Regional Government," as it is comprised of five distinct, ethnically defined regions, the population of which agreed to consolidate into one region.

28. The 1994 Constitution uses the term "nation," which it describes as "... a group of people who have or share a large measure of a common culture, or similar customs, mutual intelligibility of language, belief in a common or related identity, and who predominantly inhabit an identifiable, contiguous territory."

29. This is expected by experts: Kingsley M. de Silva, *Managing Ethnic Tensions in Multi-Ethnic Societies* (Lanham: University Press of America, 1986), p. 374; Walle Engedayehu, "Ethiopia: Democracy and the Politics of Ethnicity," *Africa Today*, XL, 2 1993), pp. 29–52; and his "Ethiopia: the Pitfalls of Ethnic Federalism," *Africa Quarterly*, XXXIV, 2 (1994), pp. 149–92.

30. These points are considered in: Paul B. Henze, "Ethiopia and Eritrea in Transition: The Impact of Ethnicity on Politics and Development — Opportunities and Pitfalls" (Paper Prepared for XIIth International Ethiopian Studies Conference, Michigan State University, September 1994).

31. These countries are: Brazil, Comoros, Nigeria, India, Malaysia, Pakistan, Mexico, Venezuela, and the United Arab Emirates. Elazar, *Federal Systems of the World*, pp. 395–97.

32. The development of the modern Mexican administrative state is described more completely by David E. Stansfield, "Decentralization in Mexico: The Political Context," in Arthur Morris and Stella Lowder, eds., *Decentralization in Latin America: An Evaluation* (New York: Praeger Publishers, 1992), pp. 111–25.

33. See: Victoria E. Rodriguez, "Mexico's Decentralization in the 1980s: Promises, Promises, Promises..." in Arthur Morris and Stella Lowder, eds., *Decentralization in Latin America: An Evaluation* (New York: Praeger Publishing, 1992), pp. 127–43.

34. Background on the 100 Cities Program is from interviews with Mr. Luis Castro, Director General for Urban Development of SEDESOL (the Ministry of Social Development) and Mr. Miguel Ramirez, External Advisor to the Director General for Urban Development of SEDESOL. "The 100 Cities Program."

35. Twenty-seven percent of the population of Mexico is in these four cities. SEDESOL, "The 100 Cities Program," p. 2.

36. Even though the Program is called the 100 Cities Program, it includes 116 localities. SEDESOL, "The 100 Cities Program," p. 12.

37. See: Merilee S. Grindle, "Altering the Relationship: Peasants, the Market, and the State in Mexico," in Riordan Roett, ed., *The Challenge of Institutional Reform in Mexico*, (Boulder: Lynne Rienner, 1995), pp. 39–56.

38. SEDESOL, "The 100 Cities Program," pp. 12–13.

39. As of October 1994, fifty-four urban development advisory councils had been formed and thirty more were being installed. SEDESOL, "The 100 Cities Program," p. 11.

40. Grindle, "Altering the Relationship," pp. 39–56.

41. See, for example: "The President, the Peso, the Markets and Those Indians," *The Economist* (December 24th 1994), pp. 43–44; "Quick Fix or

Quagmire?" *The Economist* (January 21, 1995), p. 73; "Rescuing the Sombrero," *The Economist* (January 21, 1995), pp. 18–19; "More Cracks in Mexico," *The Economist* (March 4, 1995), p. 12; "Zedillo's Hopes for Party and State," *The Economist* (April 1, 1995), pp. 36–37.

42. Francisco Gil Diaz, "Reforming Mexico's Tax Administration."

43. SEDESOL, "The 100 Cities Program," p. 13.

Synthesis and Summary

The growing complexity of the vertical structure of the public sector casts serious doubt on any simplistic forecasts of tendencies toward either centralization or decentralization.

Wallace Oates, *Studies in Fiscal Federalism*, p. xi.

FOR MOST DEVELOPING COUNTRIES, the administrative challenge is to simultaneously improve the delivery of public goods and services and substantially downsize the public sector, primarily through increased devolution and delegation. Rising to this challenge will be particularly difficult for the many countries with weak centers and limited personnel and financial resources. The task is further compounded for those countries fragmented by ethnic, religious, and nationalist demands for greater local autonomy. Meeting such challenges will require new analytical frameworks that can assist government decision-makers and professionals in designing and implementing innovative administrative reforms and interventions. The question addressed in this chapter is whether the Administrative Design Framework presented in Chapter 4 and illustrated in Chapter 5 can be useful to them.

This chapter has two main objectives. The first is to review the design of administrative systems defined as task related roles and structures. A matrix is used to demonstrate the three administrative design options based on the two dimensions: role and task. Second, it seeks to demonstrate several key roles that administrative systems perform when making a transition from one strategy of administrative design to another or when carrying out specific public sector tasks. The roles discussed here are *identification and planning, policy innovation, strategy, political leadership, financial mobilization, task management, and administration*. Additional roles that are not covered here would include operational implementation and management, performance oversight and auditing, and *evaluation* and *redesign*.

FROM FRAMEWORK AND CASE STUDIES TO GUIDELINES

Administrative decentralization is central to addressing current issues of public sector governance and performance. As discussed in Chapter 2, the current frameworks are not particularly helpful in doing this. To a large extent, this is because of their static nature, which results from their emphasis on institutional structures and their spatial relationships. Another deficiency with these frameworks has been the inability of specialists to use them to devise guidelines for improving spatially centralized and decentralized administrative systems in terms of efficiency, accountability, and effective resource mobilization. To confront these deficiencies and break the *monopoly of central design*, Chapters 3 and 4 introduced a new Framework that focuses on *administrative design* and emphasizes *administrative roles* required to carry out specific public sector tasks.

The focus on tasks and roles is important because they are dynamic, particularly as a country's strategy of administrative design moves from exclusive monopoly or deconcentrated forms of Distributed Institutional Monopoly toward devolution and expanded administrative pluralism. As such, Chapters 3–4 provide a framework for understanding how *roles* related to administrative design strategies and specific public sector tasks can be recombined with *spatially* centralized or decentralized structures to promote accountable, efficient and effective administration. These chapters also set administrative decentralization within a wider framework of administrative design that recognizes that some public sector tasks and some task related roles probably should, under most conditions, be centralized. Hence, the framework explicitly allows designers and implementors to consider administrative possibilities for centralization as well as decentralization.

The key to breaking the monopoly of central design lies in the sharing of roles related to the execution of specific public sector tasks, such as the construction and maintenance of infrastructure or the provision of refuse collection and disposal. It is the *sharing* of roles at central and non-central levels that is the hallmark of a transition toward the more devolutionary forms of Distributed Institutional Monopoly and Institutional Pluralism.

The Administrative Design Framework emphasizes the degree of role monopoly or pluralism because of its assertion that, all other things being equal, role pluralism promotes accountable administrative systems. Accountable administrative systems manage resources more efficiently and effectively. As such, they are better able to mobilize resources than administrative systems that are highly monopolistic and largely unaccountable.

Chapter 5's case studies described the design and effects of the three strategies generated by the Administrative Design Framework. The most typical administrative design approaches found in late developing countries are Institutional Monopoly and Distributed Institutional Monopoly, where roles are monopolized and structure is either centralized or decentralized. These two administrative designs will predominate for the foreseeable future in most developing countries. Case studies of the two central forms of Distributed Institutional Monopoly were presented: Kenya (deconcentration) and Ethiopia (devolution). The Kenyan case suggests that accountability, effectiveness, and efficiency are unlikely to be advanced when highly centralized administrative design strategies are pursued. This is important, because most developing countries, like Kenya, will continue to use deconcentration and central monopoly disguised as devolution and, as a result, achieve less efficiency and accountability in the execution of public sector tasks. The Ethiopian case demonstrates that while devolution can promise substantially improved accountability and enhanced production and provision of collective goods and services, it is difficult to introduce and risky when pursued by weak states with limited personnel and financial resources. The Ethiopian case is also significant because a number of ethnically or religiously fragmented states will be tempted to use federal, confederal, or devolved unitary solutions to promote political reconstruction.

Institutional Pluralism offers a strategy that has a high probability of making the public sector more accountable and efficient. The question is whether government decision-makers and professionals in developing countries can move toward this strategy of administrative design. The case of Mexico provides an example of how this can be done. Its 100 Cities Program shows the processes involved when governments commit to a gradual transition from Distributed Institutional Monopoly to Institutional

Pluralism, a transition that centers on increased devolution and delegation. It is submitted that Mexico's gradual approach is more likely to be successful if those designing and implementing the transition to Institutional Pluralism draw upon the insights into tasks and roles that lie at the heart of the Administrative Design Framework. At a minimum, the Mexican case demonstrates that achieving the third strategy of Institutional Pluralism may be possible for some strategy and task-related roles.

DESIGN OF ADMINISTRATIVE SYSTEMS

As argued in Chapter 4, the Administrative Design Framework presents three objectives of administrative design: accountability of performance, efficiency of management, and effectiveness in mobilizing and using resources. The framework assumes that accountability is the foremost objective and that efficient management and effective resource mobilization stem from accountability. Further, the framework assumes that accountability is maximized by having two or more public sector institutions and/or private sector firms and organizations share in the performance of the roles needed to promote administrative design changes or carry out a particular administratively decentralized public sector task. In particular, it argues that pluralist delivery of roles through the strategies of Distributed Institutional Monopoly's devolutionary form or through Institutional Pluralism promotes accountability and good management and that government decision-makers and professionals should seek ways to promote a transition in their public sector administration from monopoly toward expanded devolution and more extensive pluralism.

One of the major flaws in the conventional Type:Function Framework is its assumption that spatial distribution of authority will increase accountability and make management efficient and effective. The evidence reviewed in Chapters 1 and 2 demonstrates that spatial administrative decentralization does not make systems more accountable because task-related roles are monopolized and not shared.[1] The Administrative Design Framework thus stresses the analytic dimension of the concentration of administrative roles. Importantly, this does not preclude consideration of the structural/spatial dimension. Rather, it extends the spatial to the analytical. This is illustrated in Figure 3, demonstrating the analytic and spatial dimensions of administrative design.

In Figure 3, Quadrant I is the conventional approach of centralization

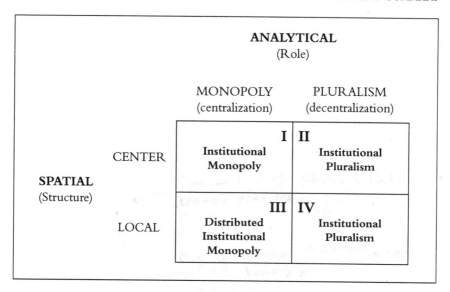

FIGURE 3: Analytical and Spatial Design Dimensions of Administrative Systems

or what Chapters 3 and 4 have defined as Institutional Monopoly. Roles are not shared. Instead they are monopolized within one central public sector institution. Quadrant III represents the most conventional approach to administrative decentralization, or what Chapters 3 and 4 have defined as Distributed Institutional Monopoly, for the roles are not shared but the responsibility for the roles is spatially distributed. Included within Quadrant III are both the deconcentrated and devolved types of Distributed Institutional Monopoly. Quadrants II and IV are examples of the third administrative strategy, Institutional Pluralism, where roles related to a specific task are shared by two or more governmental institutions and/or private sector firms or community organizations. Institutional Pluralism can be spatially centralized or decentralized.

The administrative system in most countries is comprised of a mix of these strategies. However, particular strategies dominate. In most developing countries, the strategies being implemented are largely located in Quadrants I and III. In part, this because there are strong theoretical and political reasons for centralizing stabilization and distribution objectives (Quadrant I). Pluralism does occur in some developing countries in regard to these objectives when some roles related to stabilization and distribution tasks are delegated to state-controlled enterprises and authorities (Quadrant II). However, this strategy is not common. It is far more likely that the third objective, allocation, will be spatially decentral-ized, either through deconcentration and devolution (Quadrant III) or delegation (Quadrant IV).

Examples of this mix are found in Chapter 5's case studies. In Kenya, Mexico, and Ethiopia, the central government monopolizes such stabili-zation and distribution functions as defense, foreign policy, and monetary policy, functions which are located in Quadrant I. On the other hand, all three countries pursue different strategies in regard to allocation objec-tives. Kenya's District Focus strategy is located in Quadrant III. This is because the strategy is based on a spatial deconcentration that continues to maintain central ministry monopoly control over the administrative and technical performance of field agent roles. While Kenya's strategy has led to some gains in efficiency and effectiveness, it has not led to increased accountability through the sharing of roles related to tasks through devo-lution or delegation, or increased local-level participation. Mexico's 100 Cities Program is located in Quadrants I, II, and IV because it is a cautious strategy of devolution and delegation that is focused on specific urban areas, conceived and guided by a federal agency, and dependent on sub-stantial federal funding. Ethiopia's experiment with ethnic federalism and devolution is also located in Quadrant III. This is the case even though, unlike in Kenya's deconcentrated approach, the roles related to tasks, such as education and health, will be shared between the federal line ministries and state and *wereda* bureaus. Under the new Constitution, technical and administrative execution of public sector tasks at all three levels are to be governed by popularly elected councils. In a sense, Ethiopia claims to be breaking the monopoly of central design and moving toward a form of pluralism. But devolution is not delegation. Therefore, Ethiopia's adminis-trative strategy for the allocative objective remains in Quadrant III.

By focusing on the task-related roles administrative systems perform, the Administrative Design Framework demonstrates that administrative systems are not monolithic. A spatially centralized governmental institu-tion can have a monopoly over some roles while sharing other roles with spatially centralized or decentralized governmental institutions. Over time dynamic combinations in role performance are possible.

Figure 3 also illustrates two design guidelines that can be useful to governments seeking to formulate a strategy of administrative decentrali-zation. First, there are a *variety of options* in designing an administrative system relative to public sector tasks and the roles required for them to be performed. For example, the financing role for local-level road construction could be wholly done by a local governmental institution (Quadrant III), shared between such an institution and the central government (Quadrants I and III), or done by a local governmental institution, an aid agency, international private bank, and the central government (Quadrants IV and I, or III and II, or II and IV).

Further, it is possible to have two or more administrative designs (quadrants) for the delivery of roles related to the execution of a specific public sector task. As many studies have demonstrated, spatial administrative decentralization requires complementary strength among central and non-central governmental institutions. Chapter 3 and 4's emphasis on the importance of administrative and financial capacity, and the difficulties of field administration described in the Kenyan case study, suggest that complementary strength is difficult to find in developing countries. The delivery of a task-related role, such as financing, may require not only complementary institutions but also complementary roles. For example, establishing a financing role at the local level for a particular public sector task may require a prior improvement in the central government's regulatory role of governing capital markets. In such a situation, the performance of the financing role, which can be delivered by several administrative options, also requires that a complementary role (regulation) be provided prior to and along with the financing role. There are also a variety of administrative design options in providing these complementary roles.

SEQUENCE OPTIONS IN ADMINISTRATIVE DESIGN

The second design guideline underlying the Administrative Design Framework is that options in the sequence of Administrative Design must be carefully considered. Because the Framework is not static, there are a *variety of sequences* that can occur in the transition of an administrative system's strategy for the execution of a specific public sector task and the roles related to such a task. Four different sequences of spatial (structural) and analytical (role) centralization and decentralization can be illustrated through reference to Figure 3. These are:

Sequence 1: Quadrant I to Quadrant III: From centralized role and structure to spatially decentralized structure (deconcentrated or devolved) but centralized role.

165

Sequence 2:   Quadrant I to Quadrant II, From centralized role and structure to decentralized role and centralized structure.

Sequence 3:   Quadrant III to Quadrant IV: From centralized role and
decentralized structure (deconcentrated or devolved) to decentralized (delegation) role and structure.

Sequence 4: Quadrant I to Quadrant IV: From centralized role and structure to decentralized role (delegation) and structure.

The most common view of administrative design is Sequence 1, which is to spatially decentralize a formerly centralized task-related role while retaining monopoly or central control. This sequence and its problems are well illustrated by the Kenyan and Ethiopian case studies of Distrib-uted Institutional Monopoly. Sequence 2 administratively decentralizes the specific task related roles without spatially decentralizing. Examples of this are found where countries have devolved or delegated specific roles related to particular stabilization and distribution tasks to other central institutions. Typically, this occurs when a central bank devolves or del-egates some of its task-related roles to specialized banks and financial institutions located in the capital city that are either controlled or closely regulated by the centralized government. No example of this sequence is given in Chapter 5. Sequence 3 illustrates the situation when specific roles related to spatially decentralized tasks are administratively delegated to private sector firms or community organizations. The Mexico case study provides an example of this, since devolved urban administrations are delegating some task related roles to private sector firms. Sequence 4 administratively decentralizes both the role and the structure of a cen-tralized administrative system. No example of this sequence is provided Chapter 5's case studies. Examples of this sequence are, however, not hard to find. For example, roles and structures of centrally controlled medical, veterinary, or agricultural research can be contracted out to private sec-tor firms, a strategy aid agencies are pressing a number of financially weak governments to consider. There are several other sequences that are logically possible.

Providing governments with guidelines for designing administrative systems that include designs that administratively decentralize structures and roles involves two tasks. The first is to outline the options for deliver-ing roles. The second is to suggest sequences in administrative design.

Again, Figure 3 provides insights into such tasks. To illustrate the utility of this framework, the three cases are briefly revisited.

The District Focus strategy and the 100 Cities Program in Mexico involve most of the roles in Chapter 4. These roles are: policy innovation, leadership, planning, financing, management, and task administration. In the discussion that follows, these roles will be discussed primarily in regard to the administrative strategies set forth in Figure 3 and to the sequencing of such strategy roles outlined above.

Leadership is arguably the most central role in a reform related to a administrative decentralization. National-level leadership is essential to carrying out administrative reform. Several studies and conferences on administrative decentralization have concluded that without strong political commitment, reforms or programs aimed at decentralizing public sector tasks and related roles are unlikely to succeed.[2] In the early stages of an administrative decentralization reform, when the benefits of reform are not widely valued and are viewed by many as threatening, national-level leadership is critical. Leadership also has to lay the groundwork for other, more task-related roles such as strategy, financing and regulation.

In the Kenyan case, the leadership was committed to maintaining strong central control over the administrative decentralization process. The misleading rhetoric over the objectives of Kenya's District Focus strategy is an example of a reform that follows Sequence 1: Quadrant I to III. Despite presidential rhetoric about greater involvement of rural and urban people in the identification and selection of projects and programs carried out in their districts as well as oversight over the effective and efficient performance of public sector tasks by civil servants, the senior Government decision-makers in Quadrant I never had any intention of eventually following a sequence from III to IV. Aid agencies that are aware of this position are at a loss to suggest a strategy that will move the Government toward a meaningful consideration of Sequence 3.

The administrative design of the leadership role in the 100 Cities Program came from the federal government in Mexico City and so was located in Quadrant I. As the program has gained momentum and the municipios have embraced the reform, leadership roles have come to be increasingly shared between the spatial center and deconcentrated and devolved local governmental institutions (Quadrants I and III). Raising the level of participation by private sector firms and organizations (Quadrant IV) in the performance of leadership roles must increase and support officials in the non-central governmental sector. This is because leadership commitment by central leaders in hard-pressed late developing countries is often short-lived.[3]

The move toward ethnic federalism in Ethiopia is an example of Sequence 3. This move has been led by a victorious group of regional secessionists. Upon defeating the military regime, the leaders of this group of guerilla fighters suddenly found themselves holding power over a country that was fragmented by ethnic regionalism. Since taking control of the Government, they have been strongly committed to a federal solution involving substantial devolution. The country's new Constitution establishes a system of governance that moves from seventeen years of military rule based on Haile Selassie's Imperial system (Quadrants I and III) into a highly devolved federal system where task-related roles are shared by central and non-central governmental levels. Under the Constitution and supporting legislation issued between 1992 and 1994: (1) roles related to tasks, such as education or health, will be shared between the federal Ministries of Education or Health and state and district educational or health bureaus and offices; and (2) technical and administrative execution of public sector tasks at all three levels are to be governed by popularly elected councils. As a result, the breaking of the monopoly of central design is more far reaching in Ethiopia than in Mexico's 100 Cities Program. But Ethiopia still represents a case of Distributed Institutional Monopoly.

Closely related to the role of leadership in an administrative decentralization intervention, is the role of *strategy*. A strategy is a vision of a preferred outcome coupled with practical steps to achieve that vision. The 100 Cities Program is a strategy which combines economic and political objectives. The Program seeks to promote rapid economic growth and increased political legitimacy in the key constituencies of the Program's municipios.

It is typical for reform strategies to be developed and promoted by the center, for they benefit the center (Quadrant I). The Transitional Government of Ethiopia is largely following a political strategy formulated at the center, for as pointed out in Chapter 5, ethnic conflict can place substantial constraints on the country's efforts to achieve economic progress. So too, Kenya's District Focus initiative is a political strategy formulated at the center to protect central control, regardless of the statements of politicians that it will gradually lead to devolution and greater participation. The country's economic strategy is largely confined to using District Focus to gain greater budgetary efficiency in the center's limited budgetary allocations to districts. To be sure, the strategy can lead to more equitable economic growth, but this is not its primary objective.

In most administrative decentralization reforms and programs, the role of *regulation* is often done by the center and not shared or delegated spatially to non-central governmental institutions or analytically through assigning some aspects of the regulation role to local governmental institutions. Thus, this role often remains within Quadrant I. If a government decides to move its administrative design for administrative decentralization toward Institutional Pluralism and engage in brokering roles (Quadrant IV), rules are needed to ensure that the distributed administrative systems promote linkages with non-public institutions and organizations. For the allocation objective, the role of the spatial center then increasingly becomes one of a regulator that ensures that the playing field is not only level, but that it exists at all. The role of regulation is not efficiently executed when multiple actors are involved, as is the case in Quadrant II, for there needs to be a unity of policy.

In this regard, the absence or weakness of regulations governing private involvement in roles related to the provision of public goods and services is one of the principal concerns Mexican officials face in achieving the objectives of the 100 Cities Program. In Ethiopia, there is a great need to formulate regulatory provisions that clearly specify the task-related roles that will be shared by the federal government, states, and *weredas*.

The *oversight* role is frequently shared between spatially centralized and decentralized structures (Quadrants I and III or IV). In the Kenyan case, oversight is located in the Office of the President (Quadrant I) and the District Commissioner (Quadrant III). However, this oversight in aimed more at maintaining political control and gaining rents than it is toward ensuring that development and welfare tasks are effectively and efficiently carried out. From the inception of the 100 Cities Program, oversight was provided by SEDESOL (Quadrant I) and the local citizen advisory committees (Quadrant IV). The role of oversight in Ethiopia is currently unclear. The intention is to place it in popularly elected federal, state, and *wereda* councils (Quadrant III) organized by parties (Quadrant IV), which by definition are outside the public sector. The intention has not been met.

The effectiveness of oversight depends on the relative capacity and authority at different levels. It is especially hard to develop technical capacity and credible authority at the non-central governmental or private sector levels. In the case of the 100 Cities Program, the sequence of the administrative design relative to oversight is not clear. This is largely due to the fact that the oversight role is closely tied to the financing role and the structure of financing, which in Kenya and Ethiopia is centrally controlled while in Mexico there is greater balance. As long as public sector tasks are funded wholly or largely by central revenues through national budgets, oversight will continue to be done from the center.

There are many options in the administrative design of the *finance* role. In the 100 Cities Program it is shared relatively equally by the center, the local government, and local private investors (a strategy of Quadrant I and IV). The Program is unique in adopting a pluralist local financing strategy (Quadrant IV) rather than the typical strategy of entirely publicly funded local financing (Quadrants I and III). The majority of cases show financing either being completely funded through the center, as in Kenya, or with the center dominating revenue, as in Ethiopia. The intention of the 100 Cities Program is to evolve to a wholly locally funded strategy with increasing Quadrant IV participation by international capital and perhaps Quadrant II involvement with international multilateral financial institutions. Redefining the financing role from the conventional design pair of Quadrant I and III, which is the case under Kenya's District Focus strategy, to a pluralist approach as suggested by Quadrant IV, illustrates the argument that pluralism will improve the mobilization of capital and make its use more accountable and efficient. A pluralist approach to the finance role promotes such creative solutions as debt financing of infrastructure and concessionary investment. A variety of approaches are available for developing countries to consider, including build-own-operate (BOO) and build-own-transfer (BOT) schemes.[4]

The *planning* role is often shared from the inception of an administrative reform. In the 100 Cities Program, strengthening the planning process was a critical part of the reform. In the initial stages, the central ministry, SEDESOL, took the lead in defining the new planning techniques to be used and in training local planners in their application. The local planners in Mexico were employees of the municipios, whereas the District Planning Officers in Kenya were employees of the central planning ministry. In Mexico's case, the administrative design of the planning role was principally in Quadrant I. But the program aimed at increasing the municipios' participation in planning (Quadrant III). The reform quickly developed local planning capacity, so the design is currently both Quadrant I and

Quadrant III, with the role of local planners increasing. As central financing is phased out and replaced by local sources, the role of local planning will increase.

The *brokerage* role is the defining feature of the Institutional Pluralism strategy. The brokerage role is where both central and devolved local-level governmental institutions attempt to harness both the market and civil society organizations by delegating roles related to the provision of collective goods and services to private sector firms and organizations. In the case of Kenya's District Focus strategy, there is no brokerage role because the central government has never planned on devolving strong powers to local-level governmental units or allowing the transfer of public sector tasks or roles related to such tasks to private sector firms or organizations. However, as noted in Chapter 5, the government often looks the other way when such firms and organizations take on activities it lacks the resources or commitment to carry out. This is to be expected, for meaningful devolution and delegation is the exception under Institutional or Distributed Institutional Monopoly strategies.

In contrast, in the case of Mexico's 100 Cities Program the administration of the *municipios* has worked with private investors to fund one-third of the low-income housing and invest in waste treatment plants. As such, the 100 Cities case illustrates several features of the brokerage role. First, it involves considerable complementarities amongst other roles to create the enabling environment to induce private investment. Some of the key complementary roles were leadership, financing, regulation and planning. Leadership was essential. The President and top-level federal ministries made the program a national priority. Financing was central, for public funds reduced the risk for private investors. Regulation was essential, for it created new opportunities for investment. Planning was also important, for it provided private investors information about investment opportunities and also provided a creative strategy for intensifying land use. In sum, the experience of the 100 Cities Program underscores the role of a capable and committed center to create the enabling environment needed for local public agencies to perform a brokerage role. A brokerage role need not rest at the local level (Quadrant IV), but can also be exercised at the center (Quadrants I and II).

GUIDELINES FOR ADMINISTRATIVE DECENTRALIZATION

The key roles that administrative systems need to effectively perform to execute public sector tasks have now been reviewed, and the design options and the sequence of designs have been illustrated using the cases of Kenya's deconcentrated District Focus strategy, Ethiopia's devolved experiment in ethnic federalism, and Mexico's 100 Cities Program and its creative use of administrative delegation. Clearly, the Kenyan case represents the patterns of decentralization that are found in a large number of developing countries. On the other hand, the Ethiopian and Mexican cases stand on the frontier of innovation, Ethiopia in regard to devolution (Sequence 1) and Mexico in regard to delegation (Sequence 3). As such, they cannot yet generate definitive guidelines for introducing strategies of either Distributive Institutional Monopoly or Institutional Pluralism. Still, it is possible to identify some emerging guidelines that are more broadly applicable.

First, a strong center is a prerequisite to meaningful and effective spatial decentralization. While the allocation objectives may be spatially decentralized, as prescribed in the theory of public finance, an enabling environment provided at the center is needed for their effective delivery. The Ethiopian case illustrates the risk that emerges when the center is weak, financial resources are limited, and the center controls most revenue.

Second, a strong center is needed for role decentralization. In Kenya, the center is strong enough to deconcentrate task specific roles because personnel carrying out such roles are under the technical and administrative control of line ministries.

In light of the first two guidelines, a key question arises: what can be done if the center is not accountable or uses administrative decentralization to increase its control, as is the case in Kenya? Under such circumstances there is limited room for maneuver, although two strategies are possible. One strategy would be for reformers to try and make the center itself more accountable by making it pluralist (Quadrant II). A second strategy would be for them to strengthen a spatially and role decentralized administrative system (Quadrant IV). In regard to this second strategy, one specialist notes:

Giving sub-national governments autonomy to tax and spend may be considered a hallmark of trade liberalization, with central government agencies abandoning their monopolies in the provision of public goods and services, allowing markets for public goods to emerge.[5]

Aid agencies could assist reformers by providing technical assistance and capital directly to non-central governmental institutions.[6] These prescriptions assume, however, a center that is willing to respond positively to reform and reduce its monopoly over tasks and task-related roles. If the center is not progressive and is unwilling to release its administrative monopoly on public sector roles, especially those related to finances, the prospects for accountable, efficient, and effective decentralization are dim.

A third principle is that there are considerable obstacles in the way of reforms aimed at promoting spatially decentralized Institutional Pluralism. Managing task-related roles either within a hierarchy (Distributed Institutional Monopoly) or between hierarchies or devolved governmental units, markets, and civil society organizations (Institutional Pluralism) involves coordination costs. One cannot assume a priori that Institutional Pluralism has higher coordination costs, but it is possible. Another obstacle that Institutional Pluralism confronts when it attempts to harness the market through delegation is that in emerging economies there may be considerable imperfections. Market solutions may offer a worse solution than providing services through governmental institutions.[7] So too, devolved local governmental units and civil society organizations may lack the personnel and financial resources required to carry out the demanding task-related roles assigned under a strategy of Institutional Pluralism.

CAVEAT AND QUESTIONS

The Administrative Design Framework presented in Chapters 3 and 4 has not been extensively tested. However, cases are beginning to appear of experiments by late developing countries that pursue greater involvement of actors in the execution of decentralized public sector tasks.[8] Still, more work is required in grounding the Framework, especially in addressing two difficult questions:

- As spatially centralized roles are devolved and delegated (a transition from Quadrant III to IV), what complementary roles need to be strengthened at the center, either as a precondition or concurrently?

- How are central roles devolved and delegated during the transition from Quadrant I to IV?

Both of these questions raise an even more fundamental question:

- How do governments move from conventional administrative structures, where roles are monopolized, to new structures where roles are shared through devolution and delegation?

This question is at the very heart of current debates on administrative reform in developed and developing countries alike. At issue are the three principles of administrative design: accountability, efficiency, and effectiveness, and their impact on resource mobilization. While Institutional Pluralism may not be the dominant administrative strategy in the future for developing countries, some governments are anxious to incorporate, if only partially, the features of this design to promote accountable, efficient and effective administrative systems. Administrative end states are easy to prescribe. The far harder task is to develop workable strategies for introducing change within existing administrative systems that combine different design guidelines yet change outcomes and, eventually, behavior. Designing and managing transitional and mixed administrative systems is very difficult. The challenge of administrative design in the 1990s and beyond is to develop analytical tools that can assist government decision-makers in developing countries to initiate and sustain the transition from monopolistic to pluralistic administrative systems.

CHAPTER 6
NOTES

1. For example: Olowu, "The Failure of Current Decentralization Programs in Africa."

2. United Nations Development Program, *Workshop on the Decentralization Process*.

3. Baumgartner and Jones have argued that the American political system has "lurches and lulls" and that the policy priorities change often: *Agendas and Instability in American Politics*, p. 250.

4. For suggestions on alternative financing strategies see: David Gisselquist, "How to Encourage Government Decentralization: Interesting Ideas for Redirecting Lending," *Transitions*, V, 7 (1994), pp. 7–8.

5. *Ibid.*, p. 7.

6. For example, international assistance could include facilitating the development of capital markets (bond and equity) and the management of concessions that would expand the financing alternatives for local governments and lessen their dependency on the center.

7. Vladmir Benacek, *Market Failure versus Government Failure: The Ways of the Emerging Market Economies*, (Prague: Charles University, Center for Economic Research and Graduate Education, Working Paper No. 5, 1992).

8. For example: Judith Tendler and Sara Fredheim, "Trust in a Rent-seeking World: Health and Government Transformed in Northeast Brazil," *World Development*, XXII, 12 (1994), pp. 1171–91.

Bibliography

Acuna, Luis Fernando Ramierz. "Privatization of Tax Administration." In *Improving Tax Administration in Developing Countries*, Richard M. Bird and Milka Casanegra de Jantscher, eds. Washington, D.C.: International Monetary Fund, 1992.

Adamolekun, Lapido. "Promoting African Decentralization." *Public Administration and Development*, XI, 3 (1991), pp. 285–91.

Alderfer, H. F. *Local Government in Developing Countries.* NewYork: McGraw-Hill, 1964.

Allen, Hubert J. B. "Enhancing Administrative and Management Capacity in the Area of Local Government." In *Seminar on Decentralization in African Countries: Banjul, Gambia, 27–31 July 1992.* New York: United Nations Department of Economic and Social Development and African Association for Public Administration and Management, 1993, pp. 94–114.

Apthorpe, Raymond and Diana Conyers. "Decentralization, Recentralization and Popular Participation: Towards a Framework for Analysis." *Development and Peace*, III, 2 (1982), pp. 47–59.

Bahl, Roy and Linn, Johannes. *Urban Public Finance in Developing Countries.* Oxford: Oxford University Press, 1992.

Barkan, Joel D. and Michael Chege. "Decentralizing the State: District Focus and the Politics of Reallocation in Kenya."*Journal of Modern African Studies*, XXVII, 3 (1989), pp. 431–53.

Barrons. "Auditing the IRS." December 23, 1996, p. 35.

Barzelay, Michael. *Breaking Through Bureaucracy: A New Vision for Managing in Government*. Berkeley: University of California Press, 1994.

Baumgartner, Frank R. and Bryan D. Jones. *Agendas and Instability in American Politics*. Chicago: University of Chicago Press, 1993.

Benacek, Vladmir. *Market Failure versus Government Failure: The Ways of the Emerging Market Economies*. Prague: Charles University, Center for Economic Research and Graduate Education, Working Paper No. 5, 1992.

Bienen, Henry et al. "Decentralization in Nepal." *World Development*, XVIII, 1 (1990), pp. 61–75.

Binswanger, Hans. "Decentralization, Fiscal Systems, and Rural Development." Request for Research Support Budget Funding to The World Bank Agricultural Division, March 18, 1994.

Blair, Harry W. "Participation, Public Policy, Political Economy and Development in Rural Bangladesh 1958–85." *World Development*, XIII, 12 (1985), pp. 1231–47.

Bratton, Michael. "Civil Society and Political Transition in Africa." *Institute for Development Research*, XI, 6 (1994).

Brennan, Geoffrey and James Buchanan. *The Power to Tax: Analytical Foundations of a Fiscal Constitution*. Cambridge: Cambridge University Press, 1980.

Brown, Charles C. and Wallace E. Oates. "Assistance to the Poor in a Federal System." *Journal of Public Economics*, XXXII, (1987), pp. 307–330.

Bruyn, S. T. and J. Meehan, eds. *Beyond the Market and the State: New Directions in Community Development*. Philadelphia: Temple University Press, 1987.

Buchanan, J. M. and G. Tullock. *The Calculus of Consent*. Ann Arbor: University of Michigan Press, 1962.

Caiden, Gerald E. *Administrative Reform Comes of Age*. Berlin: Walter de Gruyter, 1991.

Cheema, Shabbir G., ed., *Institutional Dimensions of Regional Development*.

Nagoya: United Nations Centre for Regional Development, 1981.

———— and Dennis A. Rondinelli, eds. *Decentralization and Development: Policy Implementation in Developing Counties.* Beverly Hills: Sage Publications, 1983.

Clapham, Christopher. *Transformation and Continuity in Revolutionary Ethiopia.* New York: Cambridge University Press, 1988.

Cohen, John M. and Richard M. Hook. "Decentralized Planning in Kenya." *Public Administration and Development,* VII, 1 (1987), pp. 77–93.

Cohen, John M. and Norman T. Uphoff. *Rural Development Participation: Concepts and Measures for Project Design, Implementation and Evaluation.* Ithaca: Cornell University, Rural Development Committee, 1977.

Cohen, John M. and Peter H. Koehn. "Rural and Urban Land Reform in Ethiopia." *African Law Studies,* No. 14 (1977), pp. 3–62.

————. *Ethiopian Provincial and Municipal Government: Imperial Patterns and Postrevolutionary Changes.* East Lansing: Michigan State University, African Studies Center, 1980.

Cohen, John M. and David B. Lewis, "Development from Below: Local Development Associations in the Yemen Arab Republic." *World Development,* IX, 11/12 (1981), pp. 1039–91.

Cohen, John M. *Integrated Rural Development: The Ethiopian Experience and the Debate.* Uppsala: Scandinavian Institute of African Studies, 1987.

————. "Importance of Public Service Reform: The Case of Kenya." *Journal of Modern African Studies,* XXXI, 3 (1993), pp. 449–76.

————. "Capacity Building in the Public Sector: A Focused Framework for Analysis and Action." *International Review of Administrative Sciences,* LXI, 3 (1995), pp. 407–22.

————. *Transition Toward Democracy and Governance in Post Mengistu Ethiopia* (Cambridge: Harvard Institute for International Development, Development Discussion Paper No. 493, June 1994), pp. 9–17.

————. "Ethnic Federalism in Ethiopia." *Northeast African Studies,* II, 2 (New Series) (1996), pp. 157–88.

Cohen, Stephen, John Dykman, Erica Schoenberger, and Charles Downs.

"A Framework for Policy Analysis." Paper prepared for the Project on Managing Decentralization, University of California at Berkeley, Institute of International Studies, 1981.

Cointreau, S. J. "Environmental Management of Urban Solid Wastes in Developing Countries: A Project Guide." Paper prepared for The World Bank, Washington, D.C., 1982.

Colburn, Forest D. *The Vogue of Revolution in Poor Countries.* Princeton: Princeton University Press, 1994.

Conyers, Diana. "Decentralization for Regional Development: a Comparative Study of Tanzania, Zambia and Papua New Guinea." *Public Administration and Development*, I, 2 (1981), pp. 107–20.

————. "Decentralization: The Latest Fashion in Development Administration?" *Public Administration and Development*, III, 2 (1983), pp. 97–109.

————. "Decentralization and Development: A Review of the Literature." *Public Administration and Development*, IV, 2 (1984), pp. 187–97.

Cook, Cynthia C., Henri L. Beenhakker, and Richard E. Hartwig. *Institutional Considerations in Rural Roads Projects.* Washington, D.C.: The World Bank, Staff Working Paper No. 748, 1985.

Currid, Cheryl. *Computing Strategies for Reengineering Your Organization.* Rocklin, California: Prima Publishing, 1994.

Davenport, Thomas H. *Process Innovation: Reengineering Work through Information Technology.* Boston: Harvard Business School Press, 1993.

Davey, Kenneth J. *Financing Regional Government: International Practices and Their Relevance to the Third World.* Chichester: John Wiley and Sons, 1983.

Davis, Daniel, David Hulme, and Philip Woodhouse. "Decentralization by Default: Local Governance and the View from the Village in The Gambia." *Public Administration and Development*, XIV, 3 (1994), pp. 253–69.

Davis, S. and P. Lawrence. *Matrix.* Reading: Addison–Wesley, 1977.

DeMello, L. "Local Government and National Development Strategies." *Planning and Administration*, IX, 2 (1982), pp. 96–112.

de Merode, Louis. *Civil Service Pay and Employment in Africa: Selected Imple-*

mentation Experiences. Report prepared for International Bank for Reconstruction and Development, Washington, D.C., 1991.

de Silva, Kingsley M. *Managing Ethnic Tensions in Multi-Ethnic Societies*. Lanham: University Press of America, 1986.

Diaz, Francisco Gil. "Reforming Mexico's Tax Administration." In *Information Technology and Innovation in Tax Administration*, Glenn Jenkins, ed. The Hague: Kluwer Law International, 1996, pp. 27–35.

Dillinger, William. *Decentralization and its Implications for Urban Service Delivery*. Washington, D.C.: The World Bank, Urban Management Program Paper No. 16, May 1994.

DiIulio, John J., Jr., ed., *Deregulating the Public Service: Can Government Be Improved?* Washington, D.C.: The Brookings Institution, 1994.

DiMaggio, Paul J. and Walter W. Powell. "Introduction." In *The New Institutionalism in Organizational Analysis*, Walter W. Powell and Paul J. DiMaggio, eds. Chicago: University of Chicago Press, 1991, pp. 1–38.

Dubnick, Melvin J. "A Coup Against King Bureaucracy." In *Deregulating the Public Service: Can Government Be Improved?*, DiIulio, John J. Jr., eds. Washington, D.C.: The Brookings Institution, 1994.

Dwight, A. L. "A Concept of Decentralization." *Public Administration and Review*, XXX, 1 (1970), pp. 60–63.

The Economist. "The President, the Peso, the Markets and Those Indians." December 24, 1994, pp. 43–44.

The Economist. "Quick Fix or Quagmire?" January 21, 1995, p. 73.

The Economist. "Rescuing the Sombrero." January 21, 1995, pp. 18–19.

The Economist. "More Cracks in Mexico." March 4, 1995, p. 12.

The Economist. "Zedillo's Hopes for Party and State." April 1, 1995, pp. 36–37.

Edwards, M. and D. Hulme. *Making a Difference: NGOs and Development in a Changing World*. London: Earthscan, 1992.

Elazar, Daniel J. *Exploring Federalism*. Tuscaloosa: University of Alabama Press, 1987.

————. *Federal Systems of the World.* Essex: Longmans, 1991.

Engedayehu, Walle. "Ethiopia: Democracy and the Politics of Ethnicity." *Africa Today* XL, 2 (1993), pp. 29–52.

————. "Ethiopia: The Pitfalls of Ethnic Federalism." *Africa Quarterly* XXXIV, 2 (1994), pp. 149–92.

Esman, Milton J. "The Maturing of Development Administration." *Public Administration and Development,* VIII, 2 (1984), pp. 125–39.

————. *Management Dimensions of Development: Perspectives and Strategies.* West Hartford: Kumarian Press, 1991.

———— and Norman T. Uphoff. *Local Organizations: Intermediaries in Rural Development.* Ithaca: Cornell University Press, 1984.

European Centre for Development Policy Management. *Democratisation in Sub-Saharan Africa: The Search for Institutional Renewal.* Maastricht: ECDPM Occasional Paper, 1992.

Fagence, Michael. *Citizenship Participation in Planning.* Oxford: Pergamon Press, 1977.

Ferris, James and Elizabeth Graddy. "Contracting Out: For What? With Whom?" *Public Administration Review,* XLVI, 4 (1986), pp. 332–44.

Fesler, James W. "Approaches to the Understanding of Decentralization." *Journal of Politics,* XXVII, (1965), pp. 536–66.

————. "Centralization and Decentralization." In *International Encyclopedia of the Social Sciences,* David L. Sills, ed. New York: Macmillan, 1968, pp. 370–79.

Foglesong, Richard E. and Joel D. Wolfe. *The Politics of Economic Adjustment: Pluralism, Corporatism, and Privatization.* New York: Greenwood Press, 1989.

Fowler, A. *NGOs in Africa: Achieving Comparative Advantage in Relief and Micro-Development.* Sussex: University of Sussex, Institute of Development Studies, Discussion Paper No. 249, 1988.

Frankel, Francine R. *India's Political Economy, 1947–1977: The Gradual Revolution.* Princeton: Princeton University Press, 1978.

Fried, Robert C. "Prefectoral Linkages of Nation and Loyalty." In *Comparative Local Politics: A Systems-Functions Approach*, Jack Goldsmith, ed. Boston: Holbrook Press, Inc., 1973.

Friedman, Harry. "Local Political Alternatives for Decentralized Development." In *Decentralization and Development: Policy Implementation in Developing Countries*, Shabbir G. Cheema and Dennis A. Rondinelli, eds. Beverly Hills: Sage Publications, 1983, pp. 35–58.

Furness, Norman. "The Practical Significance of Decentralization." *Journal of Politics*, XXXVI, 4 (1974), pp. 958–82.

Gerschenkron, Alexander. *Economic Backwardness in Historical Perspective*. Belknap Press: Cambridge, Massachusetts, 1962.

Gisselquist, David. "How to Encourage Government Decentralization: Interesting Ideas for Redirecting Lending." *Transitions*, V, 7 (1994), pp. 7–15.

Goldsmith, Jack, ed., *Comparative Local Politics: A Systems-Functions Approach*. Boston: Holbrook Press, Inc., 1973.

Gottlieb, Gidon. "Nations Without States." *Foreign Affairs*, LXXIII, 3 (1994), pp. 100–112.

Govoyega, A. "Local Government Reform in Nigeria." In *Local Government in the Third World*, Philip Mawhood, ed. Chichester: Wiley, 1983, pp. 225–47.

Gow, David D. *Local Organizations and Rural Development: A Comparative Reappraisal*, 2 vols. Washington, D.C.: Development Alternatives, Inc., 1979.

Granlich, Edward M. "Intergovernmental Grants: A Review of the Empirical Literature." In *The Political Economy of Fiscal Federalism*, Wallace E. Oates, ed. Lexington, Mass.: Heath-Lexington, 1975, pp. 219-40.

Gran, Guy. *Development by People: Citizen Construction of a Just World*. New York: Praeger, 1983.

Grindle, Merilee S. *Bureaucrats, Politicians, and Peasants in Mexico: A Case Study in Public Policy*. Berkeley: University of California Press, 1977.

————. "Altering the Relationship: Peasants, the Market, and the State in Mexico." In *The Challenge of Institutional Reform in Mexico*, Riordan Roett, ed. Boulder: Lynne Rienner Publishers, 1995.

———— and John W. Thomas. *Public Choices and Policy Change: The Political Economy of Reform in Developing Countries*. Baltimore and London: The Johns Hopkins University Press, 1991.

Hamilton, Nora. *The Limits of State Autonomy: Post-Revolutionary Mexico*. Princeton: Princeton University Press, 1982.

Hammer, Michael and James Champy. *Reengineering the Corporation: A Manifesto for Business Revolution*. New York: HarperBusiness, 1993.

Hanf, K. and F. Scharpf. *Interorganizational Policy Making: Limits to Coordination and Central Control*. London: Sage, 1978.

Hansen, Gary, Heather McHugh, and Malcolm Young. "Civil Society and Democratic Development." Paper prepared by the Center for Development Information and Evaluation, USAID, Washington, D.C. February, 1994.

Harbeson, John W. *The Ethiopian Transformation: The Quest for the Post-Imperial State*. Boulder: Westview Press, 1988.

————, Donald Rothchild, and Naiomi Chazan, eds. *Civil Society and the State in Africa*. Boulder: Lynne Rienner Publishers, 1994.

Hart, D. K. "Theories of Government Related to Decentralization and Citizen Participation." *Public Administration Review*, XXXII, Special Issue (1972), pp. 603–21.

Healey, John and Mark Robinson. *Democracy, Governance and Economic Policy: Sub-Saharan Africa in Comparative Perspective*. London: Overseas Development Institute, 1994.

Henao, Marino. *Transparencia: Una Estrategia Para Optimizar la Productividad Social de los Recursos Publicos*. The Final Report of the Presidential Commission on Public Reform in Colombia, May 1991.

Heaphy, James J., ed. *Spatial Dimensions of Development Administration*. Durham, N.C.: Duke University Press, 1971.

Heath, J. *Public Enterprise at the Crossroads*. London: Routledge, 1990.

Henze, Paul B. "Ethiopia and Eritrea in Transition: The Impact of Ethnicity on Politics and Development—Opportunities and Pitfalls." Paper prepared for XIIth International Ethiopian Studies Conference, Michigan State University, September 1994.

Hicks, Ursula K. *Development from Below: Local Government and Finance in Developing Countries of the Commonwealth.* Oxford: Clarendon Press, 1961.

Humes, Samuel and Eileen M. Martin. *The Structure of Local Government: A Comparative Survey of 81 Countries.* The Hague: International Union of Local Authorities, 1969.

Huntington, Samuel. *The Third Wave Democratization in the Late Twentieth Century.* Norman: University of Oklahoma Press, 1991.

Huntington, Samuel P. "The Clash of Civilizations?" *Foreign Affairs*, LXXII, 3 (1993), pp. 22–49.

———. "Political Development in Ethiopia: A Peasant-Based Dominant-Party Democracy?" Report prepared for USAID Ethiopia, Addis Ababa, May 17, 1993.

Hyden, Goran. *No Shortcuts to Progress: African Development Management in Perspective.* Berkeley: University of California Press, 1983.

Israel, Arturo. *Institutional Development: Incentives to Performance.* Baltimore: The Johns Hopkins University Press, 1987.

Jackson, Robert H. and Carl G. Rosberg. *Personal Rule in Black Africa: Prince, Autocrat, Prophet, Tyrant.* Berkeley: University of California Press, 1982.

Jaques, Elliot. "In Praise of Hierarchy." *Harvard Business Review*, LXVIII (January–February 1990), pp. 127–33.

Jones, L. P. and R. Moran. *Public Enterprise in Less Developed Countries.* Cambridge: Cambridge University Press, 1982.

Kaplan, Irving, et al. *Area Handbook for Kenya.* Washington, D.C.: U.S. Government Printing Office, 1976.

Kaplan, Robert D. "The Coming Anarchy." *Atlantic Monthly*, (February 1994), pp. 44–49, 52, 54, 58–64.

Kaufman, Herbert. "Administrative Decentralization and Political Power." *Public Administration Review*, XXIX (January–February 1969), pp. 3–15.

Kaul, Mohan, Nitin R. Patel, and Khalid Shams. *Searching for a Paddle: Trends in IT Applications in Asian Government Systems*, 2 Vols. Kuala Lumpur: Asian and Pacific Development Centre, 1987.

Keen, Peter G. W. *Shaping the Future: Business Design Through Information Technology*. Cambridge, Massachusetts: Harvard Business School Press, 1991.

Kettl, Donald F. *Government by Proxy: Mismanaging Federal Programs*. Washington, D.C.: QC Press, 1988.

Kikeri, Sunita, John Nellis, and Mary Shirley. *Privatization: The Lessons of Experience*. Washington, D.C.: The World Bank, 1992.

Kind, David J. "Civil Service Policies in Indonesia: an Obstacle to Decentralization?" *Public Administration and Development*, VIII, 3 (1988) pp. 249–60.

Klitgaard, Robert. *Adjusting to Reality: Beyond "State Versus Market" in Economic Development*. San Francisco: International Center for Economic Growth, 1991.

———. *Controlling Corruption*. Berkeley: University of California Press, 1988.

Klugman, Jeni. *Decentralization: A Survey of Literature from a Human Development Perspective*. New York: United Nations, Human Development Report Office, Occasional Paper No. 13, July 1994.

Knott, Jack H. and Gary J. Miller. *Reforming Bureaucracy: The Politics of Institutional Choice*. Englewood Cliffs: Prentice-Hall, Inc., 1987.

Kochem, Manfred and Karl Deutsch. *Decentralization: Sketches toward a Rational Theory*. Cambridge: Oelgeschlager, Gunn and Hain, 1980.

Korten, David C. "Community Organization and Rural Development: a Learning Process Approach." *Public Administration Review*, XL, 5 (1980), pp. 450–511.

Korten, David C. "The Community: Master or Client? A Reply." *Public Administration and Development*, IX, 5 (1989), pp. 569–75.

Korten, David C. *Getting to the 21st Century: Voluntary Action and the Global Agenda.* West Hartford: Kumarian Press, 1990.

———— and Rudi Klauss, eds., *People Centered Development: Contributions Toward Theory and Planning Frameworks.* West Hartford: Kumarian Press, 1984.

Landau, Martin and Eva Eagle. "On the Concept of Decentralization." Paper prepared for Decentralization Project, University of California at Berkeley, Institute of International Studies, 1981.

Landau, Martin and Russell Stout, Jr. "To Manage is Not to Control: Or, the Folly of Type II Errors." *Public Administration Review,* XXXIX (March/April 1979), pp. 148–56.

Landell-Mills, P. "Governance, Cultural Change and Empowerment." *Journal of Modern African Studies,* XXX, 4 (1992), pp. 543–67.

Lang, Nicholas R. "The Dialectics of Decentralization: Economic Reform and Regional Inequality in Yugoslavia." *World Politics,* XXVII, 3 (1975), pp. 309–35.

Lantran, Jean-Marie. "Managing Small Contracts: Contracting Out of Road Maintenance Activities: Practical Guidance on How to Streamline and Manage Small Contracts for Public Works and Services." Paper prepared for The World Bank, Washington, D.C., April 1993.

Le Gendre, Bertrand. "Ethiopia Takes a Step Towards Democracy." *Manchester Guardian.* August 16, 1995.

Leonard, David K. "Analyzing the Organizational Requirements for Serving the Rural Poor." In *Institutions of Rural Development for the Poor: Decentralization and Organizational Linkages,* D. K. Leonard and D. R. Marshall, eds. Berkeley: University of California, Institute for International Studies, 1982, pp. 8–15.

Leonard, David K. "Choosing Among Forms of Decentralization and Linkage." In *Institutions of Rural Development for the Poor: Decentralization and Linkages,* D. K. Leonard and D. R. Marshall, eds. Berkeley: Institute for International Studies, University of California, 1982, pp. 193–226.

Leonard, David K. "Interorganizational Linkages for Decentralizing Rural Development: Overcoming Administrative Weaknesses." In

Decentralization and Development: Policy Implementation in Developing Countries, G. Shabbir Cheema and Dennis A. Rondinelli, eds. Beverly Hills: Sage Publications, 1983, pp. 271–91.

Leonard, David K. *African Successes: Four Public Managers of Kenyan Rural Development.* Berkeley: University of California Press, 1991.

———— and Dale Rogers Marshall, eds. *Institutions of Rural Development for the Poor: Decentralization and Organizational Linkages.* Berkeley: University of California, Institute of International Studies, 1982.

Lewis M. and T. R. Miller. "Public-Private Partnership in African Urban Development." Paper prepared for USAID, Washington, D.C., 1986.

Lindauer, David L. and Michael Roemer, eds., *Africa and Asia: Legacies and Opportunities in Development.* San Francisco: ICS Press for Harvard Institute for International Development and the International Center for Economic Growth, 1994.

Linsky, Martin. "The Realities of Making Democracy in South Africa." *The Boston Globe.* February 25, 1995.

Lipnack, Jessica P. and Jeffrey S. Stamps, *The Team Net Factor: Bringing the Power of Boundary-Crossing Into the Heart of Your Business.* Essex Junction, Vermont: Oliver Wight Publications, Inc., 1993.

Loughlin, Martin. *Administrative Accountability in Local Governments.* London: Joseph Roundtree Foundation, 1992.

Maass, A. A., ed. *Area and Power: A Theory of Local Government.* Glencoe: Free Press, 1959.

Maddock, H. *Democracy, Decentralization and Development.* Bombay: Asia Publishing House, 1963.

Makokha, Joseph. *The District Focus: Conceptual and Management Problems.* Nairobi: Africa Press Research Bureau, 1985.

Malone, Thomas W., Joanne Yates, and Robert I. Benjamin. "Electronic Markets and Electronic Hierarchies." In *Information Technology and the Corporation of the 1990s: Research Studies,* Thomas J. Allen and Michael S. Scott Morton, eds. Oxford: Oxford University Press, 1994, pp. 61–83.

Marshall, Dale Rogers. "Lessons from the Implementation of Poverty Programs in the United States." In *Institutions of Rural Development for the Poor: Decentralization and Linkages*, D. K. Leonard and D. R. Marshall, eds. Berkeley: Institute of International Studies, 1982, pp. 40–72.

Mawhood, Philip. "Decentralization: the Concept and the Practice." In *Local Government in the Third World: The Experience of Tropical Africa*, Philip Mawhood, ed. Chichester: John Wiley & Sons, 1983, pp. 1–24.

———, ed. *Local Government in the Third World: The Experience of Tropical Africa*. Chichester: John Wiley & Sons, 1983.

———. "Decentralization and the Third World in the 1980s." *Planning Administration*, XIV, 1 (1987), pp. 10–22.

Mazuri, Ali. "Planned Governance and the Liberal Revival in Africa: The Paradox of Anticipation." *Cornell International Law Journal*, XV (1992), pp. 541–2.

Mbithi, Philip and Ramus Rasmussion. *Self-Reliance in Kenya: The Case of Harambee*. Uppsala: Scandinavian Institute of African Studies, 1977.

McCullough, J. S. "Institutional Development for Local Authorities: Financial Management." Consultant Report for Ministry of Local Government, Housing, and Construction, Colombo, 1984.

Migdal, Joel. "Strong States, Weak States: Power and Accommodation." In *Understanding Political Development*, Myron Weiner and Samuel P. Huntington, eds. Boston: Little, Brown and Co., 1987, pp. 391–434.

———. *Strong States and Weak States: State-Society Relations and State Capabilities in the Third World*. Princeton: Princeton University Press, 1988.

Minis, H. P. and S. S. Johnson. "Case Study of Financial Management Practices in Tunisia." Durham: Research Triangle Institute, 1982.

Moris, Jon. "The Transferability of Western Management Concepts and Programs: An East African Perspective." In *Education and Training for Public Sector Management in Developing Countries*, W. D. Stifel, J. E. Black, and J. S. Coleman, eds. New York: The Rockefeller Foundation, 1977, pp. 73–83.

Morss, Elliot, et al. *Strategies for Small Farmer Development*. Boulder: Westview Press, 1976.

Morton, Michael S. Scott. "Introduction." In *The Corporation of the 1990s: Information Technology and Organizational Transformation*, Michael S. Scott Morton, ed. Oxford: Oxford University Press, 1991, pp. 3–26.

Montgomery, John D. "Decentralizing Integrated Rural Development Activities." In *Decentralization and Development: Policy Implementation in Developing Countries*, Shabbir G. Cheema and Dennis A. Rondinelli, eds. Beverly Hills: Sage Publications, 1983.

Musgrave, Richard A. *The Theory of Public Finance*. New York: McGraw-Hill, 1959.

Mushi, Samuel Stephen. "Strengthening Local Government in Africa: Organizational and Structural Aspects." In *Seminar on Decentralization in African Countries: Banjul, Gambia, 27–31 July 1992*. New York: United Nations Department of Economic and Social Development and African Association for Public Administration and Management, 1993, pp. 24–45.

Negarit Gazeta. "Transitional Period Charter of Ethiopia." Charter No. 1 of 1991. 50th Year, No. 1, July 22, 1991.

Negarit Gazeta. "Proclamation to Provide for the Establishment of National/Regional Self-Government." Proclamation No. 7 of 1992. 51st Year, No. 2, January 14, 1992.

Negarit Gazeta. "Proclamation to Define the Powers and Duties of the Central and Regional Executive Organs of the Transition Government of Ethiopia." Proclamation No. 41 of 1993. 52nd Year, No. 26, January 20, 1993.

Nellis, John. *Contract Plans and Public Enterprise Performance*. Washington, D.C.: The World Bank, Discussion Paper No. 48, 1986.

———, Sunita Kikeri, and Mary Shirley. *Privatization: Lessons of Experience*. Washington, D.C.: The World Bank, 1992.

Nelson, Richard and Sidney Winter. *An Evolutionary Theory of Economic Change*. Cambridge: Harvard University Press, 1982.

New York Times. "Economic Crisis Hits Mexico's States, With Some Nearly Broke." May 10, 1995, p. A13.

Nordlinger, E. and J. Hardy. "Urban Decentralization: An Evaluation of

Four Models." *Public Policy*, XX (1972), pp. 359–96.

Oates, Wallace E. "The Theory of Public Finance in a Federal System." *Canadian Journal of Economics*, I (February 1968), pp. 37–54.

———. *Fiscal Federalism*. New York: Harcourt Brace and Jovanovich, Inc., 1972.

———. "The Changing Structure of Intergovernmental Fiscal Relations." In *Secular Trends of the Public Sector*, H. Recketenwald, ed. Paris: Editions Cujas, 1978, pp. 151–60.

———. "The New Federalism: An Economist's View." *Cato Journal*, II, 2 (1982), pp. 473–88.

———. "Searching for Leviathan: An Empirical Study." *American Economic Review*, LXXV (March 1985), pp. 748–57.

———. "Searching for Leviathan: A Reply and Some Further Reflections." *American Economic Review*, LXXIX (June 1989), pp. 578–83.

———. "Decentralization of the Public Sector: An Overview." In *Decentralization, Local Governments, and Markets*, R. Bennett, ed. Oxford: Oxford University Press, 1990, pp. 43–58.

———, ed., *Studies in Fiscal Federalism*. Brookfield, Vermont: Edward Elgar, 1991.

Oliver, Dawn. *Government in the United Kingdom: The Search for Accountability, Efficiency and Citizenship.* Oxford: Oxford University Press, 1991.

Olowu, Dele. "Local Government Innovation in Nigeria and Brazil." *Public Administration and Development*, II, 4 (1982), pp. 345–57.

———. "The Failure of Current Decentralization Programs in Africa." In *The Failure of the Centralized State: Institutions and Self-Governance in Africa*, J. S. Wunsch and D. Olowu, eds. Boulder: Westview Press, 1990, pp. 74–90.

———. "Central-Local Government Relations." In *Seminar on Decentralization in African Countries: Banjul, Gambia, 27–31 July 1992*. New York: United Nations Department of Economic and Social Development and African Association for Public Administration and Management, 1993, pp. 46–76.

Olson, M. *The Logic of Collective Action*. Cambridge: Cambridge University Press, 1965.

Osborne, David and Ted Gaebler. *Reinventing Government: How the Entrepreneurial Spirit is Transforming the Public Sector*. New York: Plume Press, 1993.

Ostrom, V., C. M. Tiebout, and R. Warren. "The Organization of Government in Metropolitan Areas: A Theoretical Inquiry." *American Political Science Review*, LV, 4 (1961), pp. 831–42.

Oxford English Dictionary. Oxford: Clarendon Press, 1978.

Oyugi, Walter Ouma. *Rural Development Administration: A Kenyan Experience*. New Deli: Vikas Publishing House, 1981.

Peterson, Stephen B. "Alternative Local Organizations Supporting the Agricultural Development of the Poor." In *Institutions of Rural Development for the Poor: Decentralization and Organizational Linkages*, edited by David K. Leonard and Dale Rogers Marshall. Berkeley: Institute for International Studies, 1982, pp. 125–50.

———. "Government, Cooperatives, and the Private Sector in Peasant Agriculture." In *Institutions of Rural Development for the Poor: Decentralization and Organizational Linkages*, David K. Leonard and Dale Rogers Marshall, eds. Berkeley: Institute for International Studies, 1982, pp. 73–124.

———. "From Processing to Analyzing: Intensifying the Use of Microcomputers in Developing Bureaucracies." *Public Administration and Development*, XI, 5 (1991), pp. 491–510.

———. "Budgeting in Kenya: Practice and Prescription." *Public Budgeting and Finance*, XIV, 3 (1994), pp. 55–76.

———. "Making IT Work: Implementing Effective Financial Information Systems in Bureaucracies of Developing Countries." In *Information Technology and Innovation in Tax Administration*, Glenn Jenkins, ed. The Hague: Kluwer Law International, 1996, pp. 177–94.

———. "The Recurrent Cost Crisis in Development Bureaucracies." In *Public Budgeting and Financial Administration in Developing Countries*, N. Caiden, ed. Greenwich: JAI Press, 1996, pp. 175–203.

————. "Financial Reform in Kenya: Implementing a Public Investment Program in Line Ministries." In *Public Budgeting and Financial Administration in Developing Countries*, N. Caiden, ed. Greenwich: JAI Press, 1996, pp. 115–40.

————. "A Second Path: Mexico's Second Customs Inspection," paper presented to the Symposium on Innovations in Trade Administration: Customs in the 21st Century convened by the Harvard Institute for International Development and the International Tax Program, Harvard Law School, Harvard University, Cambridge, Massachusetts, November 14–15, 1996.

————. "Computerizing Personnel Information Systems in African Bureaucracies," *International Journal of Public Administration*, XX, 10 (1997), pp. 1865–89.

————. "Hierarchy versus Networks: Alternative Strategies for Building Public Sector Bureaucracies in Africa." In *Getting Good Government: Capacity Building in the Public Sectors of Developing Countries*, Merilee S. Grindle, ed. Cambridge: Harvard University Press, 1997.

————. "Saints, Demons, Wizards and Systems: Why Information Technology Reforms Fail or Underperform in Public Bureaucracies in Africa," *Public Administration and Development*, XVIII, I (1998), pp. 37–60.

Pinkney, Robert. *Democracy in the Third World*. Boulder: Lynne Rienner Publishers, 1994.

Prud'homme, Rèmy. "Informal Local Taxation in Developing Countries." *Environment and Planning C, Government and Policy*, X, 1 (1992), pp. 1–17.

————. *On the Dangers of Decentralization*. Washington, D.C.: The World Bank, Transportation, Water, and Urban Development Department, Policy Research Working Paper No. 1252, 1994.

Public Administration Times, "NPR Under Scrutiny," XVII, 10, October 1, 1994, p. 1.

Ralston, Leonore, James Anderson, and Elizabeth Colson. *Voluntary Efforts in Decentralized Management: Opportunities and Constraints in Rural Development*. Berkeley: University of California, Institute of International Studies, 1983.

Raper, Arthur F. *Rural Development in Action: The Comprehensive Experiment at Comilla, East Pakistan.* Ithaca: Cornell University Press, 1970.

Republic of Kenya, *Economic Management for Renewed Growth: Sessional Paper No. 1.* Nairobi: Government Printer, 1982.

Republic of Kenya, Office of the President. *District Focus for Rural Development.* Nairobi: Government Printer, June 1983.

Republic of Kenya, Office of the President. *National Training Strategy for District Focus* Nairobi: Government Printer, 1985.

Richmond, Edmund B. "Senegambia and the Confederation: History, Expectations and Disillusions." *Journal of Third World Studies,* X, 3 (1993), pp. 172–94.

Rodriguez, Victoria E. "Mexico's Decentralization in the 1980s: Promises, Promises, Promises..." In *Decentralization in Latin America: An Evaluation,* Arthur Morris and Stella Lowder, eds. New York: Praeger Publishing, 1992.

Romer, Paul. *Increasing Returns and New Developments in the Theory of Growth.* Washington, D.C.: National Bureau of Economic Research," Working Paper No. 3098, 1989.

Rondinelli, Dennis A. and John R. Nellis, "Assessing Decentralization Policies in Developing Countries: The Case for Cautious Optimism." *Development Policy Review,* IV, 1 (1986), pp. 3–23.

Rondinelli, Dennis A., James S. McCullough, and Ronald W. Johnson. "Analyzing Decentralization Policies in Developing Countries: A Political-Economy Framework. *Development and Change,* XX, 3/4 (1989), pp. 57–87.

Rondinelli, Dennis A., John R. Nellis, and Shabbir G. Cheema. *Decentralization in Developing Countries: A Review of Recent Experience.* Washington, D.C.: The World Bank, Staff Working Paper No. 581, 1984.

Rondinelli, Dennis A. *Development Projects as Policy Experiments: An Adaptive Approach to Development Administration.* New York: Methuen, 1983.

———. *Decentralizing Urban Development Programs: A Framework for Analyzing Policy.* Washington, D.C., USAID, Office of Housing and Urban

Programs, 1990.

————."Decentralization,Territorial Power and the State:A Critical Response." *Development and Change*, XXI, 3 (1990), pp. 491–500.

Roth, Gabriel. "Can Road Maintenance be Privatized"? Paper prepared for Services Group, Arlington, 1987.

————. *The Private Provision of Public Services in Developing Countries.* New York: Oxford University Press, 1987.

Roth, Stephen R. and Charles K. Mann. *Microcomputers in Development: A Public Policy Perpective.* Boulder: Westview Press, 1987.

Rowat, Donald C., ed., *International Handbook on Local Government Reorganization: Contemporary Developments.* Westport: Greenwood Press, 1980.

Rusch, William H., Fred. L. Mann, and Eugene Brausn. "Rural Cooperatives in Guatemala: A Study of Their Development and Evaluation of AID Programs in Their Support." Report prepared for USAID, Washington, D.C., 1976.

Russell, C. S. and N. K. Nicholson, eds., *Public Choice and Rural Development.* Washington, D.C.: Resources for the Future, 1981.

Sachs, Jeffrey. "The State of Economic Reforms in the Developing Countries: A Comparative Perspective." Paper presented to the Harvard Institute for International Development, Harvard University, Cambridge, October 17, 1994.

Samoff, Joel. "Decentralization: The Politics of Intervention." *Development and Change*, XXI, 3 (1990), pp. 513–30.

Sandbrook, Richard. *The Politics of Africa's Economic Stagnation.* Cambridge: Cambridge University Press, 1985.

Sanwal, Mukul. *Microcomputers in Development Administration.* New Delhi: Tata McGraw-Hill Publishing Company Ltd., 1987.

Savas, E. S., ed. *Alternatives for Delivering Public Services: Toward Improved Performance.* Boulder: Westview Press, 1977.

Scott, Maurice F. G. *A New View of Economic Growth: Four Lectures.* Washington, D.C.: The World Bank, Discussion Paper No. 131, 1991.

Schuftan, Claudio, John MacGregor, and Stephen Peterson. "Downsizing the Civil Service in the Third World: The Golden Handshake Option Revisited." *Public Administration and Development*, XVIII, I (1998), pp. 61–76.

SEDESOL, "The 100 Cities Program: A Concerted and Sustainable Regional Urban Development Strategy," Project paper prepared for SEDESOL and translated from Spanish by Dale Johnson, October, 1994.

Sherwood, F. "Devolution as a Problem of Organizational Strategy." In *Comparative Urban Research*, R. T. Daland, ed. Beverly Hills: Sage Publications, 1969, pp. 60–87.

Sherwin, W. J. *Decentralization for Development: The Concept and its Application in Ghana and Tanzania*. Washington, D.C.: Development Studies Program, 1977.

Shirley, M. M. *Managing State Owned Enterprises*. Washington, D.C.: The World Bank, Working Paper No. 577, 1983.

Silverman, Jerry M. *Public Sector Decentralization: Economic Policy and Sector Investment Programs*. Washington, D.C.: The World Bank, African Technical Department, Technical Paper No. 188, 1992.

Slater, D. "Territorial Power and the Peripheral State." *Development and Change*, XX, 3 (1989), pp. 501–31.

Smith, Brian C. *Field Administration: An Aspect of Decentralization*. London: Routledge and Kegan Paul, 1967.

———. "The Measurement of Decentralization." *International Review of Administrative Sciences*, XLV (1979), pp. 214–22.

———. *Decentralization: The Territorial Dimension of the State*. London: George Allen & Unwin, 1985.

Smoke, Paul. *Is Local Public Finance Theory Relevant for Developing Countries?* Cambridge: Harvard Institute for International Development, Development Discussion Paper No. 316 November, 1989.

———. "Local Government Fiscal Reforms in Developing Countries: Lessons from Kenya," *World Development*, XXI, 6 (1993), pp. 901–23.

Stansfield, David E. "Decentralization in Mexico: The Political Context."

In *Decentralization in Latin America: An Evaluation*, Arthur Morris and Stella Lowder, eds. New York: Praeger Publishing, 1992.

Stout, Russell Jr. *Management or Control: The Organizational Challenge.* Bloomington: University of Indiana Press, 1980.

Strassmann, Paul. *Information Payoff: The Transformation of Work in the Electronic Age.* New York: The Free Press, 1985.

Tendler, Judith and Sara Fredheim. "Trust in a Rent-seeking World: Health and Government Transformed in Northeast Brazil." *World Development*, XXII, 12 (1994), pp. 1771–91.

Thomas, Barbara P. *Politics, Participation and Poverty: Development Through Self-Help in Kenya.* Boulder: Westview Press, 1985.

Tiebout, Charles. "A Pure Theory of Local Expenditures." *Journal of Political Economy*, LXIV, (October, 1956), pp. 416–24.

United Nations. *Decentralization for National and Local Development.* New York: United Nations, Working Group on the Administrative Aspects of Decentralization for National Development, 1962.

———. *Local Government Reform: Analysis of Experience in Selected Countries.* New York: United Nations, Department of Economic and Social Affairs, 1975.

———. *Seminar on Decentralization in African Countries: Banjul, Gambia, 27–31 July 1992.* New York: Department of Economic and Social Development and African Association for Public Administration and Management, 1993.

United Nations Centre for Regional Development. *Implementing Decentralization Policies and Programmes.* Nagoya: UNCRD, 1981.

United Nations Educational, Scientific and Cultural Organization. *The Decentralization of Educational Administration.* Bangkok, Regional Office, UNESCO, 1982.

United Nations Development Program. *Workshop on the Decentralization Process: Bern, Switzerland, 20–23 April 1993.* Report on Workshop, New York, Management Development Program, 1993.

Naciones Unidas. *Descentralizacion en America Latina: Santa Cruz de la Si-*

erra, Bolivia, 3–5 Noviembre 1993. Nueva York: Departamento de Apoyo al Desarrollo y de Servicios de Gestion, 1994.

United States Agency for International Development. *Local Organizations in Development.* Washington, D.C.: USAID, 1984.

————. *Democracy and Governance.* Washington, D.C.: Directorate for Policy, USAID, November 1991.

————. "USAID, Civil Society and Development." Washington, D.C.: Center for Development Information and Evaluation, USAID, December 1992.

United States General Accounting Office. "Promoting Democracy: Foreign Affairs and Defence Agencies Funds and Activities: 1991–93." Washington, D.C.: GAO, January 1994.

Uphoff, Norman T. *Local Institutional Development: An Analytical Sourcebook with Cases.* West Hartford: Kumarian Press, 1986.

———— and Milton J. Esman. *Local Organization for Rural Development: Analysis of Asian Experience.* Ithaca: Rural Development Committee, Cornell University, Rural Local Government Publication No. 19, 1974.

VanSant, Jerry. *Supporting Capacity-Building in the Indonesian Provincial Development Program.* Washington, D.C.: Development Alternatives, Inc., 1981.

Wade, Robert. *Governing the Market: Economic Theory and the Role of Government in East Asian Industrialization.* Princeton: Princeton University Press, 1990.

Walker, T., ed. *Building Capacity for Decentralization in Egypt: The Pilot Project and Beyond.* Washington, D.C.: Development Alternatives, Inc., 1981.

Wallis, John Joseph and Wallace E. Oates. "Decentralization in the Public Sector: An Empirical Study of State and Local Government." In *Studies in Fiscal Federalism,* Wallace E. Oates, eds. Brookfield, Vermont: Edward Elgar, 1991.

Wallis, Malcolm. "Local Government and Development: A Guide to the Literature." *Environment and Urbanization*, III, 1 (1991), pp. 121–29.

Wellard, K. and J. G. Copestake. *Non-Governmental Organizations and the State in Africa.* London: Routledge, 1993.

Werlin, Herbert H. "Linking Decentralization and Centralization: A Critique of the New Development Administration." *Public Administration and Development,* XII, 3 (1992), pp. 223–35.

———. "Elasticity of Control: An Analysis of Decentralization." *Journal of Comparative Administration,* II, 2 (1970), pp. 185–209.

Widner, Jennifer A. *The Rise of a Party-State in Kenya: From "Harambee!" to "Nyayo!"* Berkeley: University of California Press, 1992.

Wolfers, E. P., et al. *Decentralization: Options and Issues: A Manual for Policy Makers.* London: Commonwealth Secretariat, 1982.

Wolman, Harold. "Decentralization: What It Is and Why We Should Care." In *Decentralization, Local Governments, and Markets: Towards a Post-Welfare Agenda,* Robert J. Bennett, eds. Clarendon Press: Oxford, 1991, pp. 29–42.

World Bank. *Governance and Development.* Washington, D.C.: The World Bank, April 1992.

———. "Planned Study Series on the Relationship between NGOs and the State." Interoffice memorandum. September 14, 1992.

———. *Handbook on Technical Assistance.* (Washington, D.C.: Operations Policy Department, 1993.

———. *World Development Report 1994: Infrastructure for Development.* New York: Oxford University Press, 1994.

———. *Assessing Aid: What Works, What Doesn't, and Why.* Oxford: Oxford University Press, 1998.

Wright, W. S. *Understanding Intergovernmental Relations.* North Scituate: Duxbury Press, 1978.

Wunsch, James S. and Dele Olowu. *The Failure of the Centralized State: Institutions and Self-Governance in Africa.* Boulder: Westview Press, 1990.

Wunsch, James S. "Sustaining Third World Infrastructure Investments: Decentralization and Alternative Strategies." *Public Administration and*

Development, XI, 1 (1991), pp. 5–23.

Zartman, I. William, ed. *Collapsed States: The Disintegration and Restoration of Legitimate Authority*. Boulder: Lynne Rienner Publishers, 1994.

Zax, Jeffrey S. "Is There a Leviathan in Your Neighborhood?" *American Economic Review*, LXXIX (June 1989), pp. 560–67.

Index

About the Authors

John M. Cohen

John was an Institute Fellow of the Harvard Institute for International Development for eighteen years until his death in 1997. He was a specialist in rural development and development administration. John designed and managed numerous development projects principally in Africa spending over twenty years in the field. An expert on rural development in Ethiopia and Kenya, John wrote extensively about the development process in both countries. He also wrote about the process of economic reform and the role of foreign assistance. John held a juris doctorate and a doctorate in political science from the University of Colorado.

Stephen B. Peterson

An associate of the Harvard Institute for International Development for thirteen years, he is a specialist in public finance and management. He has designed and managed development projects in Africa for over ten years and has consulted on public finance and management in Eastern Europe, Latin America, and the Middle East. He is currently managing a project to reform Ethiopia's financial systems under that country's civil service reform. Steve holds a masters degree in finance and a doctorate in political science from the University of California Berkeley.